The Mind Possessed

The Mind Possessed

The Cognition of Spirit Possession in an
Afro-Brazilian Religious Tradition

EMMA COHEN

OXFORD
UNIVERSITY PRESS

OXFORD
UNIVERSITY PRESS

Oxford University Press, Inc., publishes works that further
Oxford University's objective of excellence
in research, scholarship, and education.

Oxford   New York
Auckland   Cape Town   Dar es Salaam   Hong Kong   Karachi
Kuala Lumpur   Madrid   Melbourne   Mexico City   Nairobi
New Delhi   Shanghai   Taipei   Toronto

With offices in
Argentina   Austria   Brazil   Chile   Czech Republic   France   Greece
Guatemala   Hungary   Italy   Japan   Poland   Portugal   Singapore
South Korea   Switzerland   Thailand   Turkey   Ukraine   Vietnam

Copyright © 2007 by Oxford University Press, Inc.

Published by Oxford University Press, Inc.
198 Madison Avenue, New York, New York 10016

www.oup.com

First issued as an Oxford University Press paperback, 2010.

Oxford is a registered trademark of Oxford University Press

Library of Congress Cataloging-in-Publication Data
Cohen, Emma, 1979–
The mind possessed : the cognition of spirit possession in an Afro-Brazilian religious tradition/
Emma Cohen.
    p. cm.
Includes bibliographical references.
ISBN 978-0-19-976744-1
1. Psychology, Religious.   2. Spirit possession–Brazil.   3. Afro-Brazilian cults.   I. Title.
BL53.C643 2007
266.6'12160981–dc22   2006032578

Printed in the United States of America
on acid-free paper

To Renato Cohen and Flávia Bassalo,

in appreciation of your love, kindness,

and support in Belém and beyond

Preface

This is a book about spirits who possess bodies. More precisely, it is a book about various people's beliefs about spirits who possess bodies, with a particular focus on an Afro-Brazilian religious community. In this community, as in many others across the world, people maintain that bodiless agents, or spirits, may temporarily possess the bodies of living people. Some of these spirits never had bodies of their own. Some of them did, having once been ordinary mortals. In some cases, these spirits are perceived as unwelcome intruders, and in others, they are warmly and excitedly received after long weeks and months of preparation and waiting. Why do such beliefs occur at all? That is the central question this books sets out to answer.

We must start with people's fundamental notions about bodies, persons, and spirits and the cognitive capacities that give rise to these notions. Understanding these mental processes is crucial to explaining the idea that a person's control over his or her body may be replaced, or eclipsed, by another controlling agent. What sort of mind would conceive of its own eviction from the body? Drawing on recent theories and findings in the growing field of cognition and culture and on ethnographic fieldwork in Brazil conducted during eighteen months in 2002–2004, I seek to explain how possession beliefs come about.

For anthropologists and scholars of religion, the originality of this account lies in its integration of ethnographic description with recent explanatory approaches in the cognitive science of religion.

These approaches seek to generate generalizable, cognitively informed accounts of the transmission of religious concepts and practices. When scholars in this area encounter an item of culture that has recognizably cross-culturally widespread features (whether a ritual, concept, or artifact), they consider how (and which) mechanisms and processes of our minds may be implicated in the generation and spread of the item. Memory, early emerging and deep-seated intuitions about how the world works, emotions, and motivation (among many others) are all potentially significant factors in cultural transmission. They mediate the production and the ebb and flow of cultural elements in broadly similar ways across all cultural landscapes. As such, they possess considerable explanatory utility in generalizable accounts of cultural phenomena. For the cognitive sciences, the originality of the account lies in the application of these largely lab-based cognitive approaches to a real empirical, ethnographically rich case, namely, the Afro-Brazilian religious traditions of the northern Brazilian city of Belém. For those readers who have neither (or no) scholarly perspective on the topic, but are curious to find out more, I encourage you to read on. This book was written for nonspecialist readers also. Its focus, Afro-Brazilian religion, is a particularly colorful, vibrant, entertaining, yet relatively little-known cultural tradition with a proud but harrowing past. For these reasons, and more to be outlined in the following chapters, Afro-Brazilian religionists are hopeful, and currently "struggling" (as they often said) for an equally proud, but more acceptant, future. For those who are at the forefront of this struggle, communicating their religion to those who as yet know little of its color, vibrancy, and past is no longer merely a novel privilege, but a priority.

This book is based on doctoral research at Queen's University Belfast (2001–2005), funded by a research studentship from the Department of Employment and Learning, Northern Ireland. It could not have been written without the additional support, interest, and expertise of many colleagues and friends. Many of these I have met as a consequence of the research. Their generosity and friendship, however, has often extended beyond matters directly relating to the research process.

I particularly want to thank my former primary supervisor, Harvey Whitehouse, and my secondary supervisor, Kay Milton, for their dedication, encouragement, patience, and advice on both practical and academic issues, as well as my examiners Pascal Boyer and Fiona Magowan for their constructive criticisms of my work. I have also benefited enormously from the support of a number of colleagues working within the Centre for Anthropology and Mind, University of Oxford and the Institute of Cognition and Culture at Queen's. To those in residence, whose company has been a daily pleasure, and to those affiliates with whom I have enjoyed e-mail dialogue, I thank you, particularly Justin Barrett, Jesse Bering, Claire Cooper, E. Thomas Lawson, Pierre Lienard, Luther Martin, Joel Mort, Jesper Sørensen, and Paulo Sousa. Many of you took the time to read parts of an earlier manuscript and listened to me "rabbiting on" about it at various times. I wish to convey my appreciation to you and to two anonymous reviewers for very helpful suggestions for improvements and future lines of enquiry. For discussion and advice on many different aspects of sourcing and gathering data, I am grateful to Erika Bourguignon, Mundicarmo Ferretti, Nicola Knight, Seth Leacock, James Lett, Ken Livingston, Stephen Nugent, and Dan Wright. I also wish to thank family and friends who have offered practical and emotional support and who have followed the research with keen interest since its beginnings.

In Belém, I met hundreds of truly generous people. I have incurred a huge debt to all those who contributed to the quality of my research and experience. Sadly, it is not possible to mention them all by name, simply because so many people played a part, and also because it is my duty to protect the identity of those participants who took me into their confidence and whose lives and thoughts are presented in this book. Nevertheless, my deepest gratitude to the staff and student community of the Department of Anthropology at the Federal University of Pará, particularly, Andrezza Barbosa, Marilú Campelo, Denise Cardoso, Taíssa Luca, Heraldo and Angelica Maués, and Anaiza Vergolino-Henry; to my dear friends in the ilè and the culto afro, especially Pai and the core members of the terreiro–que saudades; to all my neighbors, "family," and friends: Claudia, Valmir and Fatima, Louis and Márlia, Paulo and Anna, Dona Rita and Carlinhos, Danilo and Rosa, Miguel and Maria Clara, Catarina, Santiago, Dotoura Eva, Flávia, Mara, Lorena, Taíssa, Bruno, Benjamin, Paulinho, Maurício, Minori, Roffé, Rui, and Vinícius; and to the families represented by all these individuals, for countless enjoyable lunches, coffees, and conversations; to my husband, Renato, whom I met after twelve months in the field, for unreservedly supporting this research since that time.

Finally, I would like to thank Gwen Colvin, Daniel Gonzalez, and Cynthia Read and the whole editorial team at Oxford University Press for all their assistance in the preparation and publication of this book.

I am greatly indebted to all those at home and abroad who have assisted in the various stages of this research both practically and intellectually and even inadvertently. There are times in the field when a good hug (conventional or electronic) is as welcome as a good interview. To all those who played a part, your contribution was invaluable, whether or not it is expressly registered in the following pages.

Contents

Note on Translated Sources

Unless otherwise stated, published sources marked with "my translation" have been translated from Portuguese.

Where I have included research participants' statements in English, I have added where appropriate and possible (i.e., where statements were audio recorded for transcription) participants' verbatim statements. The names of all research participants have been changed.

The Mind Possessed

I

Introducing Possession

Early in September 2002, I was making my way to Pai's[1] house for the second time since arriving in Belém. I had received an invitation to attend a week of events in homage to an indigenous Brazilian family (*linha*) of spirits at his cult house, or *terreiro*, and this Tuesday evening had been set aside for a seminar on the *culto indígena* (indigenous cult). Having attended a number of ceremonies and ritual events in this and other *terreiros* around the city since arriving in late July, and still a little hesitant to test my Portuguese skills in one-to-one interview situations, I hoped that this might be a good opportunity to take in some of the teachings of relevance to my observations thus far. The plan was quietly to slip into the background and listen to what was said.

On arriving, I was led to a small room about halfway through the typically elongated Belenense[2] dwelling-place. Pai was sitting behind a little square study table that occupied most of the closet-sized space known as his "consultation room" (*sala de atendimento*). The table was covered in a carefully arranged collage of paper money in various currencies, self-portrait prints, images of Catholic saints, and other drawings, diagrams, and symbols, all sealed under a transparent sheet of plastic. Despite what I considered to be an almost unbearable level of heat, exacerbated by the tight confines of the tiny room, he was sporting an old, tatty brown hat and was enjoying a freshly lit cigar. He motioned to me to have a seat. "*Oi, minha filha*" (Hi, my daughter), he smiled, lulling me into a false sense of ease before announcing that *he* was going to interview *me*. Nevertheless, my unease would prove to be uncalled for as, in what was to become characteristic fashion, Pai commanded conversation and I listened, intrigued and at times more than a little confused, for as long as he could spare the time.

As I was showered with names, dates, and places that placed Pai's house and lineage in its Afro-Brazilian historico-religious context, I became increasingly aware that there was something a little unusual about Pai's behavior. Not only did I feel like I was drowning in this constant stream of information, but I was struggling with the way that Pai spoke about himself, as if he weren't actually there. He used the third-person singular, saying things such as, "The *pai-de-santo* was about to turn four years of age when..." and "The *pai-de-santo* has really been studying his religion" and so on.

"Pai-de-santo X?" I quizzed, mentioning a close colleague of his from another *terreiro*. "No, no," he answered, "Pai!" returning to take up his original point. Perhaps it had something to do with his use of Portuguese, I pondered, when suddenly the uncanny realization dawned on me: Pai was possessed. A host of questions arose in my mind. Is it Pai, or is it not? Is he pretending? If it's supposed to be a spirit, why does he seem so like Pai? Is Pai conscious? Will he even remember this conversation? How does he recognize me? Should I behave differently in some way? Have I behaved appropriately? Have I been disrespectful? Why didn't he introduce himself? Is it a test of some sort?

"I am Zé Pelintra," he finally announced toward the end of the conversation. "I am known throughout Brazil as a marijuana smoker and *cachaça*[3]-drinker, anything at all you want to call me. In this house I work doing charity, doing good, taking out *feitiço* [i.e., undoing sorcery],[4] healing, and giving guidance. I don't drink, unless it's coffee, tea, or soft drinks—I don't drink any alcoholic beverage. I smoke *tawari* cigars, the curer's cigar, and I work in the way that you are seeing, this simplicity. . . . I am a *caboclo*, my daughter, I am black, of African descent." He went on, talking about the week's activities in homage to an indigenous family of *entidades*—spirit entities—known as the *Juremeiros*, and classing himself as a legitimate participant by virtue of his ceremonial birthplace in the northeast of Brazil during a ritual ceremony known as *Catimbó* or *Mesa de Jurema*.

It was soon time to prepare for the seminar. I realized I was somewhere at the bottom of a very steep learning curve, with a more muddled and incoherent picture of this Afro-Brazilian-Amazonian cult house and its inhabitants than I had imagined possible. That I could even begin to construct sensible questions seemed a remote possibility. But I was encouraged by the fact that I had been given an opportunity to start by listening and had achieved some level of acceptance by both Pai and Zé, two gatekeepers in one.

Around twenty people came to the house that night to hear Pai's seminar on the indigenous religious tradition that was to be the focus of the week's ceremonial activities. As with all major ceremonial activities, the events surrounding the *culto indigena* were preceded by weeks of financial planning and practical preparation. In the few days leading up to the week of homage to the indigenous spirit families, the *casa* (house), and in particular the main dancing and ritual area, were transformed into a rainforest grotto with foliage and greenery collected from the garden and yard to the back of the house. A "mast" was erected in the middle of the *casa*, and it, too, was decorated with greenery and local tropical fruits. Men, women, and children gathered and chatted casually with one another as they sat and waited for Pai to open the meeting.

The seminar commenced about two hours behind schedule. I felt that I had probably failed to get relations with Pai's community off to a good start by detaining him with the conversation beforehand. I was soon to learn, however, that strict timetabling was to become a thing of the past. Just as I would never be blamed for keeping Pai back, so, too, I had to be prepared to accept frequent delayed starts, late arrival at interview sessions, or failure to show up altogether as normal, acceptable behavior for which blame is not apportioned and reasons rarely volunteered.

Pai (who now appeared to be *puro*, or not possessed) opened the proceedings with Catholic prayers, followed by a summary of the month's financial comings and goings. The unhealthy imbalance prompted him to issue a frank and clear demand that each of those present should pay their backlog of monthly contributions as soon as possible to allow him to buy the necessary provisions for the events of the week. As was customary, suppers would be provided for them and for members of the public who wished to attend the ceremonies, and he could hardly turn up at the supermarket without any money. As this was an *obrigação*[5] of the *casa*, and not anybody's personal responsibility, it was up to the whole *casa* to contribute.

Turning to the evening's main business, his talk took as its starting point the Aruã tribe of the island of Marajó. Located at the mouths of the Amazon and Tocantins rivers, and bigger than Switzerland at 50,000 square kilometers, this enormous fluvial island is worthy of its name, meaning "barrier to the ocean." As Pai spoke proudly of the Amazonian origins of the *culto indigena* practiced in his *casa*, I was reminded of one of the key factors that had influenced my decision to carry out fieldwork in Belém.

The first time I read about the spirit-possession cult that I later came to make the focus of my fieldwork was in George E. Simpson's *Black Religions in the*

New World (1978). Simpson drew from Seth and Ruth Leacocks's ethnography, *Spirits of the Deep* (1972), in his summary of the Belenense tradition they called "Batuque." In a table of religious cults of South America, Simpson classified cults found throughout Brazil, Surinam, French Guiana, and Venezuela into four categories: Neo-African, African-derived, Spiritualist, and Independent (1978: 15). Batuque stood alone in the final category. Setting aside the question of whether or not these cults could or should be boxed within such exclusive categories, I wondered about the lack of representation in this final category and was drawn to investigate further. It became apparent that its classification was more a reflection of the interests and agenda of Brazilianist anthropologists and sociologists at the time, than the popularity of this category of Afro-Brazilian cult.

The Leacocks emphasized the Brazilianized character of Batuque, in contrast with Candomblé in Bahia, Casa das Minas in Maranhão, and Xango in Recife, that had attracted much scholarly attention throughout the forties and fifties (Landes 1947; Carneiro 2002 [1948]; Ribeiro 1952). The cults subsumed under these umbrella terms had indeed retained a great deal of African content, and these in-depth studies were part of a rise in interest at the time in the sociological analysis of African acculturation in the New World. Traditions such as the Batuque had been sidelined by the nature of this approach. Labeled as "syncretized" and "disorganized," they were believed to be anemic imitations of the original African lifeblood. The Leacocks, however, found such claims to be misleading. Batuque, they pointed out, was not Candomblé. "It seemed clear that far from being some kind of imperfect copy of the Candomblé, it was in fact an independent, coherent religious system that deserved recognition in its own right" (1972: 317).

This necessitated a departure from the common lines of questioning that stressed the preservation and modification of "Africanisms" among the descendants of the African slaves. Turning their attention away from such concerns, the Leacocks were able to document a wealth of non-African–derived elements that formed part of the Batuque tradition. Indeed, before 1900, the main non-European ritual focus in the city was *pajelança*, a curing ceremony originating in the Amazonian interior. Located on the edge of the Amazon basin, Belém's popular culture had absorbed and assimilated such elements, imported by steady rural-urban migrations of people. As I still found to be true in my first full week of fieldwork in this Belém cult house, the activities of the *pajés*, or shamans, that were incorporated into the African-derived traditions introduced to the city at the turn of the century, had lived on in Batuque and other cults, religions, and cultural expressions.

Pai's house became the focus of my research activities. The full timetable of ritual and everyday events surrounding the *terreiro* and the core community that frequented it would not have permitted a sole researcher to accompany the lives of two or more religious communities. I have no doubt that questions of divided loyalties would have arisen had I even attempted to do so. Most larger, public ceremonial events occurred in the *terreiros* on Saturday nights; and with the ritual timetable overlapping closely from *terreiro* to *terreiro*, I realized from the outset that it would be impossible to win the trust and respect, as well as to achieve some level of membership, of more than one community. When time allowed I attended ceremonies in other *terreiros*[6] and arranged appointments for interview sessions. In all these comings and goings throughout my eighteen-month fieldwork period, I heard neither participants nor nonparticipants use the label Batuque in the sense that the Leacocks did. They did, however, still employ other terms mentioned by the Leacocks, such as Mina, Nagô, and Macumba. Although these and other terms continued to be used interchangeably by outsiders, aspirations to define more clearly one's cult practices according to certain labels, or *nações* [nations], had become popular among cult leaders in the thirty years since the Leacocks carried out their fieldwork. Hence, Pai's seminar on the *culto indígena* demonstrated his extensive knowledge of the origins of his personal practice of *pajelança*, or curing, as a set of practices separate from other "lines" [*linhas*] practiced in the *casa*. Gods, spirit families, origin stories, rituals, clothes, songs, dances, rhythms, and instruments were presented as exclusive elements of an autonomous part of the whole spectrum of religious practice, which included other similarly defined, distinct *nações*.

After the seminar, I was invited to return the following evening to see the *culto indígena* in practice. According to my informants, this Wednesday night's *pajelança* ceremony was the only one of its kind to be found in the hundreds of cult houses throughout the city. As the people gathered, those who were there for treatment (*tratamento*) found somewhere to sit and chat while the *filhos-de-santo*, or *terreiro* members,[7] prepared to assist Pai, taking showers of ritual purification, dressing appropriately for the occasion, and seeing to some last minute practical aspects of the preparations. Donated fruits were now being bunched together and hung from the wooden mast that had been erected in the center of the main room—apples, sweet potatoes, oranges, coconuts, maracujá, uxí, and other local varieties. A small brazier suspended by a long handle was prepared with charcoal and some other potently scented seeds and barks and was carried through the house, smoke billowing out and filling every corner of the dwelling from the back door, through the kitchen, living area, main ritual room, to the front of the house. Beside each of the white patio chairs lining the walls of the main room was a section of a tree trunk about half a meter in height, decorated with a length of brightly colored material knotted into a bow at the front. At the base of the trunks was a bed of sand on which rested a *cuia*, or bowl made from a dried gourd shell, containing a herbal infusion for ritual cleansing, as well as two yellow and two green candles and one larger "seven-day candle." On commenting that the colors matched those of the Brazilian flag, I was informed of the more relevant referent for the context, namely the *nação* of Jurema and the Juremeiro spirit entities. On top of each trunk was a small painted bowl containing Brazilian rum, alongside a cigar and a small image of either Saint Lazarus or Bom Jesus.

An elderly man was helped to a raised area at the front of the room that usually hosted the three drums used in all ceremonies of African origin. The drums had been replaced with a low camp-bed, a high-backed, decorative wooden chair from which Pai would lead the proceedings, and a small flat stool that had been consecrated for use by his curing entity. The man was instructed to recline in the bed—he would be treated personally by the *pai-de-santo*. When I enquired about the man's condition, I was told that he was "only there for spiritual treatment." Other more able-bodied clients were instructed to take any one of the seats in the main room. As I could see that everyone was occupied with their various tasks, I decided just to wait and see what "spiritual treatment" looked like in practice. Pai announced:

> We are here for the purpose of practicing *pajelança* in benefit of ourselves and of those people who are dear to us. In front of you, you will find two yellow candles and two green candles. You are going to light these candles at the point at which I tell you to do so—a yellow one for a friend of yours who may be passing through serious financial difficulty, and one for you to light for your own financial difficulty. The green one is for your health problem, and the other green one is for someone you know, a friend, who may need some help. . . . The little saint that is in front of you—you may notice that some are Saint Lazarus, and the others are Bom Jesus. When I pray for Saint Lazarus, those of you who have Saint Lazarus will take the saint and request your protection. Those of you who have Bom Jesus, say your prayer and request protection.

So he continued to talk them through the function and significance of the various materials to be used. The *filhos-de-santo* who were attending each of the clients were also informed of how and when they should work with the cigar and the infusion for ritual cleansing. Before the ceremony proper was initiated, a new client was welcomed and a more experienced *filho* was chosen to give her particular assistance.

The first part of the ceremony consisted of a sequence of prayers and songs, or *doutrinas*, with the wording and structure closely modeled on Catholic liturgical prayers. Pai led the group in petitions of permission, invitation, protection, and healing to the *povo da floresta*, the people (spirit entities) of the forest and of the deep (animal spirits associated with curing and *pajelança*). The images of Saint Lazarus and Bom Jesus in fact represented the great curer Tuparaci, who was "from the village of Tupinambás and was touched with all kinds of illness, but cured by the herbs and animals of the forest, observing how the animals cured him, becoming the greatest of the curers," and Inhandijara, "the white spirit of the forests." Although these spirits were believed to be present in the gathering, listening, and answering requests for spiritual and physical blessing and health, other spirits made their presence much more visible. Cobra Coral, Tibiriça, Pena Vermelha, Jaguaraciema, Caboclo Arruda, Andiraíba, Tupinambas, and Cabocla Tava, among others, were called individually to "come and fetch" their *filho-de-santo*. Pai repeated the song of invitation, substituting the names of the *caboclo* spirits he was calling as he moved from *filho* to *filho*, creating a rain-like sound with his maraca as he shook it around their heads. Through the dimmed, smoky light and above the slow steady singing of the refrain and the rattling of the maraca, I looked on as bodies, one by one, writhed, jolted, trembled, and grunted into a state of possession trance. Some regained their composure and balance readily, taking a seat on the ground or standing. Others continued to stumble and shake tensely until finally reaching full transition into this new role. Clients remained seated throughout, awaiting the unique treatment and its results.

"I begin my work in the name of the all-powerful God," Pai announced, having returned to the raised platform at the front of the room. The newly arrived *caboclo* entities were instructed to stand in front of the clients, placing their hands outstretched and resting on their heads. He continued his beseeching prayer,

> I entreat thee, by thy sublime name, by thy light and by thy grace,
> by the force of the virgin forest, by the *encantados* (spirits) of the
> forest, that at this moment, thy power would fall upon each one of
> these people, healing their pains and relieving their sufferings, that
> in this moment, the sacrosanct, divine substance of the herbs and
> the essences of the forests may pass right through into the circu-
> lation of their blood, taking into their bodies a vital energy, capable of

removing any kind of infection, inflammation, and sickness, whether it be materially provoked or whether it be provoked by their enemies, by evil forces. O, fall upon me, Lord, in thy power, and I will have the power to transform the lives of those who trust in me. Free me from anguish and inspire me in this moment in thy goodness, so that I can share with my brother the gift of charity. Defend me and help me in this accomplishment. Amen.

I had been given a premium place at the side of the platform from which to watch and record all that was taking place. Although healing and curing practices are common in *terreiros* around the city, Pai claimed to be one of few remaining authentic *pajés*, or Amazonian curers, in greater Belém. So, as the last prayer was recited for the lighting of the final yellow candle, I was pleasantly satisfied that I had observed a unique event, not only in the ritual calendar of this *casa*, but in the whole of Belém.

But things were only just beginning. Pai instructed each *caboclo* to continue individually with their "personal work." They prayed with the clients in what is known as a *passe*, a procedure in which positive, strengthening energies are believed to be transmitted through the fingertips to the participant. Pai bowed his head, resting his forehead on one hand while continuing to use the other to shake the maraca, clearly feeling the first approximations of the spirit that would come to work through him. Stillness fell on the room. The shake-shake-shake of the maraca became slower, sometimes stopping altogether and then breaking into a continuous rain-like rattle until suddenly Pai appeared to be jolted forward on his stool, and with a grunt was . . . possessed.

Sighing and wiping his brow, Rompe Mata announced his arrival in song, introducing himself as a curer and sorcerer. His voice was remarkably gruff yet frail, and as he rose to his feet, he took on the appearance of an old, stooped man of about twice Pai's forty-six years. He was aided down the steps toward me. A young woman was called from the back of the room to stand by my side against the wall. One of the participants handed me a battered tin bowl and instructed me to stay put. Rompe Mata moved toward us. Leaning forward he asked the woman beside me to locate the source of her pain. After prodding around the area at the side of her neck, he called for a lit cigar. He inhaled deeply and then blew the smoke directly onto the area he had just inspected. He drew close to her neck and began to suck gently. After three or four seconds he turned toward me and spat into the bowl I was holding. Blood, spittle, and four pointed objects slightly longer than matchsticks were expelled into the bowl. Again he sucked, and for a second time about three of the sharp objects fell into the bowl. A third and a fourth time he repeated the procedure until only spittle and blood appeared. The woman, who had clearly felt no pain and was displaying little emotional reaction, was led to a stool to sit down. The bowl was taken from me and placed on a nearby ledge. I was later informed that a total of thirteen bones from a species of catfish had been taken out of the woman's neck, leaving no mark whatsoever.

His work completed, Rompe Mata offered some words of comfort and blessing to the workers and to their clients, instructing them all to keep well and to wish him a good journey. He was being called to return to the city of the spirits. He sang a *doutrina* song to that effect then breathed in deeply, trembled, and left. Zé Pelintra arrived almost simultaneously and led everyone in final prayers to close the ceremony.

Later on, as I pondered over what I had witnessed, I was perplexed by my ignorance surrounding certain features of the evening's activities. I had a sense of partially sharing with others present some understanding of the proceedings, but I was in no doubt that the cultural context of people's intentions, motivations, and attitudes was, for me, far from being fully transparent. Why did the woman not appear to be nervous? Why did she not get angry on discovering that the source of her discomfort had indeed been caused by someone else? Why was I asked to hold the bowl? Why did some people appear to enter possession with ease while others appeared to be in pain? Why do people participate in such activities?

Spirit Possession as a Cross-Disciplinary Field of Enquiry

Questions surrounding spirit possession, arising both from personal experiences, such as those described above, and from more detached observation, have prompted many scholars to investigate various aspects of the phenomenon more deeply. A vast literature addresses spirit possession phenomena from many different angles, reflecting not only the high level of interest in the practices involved, but also their relevance to numerous disciplines that investigate human experience from different perspectives. The continued and increasing (Smith 2001: 204) practice of possession throughout the world has held the gaze of anthropologists, psychologists, psychiatrists, sociologists, neurobiologists, historians, and others. Most scholars adhere closely to disciplinary concerns and biases. Notably few seek to integrate different theoretical perspectives and research in their examinations of possession trance behavior and experience.

Recently, however, some worthy attempts have been made to consider key questions surrounding spirit possession from an interdisciplinary perspective, bringing together psychological and anthropological theories and findings. In his attempt to formulate a new analytical framework for investigating spirit possession, Morton Klass insists that it is crucial for all involved in such projects to keep abreast of the developments in relevant research in sister disciplines and the usage and usefulness of analytical terms and concepts that we borrow and introduce into our analyses. "We anthropologists ... often de- often despair when well-meaning scholars in other disciplines exhibit an out- dated or superficial understanding of our discipline's subject matter. It is equally important if we are to use such terms as *dissociation* and *trance*—and even *mind*—meaningfully and accurately, to consult the most recent litera- ture" (Klass 2003: 77). Klass updates and redefines our taxonomic categories and concepts in order to develop more accurate and precise analytical tools for answering the question of what really is happening when someone claims to be possessed by a spiritual entity.

But what does *possession* mean? The term *possession* has been used to de- scribe a broad spectrum of practices across time and cultures. Yet, do we as anthropologists converge on a clear, accepted, universal definition of posses- sion for comparative purposes? For the past three decades many anthropol- ogists have taken Erika Bourguignon's distinction between possession and trance as their point of departure. Distinguishing between possession and pos- session trance, Bourguignon writes:

> We shall say that a belief in *possession* exists, when the people in question hold that a given person is changed in some way through the presence in or on him of a spirit entity or power, other than his own personality, soul, self, or the like. We shall say that *possession trance* exists in a given society when we find that there is such a belief in possession and that it is used to account for alterations or dis- continuity in consciousness, awareness, personality, or other aspects of physical functioning. (1976: 8)

According to Bourguignon, dissociative (or "altered") states of conscious- ness that are not attributed to possession can be termed *trance*, a "universal psychobiological capacity" (1973: 11). Possession trance, then, is a dissociative state that is believed to be caused by the possessing presence of a spirit entity. Its incidence is confirmed by means of ethnographic enquiry into local beliefs about trance and possession.

Although many researchers have recognized the importance of Bourgui- gnon's distinction between possession phenomena and nonpossession al- tered states of consciousness, some have expressed concerns that it provides no more than a heuristic model that leads to superficial analyses and misleading lines of enquiry. Michael Lambek alerts us to the general danger of dissembling social wholes and forcing the fragments into our preconceived categories (1989: 38; Dumont 1975). Such categories, he claims, may only remain useful if they are reconceptualized as polythetic, thereby allowing terms such as *possession trance* to encompass the diverse range of phenomena that one encounters on the ground. Lambek describes spirit possession on the island of Mayotte as a "complex, subtle, and supple phenomenon," arguing that "the subtleties are basic to what spirit possession in Mayotte, or anywhere else, is" (1989: 37). Imposing monothetic, decontexualized categories onto the variable beliefs and practices of Mayotte and other societies, he claims, creates the danger of reifying something that is heteroglossic, continuously changing, and part of a wider context.

Lambek also argues that it is impossible consistently to employ *trance* as a term that defines only a part of the whole complex of *spirit possession*. The distinction between trance behavior and the belief in possession, he argues, is easy to make in theory but is confounded by possession phenomena one may observe on the ground. By reducing possession trance to psychophysiological processes and susceptibilities, naturalizing paradigms have relegated possession to an after-the-fact (of trance) phenomenon, detachable from and superfluous to the universal, biological, fundamental trance component of the whole possession-trance complex for the purpose of explanation. Lambek claims that the form, meaning, and incidence of trance are guided and mediated by the cultural model, arriving at the conclusion that "trance is not prior to spirit possession in either a logical or causal sense. . . . Where it is meaningful, trance, like any other regular human activity, is shaped by culture. Hence, the 'possession' and the 'trance' in any given system of 'possession trance' cannot be consistently isolated from each other in practice" (ibid.: 40).

Nevertheless, if, as Lambek claims, the subtleties are basic to what spirit possession is, then there is by implication a generalizable aspect to the phenomenon that demonstrates regularity across cultures and that can potentially provide a basis for comparative analysis and explanation. The chief concern of Lambek's approach is to "account for the diversity of trance phenomena" (ibid.: 36); hence, "the lowest common denominator cannot tell us very much" (ibid.: 37). A comparative agenda would look rather different. Comparative approaches do not necessarily deny that certain aspects of trance states, such as the particular form and meaning they take and the context in which they appear, are indeed variable or cultural (ibid.: 38). Bourguignon, for example, recognized the limitations of heuristic models and generalizations. She appealed to the crucial importance of ethnographic methods of investigation to discover how altered states are interpreted and understood within their local cultural context. Nevertheless, a method was required for carving up the subject matter that best reflected distributional patterns on the ground—separating trance from possession as distinct categories of behavior, for instance, was necessary for recording incidences of institutionalized trance that occurred without possession beliefs, of possession that occurred without trance, and of trance and possession occurring simultaneously.

The approach I take in this book addresses these fundamental theoretical issues from a fresh angle. I argue that possession is not secondary to trance, nor is its appearance wholly determined by culturally constructed meanings with which it is endowed and in which it is embedded. For our research participants, where trance and possession occur together, both are fused in processes of perception, categorization, and interpretation. Furthermore, these mental processes (e.g., perception, representation, interpretation), largely mobilized outside conscious awareness, are informed by universal mechanisms of cognition. By ignoring them, the cultural constructionist position has exaggerated the importance of public culture on the meaning, form, and incidence of spirit possession.

Biological reductionism has also failed to appreciate the cognitive component of possession trance as a subject for causal enquiry. Both approaches tend to exaggerate the explanatory potential of their constructs and hypotheses. One focuses wholly on physiological responses to certain stimuli, to which the possession-trance complex is often claimed to be ultimately reducible; the other on the systems of meanings that, it is claimed, are continually reformulated in ways that only the semantic content of the existing cultural model constrains. Closer investigation of the architecture of the mind shows us, however, that "cultural meaning" and the form and incidence of cultural phenomena are informed and constrained by tacit mental operations. The cognitive tools responsible for the generation and acquisition of ideas, and the spread of culture, constitute a relatively fixed, generic mental architecture, the product of human evolution. Insofar as these processes are generalizable across all humans, they provide instructive insights into the causes of cross-cultural recurrence and spread of spirit beliefs and related practices.

The detailed descriptions of ethnographers enhance our appreciation of the complexity and variability of spirit possession as it arises in different contexts. Through comparative analysis, however, clear patterns and regularities become apparent. Aspects of people's representations of possession, for instance, display striking cross-cultural regularities, for example, in the form that the spirits take, the properties that they possess, the contexts in which they are invoked, the functions they fulfill, and so on. It is only by producing and testing generalizable hypotheses about the causal mechanisms at work that one can make judgments about how much the "lowest common denom-inator" can tell us about culture.

Following a survey of institutionalized forms of trance across 488 socie-ties, Bourguignon concluded that she was dealing with a matter of major im-portance, not merely a bit of anthropological esoterica; 437 of the societies in her sample were reported to have at least one institutionalized form of trance (1968: 40). The presence of possession belief in 360 societies (74 percent of the sample) similarly suggests that possession concepts and practices are by no means a trivial curiosity, a mere remnant from an ancient proto-religion, or the stuff of Hollywood thrillers. What promotes the persistence and spread of these concepts? How variable are they cross-culturally? What, if any, are their cross-culturally recurrent features? Why *do* they make for great movie material?

What This Book Is About

This book by no means aspires to provide comprehensive answers to all or any of the above questions. It does, however, offer an explanatory approach that at the very least prioritizes these kinds of global questions. It combines ethno-graphic data with recent scientific research into the cognitive foundations of cultural forms. Appropriating some of the pertinent predictions and evidence from cognitive approaches of cultural transmission, and generating novel hypotheses, it attempts to explain some basic aspects of the complex set of phenomena associated with possession beliefs and practices—in particular, the form, spread, and relevance of cross-culturally recurrent spirit concepts and possession practices. It initiates a research program that will ultimately demand the use of various methodological tools for the cumulative building of a scientific account of the emergence and spread of (and resistance to) possession.[8]

The central claim is that the emergence, communication, acquisition, and storage (e.g., remembering) of ideas about spirits and possession are both pro-moted and constrained by ordinary cognitive mechanisms and processes. Cog-nitive anthropologist Pascal Boyer (e.g., 2001) and psychologist Justin Barrett (e.g., 2004) among others (e.g., Slone 2004b; Whitehouse 2004) have offered novel, cognitively informed, testable hypotheses and findings concerning the spread of cross-culturally recurrent religious concepts (e.g., about knowing gods, vengeful spirits, crying statues, sacred artifacts, etc.) that form the basis of this claim. They propose that the form, content, and transmission of such concepts are shaped and constrained by tacit, intuitive ontological knowledge about the world, which begins to develop from very early childhood. They claim, and have begun to demonstrate experimentally, that this kind of intuitive ontological knowledge—for example, for physical, biological, and psychological domains—provides much of the information contained within notions of special objects, persons, and events. The most easily transmittable (religious) ideas diverge only minimally from this basic knowledge about how the physical, biological, and social domains work. Ideas that are largely consistent with intuitive expectations for ontological categories (e.g., persons, artifacts, animals), but that violate one category-level property (e.g., an animal that talks), have been termed Minimally Counterintuitive concepts (MCI concepts). Spirits, for example, may be only minimally counterintuitive, in that they are largely consistent with the category of "person" but lack bodies (the property of physicality). Given that spirits are often presumed to be like persons in most other regards, the content of spirit concepts is readily transmitted. It is not necessary to explain that spirits think, have feelings, know, see, and so on and act on the basis of their beliefs and intentions. Spirit and ghost concepts may also demonstrate counterintuitive biology. For example, in some places it is believed that spirits never die or never age and never get hungry. The transmissive success of such ideas depends upon the activation of a wide range of intuitive assumptions that are attached to a particular domain concept (e.g., persons, objects) *and* upon the violation of one or more of those assumptions (e.g., invisible person, seeing stone). Because the new concepts already largely fit with intuitive or existing knowledge, little novel information has to be learned and rehearsed in memory.

These claims are described and developed in the second part of this book, following an introduction to the ethnographic and topical fields in chapters 2–5. The original claims of Boyer, Barrett, and others are applied to the spirit and possession concepts of the Afro-Brazilian religious traditions, and a range of novel claims is developed concerning the social cognition and social relevance of possession as well as its variable spread. These themes, and the structure and content of the book, are outlined below.

Outline of Chapters

The following chapter provides historical and ethnographic background to the "*culto afro*"[9] (as I refer to the various Afro-Brazilian religious practices in subsequent chapters). Belém's position on the edge of the Amazon Basin, thousands of miles from the more cosmopolitan and intellectually and economically prosperous conurbations of Rio de Janeiro and São Paulo in the South, and its geographical and cultural remoteness from the African heart of Brazil—Bahia—have contributed to its status as a relatively unfamiliar and unexplored site of Afro-Brazilian religious activity. It has been widely (but mistakenly) assumed by both academics and even the local population that such activity is rare in Belém. The *culto afro*'s relative obscurity, along with other factors, has contributed to public misconception, discrimination, and prejudice toward its more visible members. At the time of my field research, *culto* leaders were taking steps, assisted by the local city council, openly to engage with the public, in the parks and squares, in the media, and in political and legislative councils, that had until then maligned, stigmatized, and condemned them, and, until relatively recently, outlawed their religious practices. I describe some aspects and activities of this public, and allegedly, increasingly united face of the *culto afro*.

In chapter 3, I introduce the *culto* as it was revealed to me through interviews, informal stories, personal histories, and daily activities by the frequenters, lodgers, and leaders of one *terreiro*. Here we find a different level of political dynamics—one that is characterized not by the inhibiting force of judicial law, but by gossip, sorcery, slander, opportunistic alliance, secret knowledge, and its revelation, blessing and cursing, merit and disapproval. The context of the social arena in which *filhos* and I participated is presented through a description of the *terreiro*'s distinctive historical development and of the basic doctrinal tenets as delivered by its head (*dono*), priest (*sacerdote*), and father (*pai*), Pai.

Chapters 4 and 5 review past and present approaches to possession cults and spirit phenomena and introduce the approach taken in the remainder of the volume. Anthropological, sociological, medicalist, and biological perspectives have variously described, interpreted, and offered explanations for various aspects of possession as it appears across many of the world's societies. In the first of these chapters, we look at ethnographic description and anthropological interpretation of spirit-possession phenomena, considering the roles of both rich description and faithful representation of cultural meaning for the generation of scientific theories. In chapter 5, I review medicalist, physiological, and sociological approaches to possession. Early medicalist attempts to explain spirit-possession phenomena focused on their presumed parallels with mental illnesses and psychotic disorders. Recent neuroscientific perspectives have endeavored to identify the biological processes that underpin possession states and how these may be positively understood and characterized against scientific evidence on the neurophysiological processes underlying other "altered states of consciousness," such as meditation, as well as evidence on the effects of these states (e.g., physical and emotional well-being). Sociological theories converge on certain fundamental assumptions regarding the functional role of possession cult activity, characterizing such practices as the effect of—and the means to upgrade—peripheral social status.

I assess the usefulness of these approaches—descriptive, interpretive, and explanatory—against the evidential standards required for scientific investigation. As will become apparent, few theorists within academic anthropology have sufficiently elaborated their claims about possession to allow for precise delineation of what could count as evidence for and evidence against the theories' predictions and to enable investigations to proceed accordingly, employing appropriate methodologies. I argue that a return to scientifically grounded explanation necessitates cross-disciplinary collaboration between traditionally disparate bodies of knowledge, as well as the sharing of methodological tools of investigation.

In order to answer specifically questions concerning the form and spread of spirit concepts, I propose to begin with the rich ethnographic database provided by decades of anthropological enquiry into spirit phenomena, taken together with the evidence generated by cognitive and psychological investigations into the structures and processes of the human mind. Our minds comprise complex sets of systems that process, interpret, distort, and rearrange information they encode. But they do not do so randomly. Increasingly we are acquiring a detailed picture of the ways in which our minds tend to generate certain kinds of outputs, given certain kinds of perceptual inputs. Chapter 6 introduces some cognitive mechanisms responsible for mental representation and for the formulation and acquisition of ideas. I consider the question of why some concepts are more or less likely to become widespread within and between cultures. I suggest (following recent predictions and data from the cognitive science of culture) that we can predict which ideas are more likely to be remembered and invoked by considering their basic properties and how these properties fit with the intuitive assumptions generated by panhuman mental tools.

Because these mental tools are the product of our species' evolution and are therefore relatively stable among all humans, the tacit mental processes that these devices facilitate display considerable regularity across cultures. Predictions about cultural transmission that are informed by evidence about mental tools and processes are therefore potentially universally applicable. An important characteristic of cognition is that objects are categorized as members of conceptual categories. People conceptualize spirits (as they do any other object or event), though each is individually different, as members of a group. But what is the nature of this group? When we think of the category "spirit," how do we define it? Are there any criteria by which spirit concepts are defined that display uniformity across cultures? To answer these questions, it is helpful to consider the "spirit" category as a member of a more general parent category, such as "person." Following recent claims in the cognitive science of religion, I consider how particular notions of possession and ideas about spirits closely fit with tacit assumptions about persons. According to this view, a person is represented as a special kind of object—unlike other inanimate, physical objects, persons have agency, or the ability to think and have emotions. They also act on the basis of their thoughts, that is, they have intentional agency. Spirits are fundamentally continuous with the ontological assumptions that we hold regarding the intentionality of person-agents, but they lack one basic property that is normally assumed for persons, and objects in general, that is, physicality. Possession, as it is represented in the *culto afro*, and around the world, provides spirits with this missing property. Spirits who possess are represented as taking on corporeal form and replacing the agency of their human hosts. The host's agency is displaced and a new person is formed, one that now fits with all ontological assumptions for the person category—but with a few extra features. That spirits are typically attributed special powers to heal and punish, special access to hidden/personal knowledge, and so on, makes them particularly relevant to the explanation and resolution of personal misfortune. This issue is addressed in chapter 8, specifically in relation to the healing and counseling activities of Pai's *terreiro*.

Chapter 7 considers the cognitive and psychological processes that inform people's actual observations and perceptions of possessed hosts. In this chapter I draw upon observations and interview data from the field and from studies in social psychology and neuroscience. Together these begin to provide an account of the observer's implicit perceptions of a possessed host's actions. The behavior of a possessed host is, according to the widely accepted view of possession, wholly attributable to the intentions of the spirit now in possession of the host's body. Yet, frequently in the actual interactions between possessed hosts and observers, and in conversation about specific possessed persons, actions are attributed to the intentions of the host. This is the case even when observers apparently accept the veracity of possession and the host is said to be in a possessed state. Evidence from social psychology on the biases that inform our assessments and interpretations of other people's behaviors sheds some light on these ambiguities. Recent neuroscientific studies of person recognition can also enhance our understanding of the processes of social perception at play. These findings are crucial to explaining the ambiguities one encounters in people's behaviors and conversation concerning specific cases of possession. There are often many factors that influence how workable an idea is in practice, even when it generally fits with intuitive assumptions.

Finally, I consider the distributional patterns of possession and spirit phenomena cross-culturally. I pose the following questions: if our generic cognitive architecture constrains and predisposes us to think in certain ways, and
if concepts of spirits and possession, as they are widely represented, are the
natural outcome of these predispositions, then why are possession practices
and beliefs in spirits not evenly spread across the globe? Why, for example, is
there a preponderance of women in spirit-possession cults? Why do these practices appear most frequently among politically marginalized and oppressed
peoples? What are the mechanisms that could explain these correlations? The
variable incidence of spirit phenomena worldwide reminds us of an important
first principle. The processes of mentation, and the products of these processes
(e.g., thoughts, ideas, beliefs, and so on) are influenced by the environment
that surrounds us. Under certain ecological conditions, the natural, intuitive
outputs of our cognitive predispositions may be enhanced or inhibited. I seek
to identify these conditions on the basis of widely documented sociological,
anthropological, and psychological survey data, hypotheses, and evidence and
to consider how these factors act upon our cognitive mechanisms to produce
population-level demographic patterns of involvement in activities typically associated with spirits.

The aim of the following chapters is to take some steps toward explaining
why particular aspects of spirit possession take the form they do. Some of the
claims on which I build are already established and well substantiated through
systematic investigation. We now have at our disposal a number of well-
attested predictions and claims that have direct applicability to the problems
at hand. Some of my claims, however, are more speculative, including hypotheses for which, as yet, little or no testing has been carried out. Yet, the
accumulation of knowledge is always marked by an increasing consciousness
that there is much more to discover. One discovery can raise as many problems as it solves. Hence, by bringing pertinent scientific knowledge to bear
on the problems and questions posed by the ethnographic data (and vice versa),
this research has been characterized by the continual surfacing of novel questions and problems. I have chosen not to omit discussion of more speculative hypotheses, but to include them as untested—but potentially testable—
claims. As such, this book captures the essence of scientific investigation and
discovery. Because all knowledge is provisional, and displays varying degrees
of certainty (but is never absolutely certain), all claims here are advanced tentatively and in anticipation of further refining, reshaping, and possible re-
formulation. First steps are often faltering ones. Yet, how much we would
potentially fail to observe, learn, and discover if we didn't even get to our feet.

2

Historical and Ethnographic Setting

Eu gosto de ser afro. Eu gosto de ser uma sacerdotiza, me encontrei, me sinto feliz, não discrimino nenhuma religião.... Então eu mostro na minha cara, eu sou feliz.

I like being Afro. I like being a priestess. I found myself, I'm happy; I don't discriminate against any religion.... So, I show it on my face. I'm happy.

—A mãe-de-santo

The night of the thirty-first of August 2002 marked a momentous event in Belém's history. The *Festa das Raças* ("Party of the Races") was one of an increasing number of public events that served to bring together Afro-Brazilian religionists from across Belém and its satellite towns in occasions of cultural celebration that publicly registered the presence and vibrancy of Afro-Brazilian religiosity throughout the city. It was through these events that Belém's population was offered the opportunity to witness and participate in public musical performances and presentations, religious ceremonies, conferences, seminars, exhibitions, marches, and addresses that observed Afro-Brazilian tradition. This marked the beginning of a novel situation in which local Afro-Brazilian religionists could feel increasingly confident about taking the once-outlawed practices of their religious traditions from the privacy and protection of the cult center to audiences at the "public square" (*praça pública*).

In this chapter, I describe some of the circumstances that have precipitated these recent developments and that have shaped both the practice of and scholarly approach to the *culto afro*. This takes us back through two centuries of Belenense and Brazilian history to another series of unprecedented, reforming events. It is against this historical backdrop that, when I received the invitation to the *Festa das Raças*, two details caught my attention. First, the event was to be held in the Palácio Antônio Lemos. Second, the city's municipal government, or council, was to sponsor and co-organize the event. The significance of the occasion is especially highlighted by the irony contained in the history relevant to these two observations. As the seat of the current city council, the Palace, with its spacious, airy courtyard and balmy, tropical ambience, was the natural choice of venue for the sponsors. A brief consideration of its history, however, and the figure of its namesake, reveals that even this decision was not void of historical import.

Changing Attitudes toward African Religious Traditions

The impressive Antônio Lemos Palace, in the port district of what is now known as the "old town," took twenty-three years to build (1860–1883). Built to serve as the seat of the city's municipal government, the Palace housed the civic administration that steered the city through its most prosperous era and stands today as a testimony to the flush generated by the boom in rubber trade, at its height between 1870 and 1912. Belém's *belle-époque* was characterized by a series of socioeconomic reforms under the celebrated intendant, Antônio Lemos. These reforms coincided with similar programs in other parts of the country that would have direct implications for the everyday practices of newly emancipated African slaves, now members of the poorest sector of Brazilian society. African religious and cultural practices had been forbidden under slavery. Since the first African populations were separated from their lands, families, and fellow tribespeople, and sold and shipped by the Portuguese traders to the New World in 1534, slaves were baptized into the Catholic Church on arrival. They were stripped of everything that could ensure the survival of their religions—freedom, time, and space to practice, specialist religious knowledge, and mother-tongue communication. Yet, even in an upside-down world, in which the foreign had replaced the familiar and the commonplace was now criminal, these displaced and dispossessed populations frequently outfoxed their oppressors.

A story was often told by my friends in the field of how the slaves used to trick their supervisors by worshipping their numerous deities under the guise of the large pantheon of Catholic saints. The *orixá*[1] *Ogum* was renamed St. George, *Yemanjá* the Virgin Mary, and so on, in a subversive act so vital that the same associations between particular deities and saints continue to exist today. Furthermore, conditions of work varied from city to plantation and from the plantations to the mines, allowing for differential degrees of supervision. In the cities, where slaves had more freedom to meet compatriots, underground movements were less easily suppressed. Some slaves successfully escaped into the thick bush of the interior, establishing maroon colonies, or *quilombos*. Some of these are known to have numbered up to thirty thousand runaway slaves, descendants of slaves, and Native Americans. In such ways pockets of slaves preserved what they could of the familiar cultural traditions of their homelands in the plantations, mines, rich urban residences, and *quilombos* throughout the vast territory of Brazil.

By 1888, all men and women were free, and together with the already-escaped and emancipated ex-slaves, they acquired ample opportunity openly and routinely to practice the rituals and customs that would compose the religious traditions collectively labeled Candomblé. Under the First Republic, church and state were formally separated and the right to freedom of private religious consciousness and affiliation was paramount. A number of decrees swiftly followed, however, attaching certain qualifiers to the propositions for social equality and integration offered by the new constitutional model. These measures moderated the pronounced religious freedom, prohibiting sorcery, magic, curing, and the "illegitimate" practice of medicine (see Johnson 2002: 82–83). The elite, ruling class, however, had more than notions of order and common good on its mind. National pride was at stake. Afro-Brazilian religions were at the center of concerns surrounding a mandate for national progress that was premised on utopian notions of "whitening"[2] of both race and culture. As Paul Christopher Johnson writes, "The liberty of freed slaves to perform religious ceremonies involving drumming, sacrifice, and possession dance was an obvious site of contestation since it was in such ceremonies that difference, non-Brazilian identity, was most radically marked" (2002: 86). In the name of progress and collective interest, the response was to administer such ceremonies as falling within a broad category of public health—not religious—concerns. As Johnson observes, Candomblé was marginalized from the "constitutional 'center' of the guaranteed freedom of religion, relegated to the jurisdiction of the Penal Code's domain of illegal health practices and malevolent sorcery" (ibid.: 90). In this way, authorities justified their repressive policies toward the black, African hoi polloi, and their purported unsanitary practices.

In Belém, Lemos was busy securing international export deals and administrating the modernization of the city as the Amazon's principle gateway to the exterior. Projects that took up the challenges of sanitation and public health, communications, and architectural aesthetics rapidly transformed the appearance and infrastructure of the city. "Order and Progress," declared on the new national flag, were realized in the "aesthetic renewal of the city" (Paranaguá, et al. 2003: xix, my translation), which saw the construction of tree-lined avenues and boulevards, paved roads, parks and gardens, theatres and European-style *Café Chics*, the municipal market (*Ver-o-Peso*), railways, crematoria, drainage networks, waterworks, the waste disposal apparatus, and the inauguration of the Municipal Department for Sanitation (Sarges 2002). As in the rest of Brazil, Afro-Brazilian religious expressions were legally treated, not as religions, but as matters of public health (Johnson 2002). In Belém, Article 110 of the city's Code of Ordinances (1900) prohibited African drumming and dancing parties, and "sambas," along with "shouting without necessity" and whistling. According to official discourse, the aim was to reduce sound pollution levels. So, for the collective good, and the preservation of "order," Lemos's newly formed municipal police force was assigned the task of patrolling the city's public establishments and residences. Serving as a defense mechanism between the rich and the poor, its members' remit was to keep the "social apostates" at a safe distance from the enclaves of the elite (Sarges 2002). Maria de Nazaré Sarges, a local historian, writes:

> In this way, the *Belle-Époque* fashioned the redefinition of the urban space, the redistribution of the locales for which sanitation services were destined, and the employment of mechanisms of control over the populations. The distinction between the central area of the city, intended for the "deodorized" and "hygienic," bourgeois rich, and the "peripheral" areas, intended for the poor, working population became quite apparent. (2000: 155; my translation)

In a city in which the elite now dined on English biscuits, French champagne, and Portuguese olives and even sipped on Peking tea, and whose rich had made a hobby out of "being seen," it could be said, "The mud offends the new sensibility" (*As lamas agridem a nova sensibilidade*: ibid.: 164). The "mud" was to take numerous forms in Lemos's rose-tinted vision of a tropical Paris in Belém. Not least were the poorer classes, the presence of which, it was said, "cast an inexorable shadow over the enlightened city" (ibid.: 173). The poor, the ex-slaves, the elderly, the deranged, the contagiously ill, and the criminals were thus confined to the swampy margins of the city's landscape, far from the affluent businesses and airy residences of the elite.

In the 1930s, a nationwide shift in the Brazilian population's self-image would dramatically influence public policies and attitudes toward nonwhite

Brazilians. This was precipitated by, among other factors, the publication of Gilberto Freyre's *Casa Grande e Senzala* (1933, published in English as "The Masters and the Slaves"). Freyre's ambitious "study in the development of Brazilian civilization" (as the English translation title page presented it) offered an alternative view of national identity and economic progress to the message of "whitening" and "Europeanization" preached by turn-of-the-century intellectuals. The pervasive opinion up until this time was that a truly desirable Brazil would be one free of African and indigenous elements, symbols of what would become the backward past. The measure of Brazil's economic success as an emerging industrial force was in its supposed progression along a linear evolutionary trajectory that ultimately terminated with de-Africanization of culture and racial phenotype. The presentable, marketable Brazil was envisaged as white and European.

Freyre's view departed radically from the prevailing perspective. Indeed, he positively evaluated mixed ancestry and the culture of the *mestiço*[3] as epitomizing a distinctive, multiracial Brazilian identity. Peter Robb identifies this as Freyre's "favorite insight, that the most Brazilian things in Brazilian culture were a synthesis of indigenous, Portuguese and African elements, and like the Brazilian people itself, new and unique" (2004: 185). The impact of Freyre's message was far reaching. "It was immensely seductive.... Most seductive of all was the idea that out of Brazil's sensual and promiscuous past a new society had grown where the races flourished and racism was extinguished" (ibid.: 25).

This discourse became known as the "myth of racial democracy." Its initial appeal among the elite was in its potential to become a valuable marketing tool at a time when Brazil's growing industrial sector sought expansion and healthy trading relations with the exterior, particularly with African nations. The strategic shift in Brazilian self-portrayal, however, soon led to important changes to public policies that directly concerned the legal and social status of previously considered "African," or ex-slave, cultural expressions. Elements of African heritage were elevated from low-status, undesirable impediments to progress to the very symbols of a distinctive Brazilian identity. These were now proudly displayed in newly constructed museums and folklore centers, in dances (e.g., samba), foods (e.g., *feijoada*, the bean dish said to be an original creation of the slaves), *orixá* worship and myths, and *capoeira* (Angolan-derived martial art). These became focal attractions of foreign exchange programs and tourist parties (Santos 1998). Nevertheless, all such practices remained subject to the provisos and regulations of the repressive political regime of the New State and the subsequent military dictatorship. A system of police licensing was introduced for all Candomblé ceremonies, potentially

placing considerable restrictions on the proclaimed freedom of religious practice. Meeting the criteria for the issuing of a license was based less on the
nature of the proposed "toque" or ceremony than on personalist social links
with the authorities. Anaiza Vergolino e Silva writes:

> Until 1964, there was a great number of cult houses spread
> throughout Belém indiscriminately called terreiros, searas, tendas,
> cabanas and batuques, that operated by means of special licenses
> granted by the Police. These licenses were obtained through the fa-
> miliarity of the owners of these houses with people of prestige, of
> political and social influence, who allied themselves with the au-
> thorities in order to obtain provisional authorization to hold "toques."
> (Vergolino e Silva 1976: 90–91; my translation)

Control was the key to Brazil's progression along the path to economic
progress. The potential for the political mobilization of grassroots social units
was recognized, and repressive measures were in place to maintain order. Indeed, it was only in the late 1970s, as the military dictatorship neared its final
demise, that the system of police licensing for Candomblé ceremonies was
finally terminated.

Partying in the Palace

Despite the national legalization of Candomblé decades ago, participation in
Afro-Brazilian religious ceremony in Belém even today is generally only achiev-
able in the terreiros and cult rooms dotted around the city's swampy margins.
The majority of these remain almost hidden from view within the mazes of
potholed dirt tracks that characterize the poorest districts of the city. Yet, in
this relentlessly polarized society, the mayor of Belém had proposed to open
the doors to the Antônio Lemos Palace, the current seat of the city council,
in an unprecedented gesture of acceptance to this class of people once so
objectionable.

Buses loaded with povo de santo (lit. "people of the saint," or Afro-Brazilian
religious participants and supporters) streamed in from the periphery. Osten-
tatious and beautiful in their full ceremonial garb, they gathered in the floodlit
space at the huge front entrance to the palace, chatting and laughing excitedly,
adjusting each other's skirts and headdresses as they prepared to meet the
mayor and the newspaper photographers. Inside, in the breezy courtyard, the
scene was being prepared—drums belonging to the various groups were being erected; only minimal seating had been allocated to allow for full capacity

and mobility; and a full buffet spread of the local varieties of *salgadinhos* (popular mini-pastries), sweets, and juices was receiving its finishing touches. The city mayor, along with other councilors and politicians who had worked to bring the proposed event to fruition and to the awareness of the public, was preparing to greet his guests. When everything was as it should be, a hush fell on the entrance hall, the cameras were poised, and the large doors unlocked and opened.

With a vigorous round of applause, drumming and whistling, hugging and kissing, dancing and singing, the *povo de santo* marked their entry into a new era. Representing three religious traditions, or "nations"—Candomblé (Ketu and Angola), Mina Gege Nago, and Umbanda—groups united to present ensembles of singing, dancing, and drumming to the city council and its guest audience. Compelling speeches were followed by rapturous applauses and passionate appraisals. "No one is going to be able to hinder what you are doing," preached the mayor. "Whites, blacks, *mestiços*, Asians, Catholics, Evangelicals, and Afro-Brazilians have the prerogative to exercise their maximum right." A date was set for a yearly celebration, which met with the delight of the religious leaders gathered around the organizing committee. Forces were petitioned to protect the young mayor and his wife, and the party continued late into the fresher hours of the balmy, tropical night.

Some weeks later the event was at the center of a nationwide scandal. A popular peak-time television gossip and current affairs show, hosted by the well-known presenter, Ratinho, casually transmitted a video recording it had received from an apparently concerned member of its viewing public. The joyful scenes at the Palácio Antônio Lemos were accompanied by the voice of a narrator condemning the mayor and his guests for partaking in devil-worship. Most offensive to the participants concerned were the allegations, associated with the faces of particular religious leaders that appeared on the montage, that such people were guilty of performing cemetery rituals in which graves were desecrated and vandalized. The dances and songs that the *povo de santo* had used to dramatize the collective values of the new society, a world that would now accommodate their Afro religiosity, had been recast in a devilish dramatization of the values of a misguided and dangerous group. More than sixty years following President Vargas's decree that had removed Afro-Brazilian religions from the list of criminal acts against public health, granting religious houses, or *terreiros*, permission to practice as state-registered centers, the film poachers had highlighted the intolerance and division that continues to exist across a broad sector of Brazilian society.

The extent of public lack of awareness and suspicion surrounding local Afro-Brazilian religious practices was continually in evidence during my fieldwork period in Belém. The general consensus among many people I met outside my academic and research communities was that these people were at best deprived on multiple counts or they were mad, or both, and that their beliefs and practices clearly reflected this. At worst they were dangerous, had evil intent, and were best avoided. I was therefore probably a touch mad myself or perhaps ill advised in my choice of research area. Anyway, I was informed, I had probably come to the wrong place, as there wasn't much of that sort of thing here in Belém. Bahia, however, was rife with it and I should probably at least take a trip there to see what the real, traditional religion looked like.

At the time of my research, The Federation of Spiritist, Umbanda and Afro-religions for the State of Pará had sixteen hundred registered *terreiros* in the Greater Belém area. This was probably just the tip of the iceberg, with many nonregistered *terreiros* and other rooms used by mediums for spiritual healing and counseling sessions existing throughout the city. Although there can be no doubt that my "informants" were correct—Bahia is the African heart of Brazil and the traditional center of Candomblé—this figure was sufficient to convince at least myself that there was ample reason to stay in Belém.

The Ethnographic Setting

Compared to the conurbations on the eastern and southern coast, Belém is one of Brazil's younger cities, tracing its origin to January 1616. At the close of the previous year, a group of Portuguese settlers had been dispatched from the neighboring state of Maranhão (Northern Brazil) to set up a frontier military post that would secure control of the unprotected region of the Amazon basin against the possible occupation of the French, Dutch, or English. The party established a fort (*Forte do Presépio*) and chapel where the Guamá River flows into the Bay of Guajará. It was from this base that the Portuguese launched their exploration and colonization of the Amazon Basin and the city soon became the principle gateway for the export of minerals, dyes, woods, medicines, flavorings, and spices extracted from the forest (Leacock and Leacock 1972).

From Belém's beginnings as the colonial outpost at the mouth of an Amazonian tributary, the tides of international trade have carried a great variety of merchandise, from the importation of thousands of African slaves to the exportation of a significant portion of the rainforest. Belém, the capital of Pará state, has always served as the commercial center for the Amazon region and the construction of a highway in the 1950s, linking Belém with Brasília, over 2,350 kilometers to the south, greatly enhanced its national importance in this capacity (Leacock and Leacock 1972: 35). It was at this time that rural-urban migration began its steady rise due to the weakening prices of raw materials against manufactured goods. International agro-extractive industry has disenfranchised vast numbers of indigenous *caboclos* of rural Amazonia. In 1960, the population of Belém was 402,170. Today there are 1.8 million inhabitants occupying a total area of 1.820 sq km. This constitutes almost one third of the population of the entire state of Pará, the second largest state in Brazil.

A number of factors account for the lack of awareness that the general public of Belém demonstrates concerning the incidence of non-Catholic, non-Evangelical religions. First, Afro-Brazilian groups now present have a relatively short history in Belém and are still defined in terms of geographical references external to the city. Leacock and Leacock (1972) emphasize the relatively weak impact of African cultural forms due to the logistics of slavery in the area. Although the Portuguese crown subsidized the transportation of African slaves to the territory from 1680, only a few hundred Africans reached Belém before 1750. The total number brought to Pará was probably only a very small fraction of the four million Africans shipped to Brazil between 1550 and 1888. It is therefore unlikely that any religious cult that emphasized exclusively African traditions could have succeeded in Belém. The ethnic heterogeneity and widespread dispersal of slaves, coupled with intermarriage and joint working conditions led to considerable integration with the indigenous slaves over the centuries. "In Pará, by 1900," write Leacock and Leacock, "the ex-slaves, the freemen, and their descendants had probably been completely absorbed in the local lower-class culture that included Indian religious ideas as well as much of Indian material culture" (1972: 45). Indeed, it is widely accepted that Batuque was originally introduced from São Luis in the neighboring state of Maranhão at a time when there was little—if any—evidence of Afro-Brazilian religious activity in the city (Marks 1992). This is generally considered to have fallen around the beginning of the twentieth century.

Second, despite their current politically legitimate status and well-established presence in the city, Afro-Brazilian traditions in Belém have remained as underground and guarded as they have been unremittingly stigmatized by pervasive discriminatory opinion. The National Demographic Census recently elaborated its "other religions" category to specify Candomblé, Umbanda, and "other declarations of Afro-Brazilian religions." Also, for the first time the Census permitted registration of double or multiple religious affiliation. Despite this, it remains an inaccurate source of survey information on this point. The Atlas of Religious Affiliation and Social Indicators in Brazil suggests that the alleged virtual nonexistence of Umbanda and Candomblé in Northeast Brazil, according to the 2000 census results, is due to "a difficulty that the censused people have in declaring parallel religious practices" (2003: 101; my translation). It was thought that "religious syncretism, so common in Brazil, could now be captured by the Census" (ibid.: 9). However, in a nation of almost 170 million people, only 10,500 declared that they belonged to more than one religion, a figure that would scarcely even account for the number of self-nominated Catholics who frequently attend *terreiros* in Belém alone. Arguably, social factors contributing to such people's reticence to declare their participation in Umbanda and other Afro-Brazilian activities prevail more strongly in the backward and conservative north than in the more cosmopolitan societies of the southern conurbations. One observes how this inhibition is standard in the day-to-day life and conversation of many Belenense *terreiro*-goers.

General factors contributing to this situation are numerous. In her analysis of the Federation of Spiritist, Umbanda, and Afro-Brazilian Cults of Pará, Anaiza Vergolino e Silva reported that in the 1970 census survey all non-Catholic and non-Evangelical religious communities were lumped together under an "other religions" category. Writing of Umbanda in particular, Vergolino e Silva claimed:

> The phenomenon, however, exists in Belém, and its relevance is proven by pieces of indirect evidence, such as: the depreciative notices in the religious and political columns of the press, both written and spoken; by the number of specialist houses in the sale of Umbanda items, which increases daily in the city; by the position of a conservative wing of the Church... that adopted a position of protest before the expansion of the cult...launching "Catechisms of Alert" to the public. (Vergolino e Silva 1976: 2; my translation)

Today, religious discrimination and intolerance continue to generate abuse, direct violence, and open conflict among the Catholic majority, Evangelical fundamentalists, and members of Afro-Brazilian traditions. The various identity markers that characterize the latter category render it open to attack on more than the question of religious preferences. Afro-Brazilian religionists claim to be marginalized not only by their "demonization" by dominant religions (see Oliveira 2003), but also through their stereotypical characterization in the mind of the majority as being poor, black, and uneducated. To an extent as yet undocumented statistically, the cult practices are also largely the domain of women and homosexuals. In the provincial north of Brazil, the idea that one should take pride in belonging to any of these categories is a relatively recent concept (relative to the rest of Brazil and the

industrialized world). Dominant classist, racist, sexist, and general elitist attitudes thus combine to portray on the street, in the chat shows, on the Internet,
and the in newspapers, a religion that persists in the minds of the majority as
low status and even disreputable.

A third factor that has contributed to a distorted image of the incidence
of Afro-Brazilian religion in Belém derives from the work of some of the
first scholars to the field. Edison Carneiro, one of the foremost Brazilian researchers writes in his classic work, *Candomblés da Bahia*, "Without doubt,
the candomblé of Bahia is the most magnificent of the whole of Brazil, and
still serves as a mirror for all the other cults" (2002 [1948]: 21; my translation). Over two decades later, Roger Bastide echoed, "In Bahia the ceremonies
are more spectacular" (1971: 192). Because these researchers were primarily
interested in studying African acculturation in the New World, they included
in their studies only those traditions that seemed to have more firmly retained
their African character. New attitudes and adopted practices were understood
as "contaminants" that spoiled the authenticity and pure values of the African civilizations. Candomblé in Bahia—the largest center of the African slave
trade and the birthplace of modern, organized Brazilian Candomblé—was
therefore the benchmark reference for comparative study of all African-
derived religions throughout Brazil. Some, such as those on the fringes of the
Amazon that were considerably culturally and geographically removed from
Bahia and ultimately from Africa, fell outside the interests and agendas of
these research programs.

In Belém, the first notable exception to this trend was the work of Leacock
and Leacock, published in 1972 under the title *Spirits of the Deep*. In the absence of any existing research in the field, they went to Belém under the false
preconception that, aside from a few minor variations, they would essentially
find "people of primarily African ancestry, organized into tightly knit *terreiro*
groups, still worshipping African gods" (Leacock and Leacock 1972: 317). Instead they discovered "quite a different religion," practiced by a racially heterogeneous population, and whose pantheon included spirits with Brazilian
names and characteristics. Animal *entidades* (spirit entities) of Amazonian origin, such as dolphins, snakes, and jaguars, also populated the pantheon. Ideas
and practices had been incorporated from folk Catholicism, as well as themes
from Brazilian and Iberian folklore and history, creating "an independent,
coherent religious system that deserved recognition in its own right" (ibid.:
317). To this end, the Leacocks baptized it "Batuque," but with an important
concluding remark: "The Batuque today is far from being a completely sys-
tematized body of beliefs, and, at the rate it is still changing, this condition
seems likely to continue" (ibid.: 320).

After four decades, the body of research on the forms of Afro-Brazilian religion in Belém is still comparatively limited. Nonetheless, an increasing number of local and international anthropologists, ethnomusicologists, and historians have filled some of the gaps in our knowledge of this dynamic fusion of beliefs and practices. Anaiza Vergolino-Henry, an anthropologist at the Federal University of Pará, continues research that she commenced in 1965 as a postgraduate student at the University of São Paulo. At that time, her work coincided with the interests of Napoleão Figueiredo, the late founder of the local Anthropology Department, with whom she published the article *Alguns Elementos Novos para o Estudo dos Batuques de Belém* (Some New Elements for the Study of Batuques in Belém) (1967). As vice president of the Historical and Geographical Institute of Pará, and of the State Council for Culture, Vergolino-Henry is a widely published and recognized specialist in the long-term development of Afro-Brazilian cults in the area (see Vergolino e Silva 1976, 1987; Vergolino-Henry 1990). Her recognition among the general public as a skilled and knowledgeable lecturer, public speaker, and writer extends to many *terreiro* communities throughout Belém. Since she is the *terreiro*-members' voice to the wider academic world, it was natural, yet a privilege, for me to be introduced to my field by its chief expert.

I was not the first for whom Anaiza had performed this favor. A number of local and international students and researchers have been so introduced to the gatherings at various Belenense *terreiros*. More and less recent work on Afro-Brazilian cults in Belém, all of which exists only in Portuguese, include Furuya Yoshiako's research of the Mina-Nagô cult in the 1980s (e.g., 1986a, 1986b), Pedro Tupinambá's *Batuques de Belém* (1973), Marilu Campelo and Taissa Tavernard de Luca's work on social memory (Campelo & Luca 1999), Luca's dissertation on the history of the Afro-Brazilian cults in Belém (1999), Campelo's recent and current research on memory and Candomblé in Belém (2001, 2002), and João Simões Cardoso's dissertation *Uma Rosa A Iemanjá* (1999), in which he presents an analysis of power disputes between the Umbandist Federation in Pará and a dissident group, "Association of Friends of Iemanjá." Raymundo Heraldo Maués has also published related work on *pajelança* and popular Catholicism in the state of Pará (1990, 1995, 1999, 2001). Given the lack of local research into the presence and form of Afro-Brazilian religious forms and ritual traditions in Belém until recently, these scholars have made significant contributions to the cumulative study of the wide spectrum of popular religiosity represented across the vast Brazilian territory.

Local spiritual leaders, or *pais* and *mães-de-santo*, are also increasingly adding to the existing corpus of literature, producing an invaluable research resource in the form of informal studies, memoirs, and newsletters. In this respect, things have changed dramatically since the time the Leacocks carried out fieldwork among this unknown community. Relevant books in both Portuguese and English now line the carefully guarded shelves of the many leaders' personal libraries. These serve not only as educational resources, but also as status markers in a world in which knowledge is a valuable currency that converts into prestige credits, an enlarged clientele base, and, therefore, ultimately, increased income. For these reasons, Pai's eyes lit up when he first noticed my copy of the Leacocks' *Spirits of the Deep*. Most of the more academically aware leaders, of which he was widely reputed to be foremost, had heard of this elusive publication. That it was written in a language nobody could completely understand seemed to add to its appeal. Such a title on display would testify to the influential contacts its owner enjoyed with the wider academic world and would at least suggest command over a supplementary wealth of knowledge about this largely undocumented, oral tradition.

Pai's *Terreiro*: The "Field"

Not fully recognizing the economy of knowledge and prestige in which I was soon to become a valuable pawn, I was initially drawn to Pai principally by his love for discussion, his self-confidence, and the personal interest he took in my research. Although I considered my decision to carry out fieldwork in Belém to have hinged largely on quite arbitrary considerations, Pai explained to me rather differently the steps that had brought me right to his doorstep. "Indeed," he informed me from the outset, "the *voduns* have brought you here, and they are probably more interested in the research than you. It's a communal project that you are doing." This interpretation of events introduced an unanticipated accountability and sense of responsibility that I could only hope to honor adequately. I—along with my notebook, pen, recorder, camera, questions, and strange foreign ways—had been granted access to almost every sphere of *terreiro* activity, religious and everyday, public and private, for the collective production of a piece of research authorized at the highest level. Pai frequently reminded his *filhos* (spiritual sons), *filhas* (daughters), and clients of the supernatural and collective authorship of the research throughout the long eighteen months of questioning, interviewing, and investigation, thereby constantly rallying everyone to accommodate this new category of person in their midst.

The *terreiro* was home to Pai, his mother, and four young men between the ages of 14 and 33. Other people came and went during my research period;

some arrived by choice and others through desperate necessity. All found a welcome, but Pai made sure that his generosity was not abused or mistaken for unconditional charity. Guests, residents, and *filhos* were expected to repay the kindness shown toward them by pulling their weight with the housework, respecting the members of the household, obeying orders, and controlling their urges to eat more than their fair share. Perhaps one of Pai's most frequent complaints was that those who depended upon him most, even for the basic necessities of life, were the poorest examples of the kind of team spirit he hoped would characterize the community. Indeed, it was no surprise one day to find that the entrance to the kitchen had been barricaded with a sturdy, lockable gate.

Many of the regular attendees at the *terreiro* were young and unemployed and had few prospects in the professional arena. A number experimented with different money-spinning ventures. One woman offered a manicure service; another designed and made crochet garments and decorations; another sold jewelry sets. One of the young men depended on demand for his escorting service until he received the opportunity to train as a masseur; a number of *filhos* offered consultations with their spirit guides. It is important to note that although *filhos* who attended the *terreiro* regularly tended to be from the poorest sectors of society, clients represented all classes and walks of life. Politicians, clergymen, prostitutes, students, estate agents, restaurateurs, academics, and lawyers had visited the *terreiro* for various motives, whether to observe the vibrant dancing, drumming, and singing of the *festas* or to seek advice, guidance and physical healing from Pai, his *filhos,* and their spirit guides.

Just as at the time of the Leacocks' research, the *culto afro* in Belém today is racially[5] heterogeneous also. In a simple survey of basic personal details for ten of the core members of the *terreiro* group I asked individuals to describe their phenotype, or color. One member identified himself as *negro*, three as *moreno*, one as *moreno claro*, or "light Moreno," one as *pardo*, and four as *branco*. It is difficult to offer direct English translations for all these terms due both to their potential polysemy in the vernacular and to the comparatively limited range of color descriptor vocabulary in English. Nevertheless, the order in which they are reported here potentially represents a gradation from black (*negro*) through various shades of brown (*moreno*) to white (*branco*) (see figure 2.1). Despite the potential elasticity of the terms' meanings, and their susceptibility to variable social and historical contexts, the variability reported here certainly appears to capture a real phenotypic heterogeneity in the composition of the *terreiro* community. A more comprehensive survey of the twenty or so *filhos* who frequented the *terreiro* would unlikely diverge significantly from the percentage breakdown of this sample.

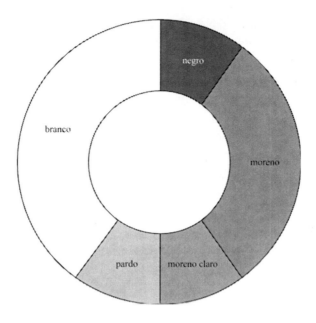

FIGURE 2.1. Breakdown of Color Descriptor Categories and Their Representation among Members

A more systematic study is needed to investigate the correspondence between participants' color categories and racial categories, and how the criteria upon which the color descriptor terms are allocated, intersect and overlap with, or diverge from, what it means to identify oneself as "afro." In the quotation opening this chapter, the *mãe-de-santo* identifies herself as Afro. More specifically, the "nation" within which she holds membership is Angola. This is by virtue of her initiation into Angolan Candomblé, however, and does not connote (biological) race as it is normally understood and as she is likely to define it for a general census. In terms of color this *mãe* would be described as white, but she is one of the Black Movement's (*Movimento Negro*) keenest supporters, and, along with all *culto afro filhos* and *filhas*, is included as a member by virtue of her cultural and religious heritage. Determining the precise breakdown of these categories, then, and their representation within the *terreiro* requires systematic investigation of the criteria by which each individual describes and defines his or her color, religious nationality and race, and how that individual's choice of identity label is influenced by the immediate social context. Furthermore, it may not necessarily be immediately obvious whether color or race categories are being appealed to in the descriptions as labels are not mutually exclusive; for example, the term *branco* may define race, but it is also a color descriptor. Indeed, *moreno* may be used as a racial category label and a color descriptor and can also mean "tanned." The results represented in figure 2.1 should therefore be understood as nothing more than a superficial indicator of the phenotypic (and only potentially the racial) heterogeneity that characterizes the *culto* (see Baran and Sousa 2001; Gil-White 2001).

It was interesting to note how participants in the survey initially seemed surprised by this question about color. Questions about name, sex, date of birth, occupation, and so on were to be expected in the "personal details" section of any questionnaire, but not questions of race and color, and especially for this ethnographer interested in religion. Race, understood as a natural-like biological category, rarely came up in conversation and everyday discourse as something that had any significant intersection with membership in the *culto afro*. One became Afro, and by extension "negro," when one became a *filho*, independent of the racial category to which one belongs. This information was largely irrelevant to the *filhos'* perceptions of fellow members and potential members.

Anthropological and sociological explanations for Afro-Brazilian religious participation, of course, traditionally turn on putative correlations with class and race categories. Many have viewed Afro-Brazilian religious arena as the exclusive domain of ex-slaves and their descendents, and therefore, of the poorest sectors of the Brazilian population. Marxist, structuralist, and functionalist theorists have offered explanations for the success of Afro-Brazilian religions and their emergent forms that have focused on sociocultural factors at the level of groups and populations. Slavery and its abolition, economic boom and bust, political instability, corruption and oppression, and racial tensions have been suggested as factors influencing the magnetism, distribution, and form of popular religion in Brazil. More recently, however, experts in the field have challenged the view of *culto afro* participants as homogeneously *anything*, questioning, most damagingly, the data from which hypotheses were constructed (e.g., Brown 1989). The heterogeneity of the *terreiro* community with which I carried out fieldwork, and the general lack in everyday discourse of evidence for any direct relevance of racial categories to religious participation, further challenges the assumptions of these models.

I intend to explain the appeal of some features of this tradition and of spirit possession, and spirit phenomena more widely through another potentially complementary, but necessarily more generalizable, approach. Accepting that the causal chain begins with the functions and constraints of the human mind in its sociocultural environment, I draw upon new developments in the cognitive explanation of cultural transmission. The overall aim is to show, through further ethnographic substantiation, how a rich body of culturally distinct idioms, concepts, and practices has sprung up against a background of general, natural cognition.

The following chapter narrows the aperture, from the wider view on historical and demographical issues concerning Afro-Brazilian religious forms, to focus on the people, activities, roles, and beliefs of the *culto afro* in Pai's *terreiro*. I describe the histories and circumstances of individuals with whom I engaged almost daily at the *terreiro* for eighteen months, paying special attention to its leader, Pai. This, I hope, provides the reader with some sense of being introduced to the community and to some of the distinctive concepts and practices that are shared by its members.

3

The Research Community

Eu sempre peço pelos orixás . . . eu queria que os orixás me dessem uma condição financeira . . . que eu não precisasse atender todos os dias como eu atendo, que eu pudesse me dedicar ao santo, aos meus filhos e principalmente a estudar a filosofia e teologia Africana . . . eu queria um tempo.

I always ask the *orixás* . . . I wish the *orixás* would grant me the financial means . . . to not have to attend [*clients*] every day like I do, to be able to dedicate myself to the *santo*, to my *filhos*, and principally to study African theology and philosophy . . . I would like some time.

—Pai

About a year after I first visited the *terreiro*, I asked nineteen regular attendees to carry out a simple exercise that, to some extent, reflects participants' motivations for their involvement and commitment in the *culto*. Each individual was presented with ten statements summarizing activities that were of considerable importance in the religious life of the community. Examples include *to pay one's ritual obligations to the orixás and spirit entities; to fulfill one's responsibilities to the egbe (community/family); to learn the fundamentos (loosely translated as theology [see below]) of the orixás; to learn the songs, dances, and language of the orixás;* and so on. They were then asked to rank them according to their importance. Each individual performed the exercise in privacy and was ensured of anonymity in the dissemination of results.

A mean ranking for the entries yielded *transmitting the religion to others* bottom of the participants' list of priorities. *Respecting and attending to* (zelar) *the pai-de-santo* was the highest ranking item. This was followed closely by *learning the fundamentos of the orixás* and *learning the rituals* (prática ritualistica)—*correct procedure* (see the appendix for full description and results). In follow-up interviews with the participants, two things became particularly clear. First— and contrary to Pai's frequent complaints—these *filhos* evidently held Pai in high regard. Both these regular attendees and the clients with whom I regularly talked while they awaited their turn to enter Pai's consultation room frequently declared their appreciation for Pai's dedication to the *orixás*, to the life of the *terreiro,* and to their individual well-being. Second, participants clearly recognized their dependence on him for the resolution of their problems. The fundamental knowledge of the appropriate rituals to be performed and of the *orixás* to be appeased, worshipped, and "cultivated" (from the verb *cultivar*) was within his custody and only revealed to them as and when they demonstrated the capacity to learn. Such knowledge was indispensable to those seeking to further their careers as full-time consultants, or *mães* and *pais* of their own religious communities. As one participant stated, "I prioritized 'to respect the *pai-de-santo.*' That's fundamental for me.... It's the *pai-de-santo* who's going to teach ... the *fundamentos* and everything that I need to learn within the *santo* (lit. *within the* orixá, or *within the* culto)" (*Eu priorizei 'respeitar o pai-de-santo', pra mim é fundamental ... é o pai-de-santo que vai ensinar ... os fundamentos e tudo que eu preciso aprender dentro do santo*). The findings accord with an earlier summary that Pai had offered of participants' motivation for attending the *terreiro*. "I think that for the *filhos,* the most important thing is the [ritual] practice because it is what brings money, power, and principally prestige" (*eu acho que pros filhos, o mais importante é a prática porque a prática é que traz o dinheiro, o poder né, principalmente o destaque*). He ponders also that the *filhos* probably feel some commitment toward him in return for his dedication to them and the *orixás*.

This chapter looks in more depth at the people, relations, practices, and beliefs that defined this *terreiro* during my research period. Unfortunately, it was not possible systematically to investigate the extent to which the structure and practices of Pai's *terreiro* are shared by other Afro-Brazilian houses in Belém. Nevertheless, through many conversations with *filhos* and leaders of other houses and visits to their larger, public ceremonies, it became clear that although each *terreiro* is autonomous and its practices and ethos are determined in large part by its leader, there are many broad similarities; for example, in the motivating factors that contribute to people's attendance, in the central importance of each *pai-* or *mãe-de-santo* for clients' and *filhos'* physical, emotional, and spiritual well-being, in the social tensions generated between *filhos* and their public expression, in the model by which the transmission of knowledge is organized, and in the structure and organization of the communities. These issues will be the focus of this chapter. Given the centrality of the *pai-de-santo* to the researcher's acceptance within this particular community, and to the identity and social morphology of the *terreiro*, I take the figure of Pai—his roles, aspirations, theology, and life history—as my point of departure. This is followed by a consideration of intra-*casa* organization and hierarchy and their articulation with the revelation and acquisition of knowledge.

Settling In

Pai was a unique character—unapologetically overpowering, domineering, and self-important, yet irresistibly charming, sensitive, and conversable, combining many of the qualities required for competent recruitment of clients and converts (and researchers), and for effective leadership. Despite the privileges granted by his social position, he frequently complained that because his days were constantly taken up with the tiresome administration of other people's concerns, time for personal schooling in the historical fundamentals of the tradition was scarce. Nevertheless, there was no viable way out of the bittersweet liaison between the personal pleasure of full-time commitment to the ancient religious traditions of the African slaves and their forefathers, and the bread-winning business of marketing the tradition's practices, mysteries, and solutions to the present-day, temporal needs of clients. As a rule, clients and even leaders-to-be were not inspired, like he was, by the so-called "deep mysteries" of the *culto* and its history. They were looking for magico-religious remedies, resolutions, and results, not the processes, premises, and teachings that were said to underlie their efficacy. The cash they paid kept the *terreiro* and its six permanent residents afloat. Hence, the hopeless fantasy of Pai receiving some support in his studies and gratitude for the thankless tasks that occupied his time was somewhat ameliorated by the arrival of the inquisitive foreign researcher onto the scene and the kudos this would bring.

It is only with these insights that I can now appreciate more completely the circumstances surrounding my swift welcome into the community of research participants. I am reminded of Johnson's humbling comment, "Whoever . . . thinks that informants entertain researchers with their stories out of respect for the social sciences or naïve good will would do well to consider Gilberto Freyre's image of a cat rubbing against a human leg. Although the cat appears to show affection, says Freyre, it is voluptuously caressing its own skin" (2002: 10). As is often the case in everyday social encounters, initial assessments of the potential for continuing relations were certainly based on mutual self-interestedness. I was concerned about the level of acceptance into Pai's world, and no doubt Pai was flattered and enthused by the possibilities that would come with the prospect of getting his *terreiro* on the academic map. To begin with, then, there was little personal or emotional interference in the mechanics of this equation. Gradually, however, some giving began to balance out the taking, and an improbable but warmhearted and affectionate friendship began to form between this young *gringa*[1] (white foreigner) researcher and Pai, an Afro-Brazilian cult priest.[2]

One lazy Sunday afternoon, as we stretched out on a mattress on the floor of the large principal room of the *terreiro*, Pai took advantage of the moments of quiet and inactivity to expound some of the key tenets of the religious "lines" practiced in his house. As was characteristic of our early conversations, he grounded his statements more in an abstract, historic past, than in actual, current *terreiro* practice. Pai, like many of his peers, regarded the tradition in the past with a strong sense of nostalgia. This was coupled with frustration with present-day corruptions to the timeless, traditional *fundamentos* on which practice is premised. Like others, Pai reminisced, complained, criticized, pointed the finger, and gossiped at every turn. But he always had some time left over for self-conscious reflection on the implications of his own shortcomings and failure to live up to his primary objective of appeasing and honoring his otherworldly superiors. Even though he was "king of his own house," accountable only to his supernatural superiors, he was first to recognize that even in his *terreiro* he fell far short of his ideal of re-creating a "little Africa" in Brazil. Referring to himself as a "sacred archaeologist," however, his attitude was far from defeatist. Although his dyed-in-the-wool traditionalism was interpreted by his enemies, and even at times by those within his house, as an excuse for a regime of arrogant and rigorous autocracy, he was widely regarded as a serious, knowledgeable, and principled *pai-de-santo*.

In some memorable conversations, like this Sunday afternoon's conversation, Pai seemed to be able to transpose his thoughts above the petty, pressing concerns that these daily tensions generated. He also uncharacteristically suspended his partiality for finer historical detail, allowing a precious opportunity to glimpse a rare, panoramic view of his personal philosophy.

> Most religions believe in a Father of Creation, whether he is called
> Zeus, or Jupiter, or Jehovah, or Olorum, or Zumbi, or Mawu-Lissa.
> They are all one. Their regional manifestation gave rise to differ-
> ent ceremonies, associated with the earth and with the historical
> events of those peoples. . . . It is the individuality, the leadership of

each person, it is the very self-interest of each religious leader that shaped them in a certain way, and everything seems different but deep down it's all the same....The Father of Creation...created primordial spirits, which we call *orixás*...he created a hierarchy and gave each one the power to govern certain events, phenomena in nature, and things to do with personality and feelings. Having done this, he turned to his project of creating the world...the planet....Some didn't want to, and never manifested themselves, never came. Others gave up some of their privileges, their life of tranquility and pleasure, a spiritual life, in order to come to earth to organize the *culto* and civilization. These that came, when they went back, were seen here on earth as very important beings.

A maioria das religiões acreditam em um Pai criador, ora chamado de Zeus, ora chamado de Júpiter, ora chamado de Alá, ora chamado de Jeová, ou ora chamado de Olorum, ou de Zumbí, ou de Mawu-Lissá. Todos eles são um só. A manifestação dele em regiões fez com que surgisse cerimônias diferentes, ligadas à terra, ligadas aos acontecimentos históricos daquele povo....É a individualidade, a liderança de cada pessoa, é o próprio egoismo de cada sacerdote, moldou de uma determinada forma porque aquilo parecesse diferente, mas, no fundo tudo é igual...O Pai criador...criou uma hierarquia e deu a cada um o poder de governar determinadas acontecimentos do lado da personalidade, dos sentimentos. Feito isso, ele se envolveu no projeto da criação do mundo...a planeta....Alguns não quiseram, nunca se manifestaram, nunca vieram, e outros cederam parte dos seus privelégios, cederam parte de uma vida de tranquilidade, de prazer, uma vida espiritual para vir à terra pra organizar o culto e organizar a civilização. Esses que vieram retornaram—quando retornaram, aqui na terra foram vistos como seres tão importantes.

In conclusion he drew some parallels with other religions—for example, Jesus leaving his heavenly home and coming to earth; the Buddha's abdication of his princely throne to lead humanity to enlightenment—and reiterated his original thought:

So, everything is equal, everything is repeated, it's only the language, the rituals that differ....The ceremonies were partly created by priests and partly transmitted by the *entidades*—according to how they wish to be worshipped, how they wish to be paid homage to. These rituals, these ceremonies diverge one from another and, because of this, diverse religions came into being.

Entao, tudo é igual, tudo é repetido. Só é a linguagem, só são os rituais que são diferentes. . . . As cerimônias em parte foram criadas pelos sacerdotes né, em parte foram transmitidas pelas entidades, como eu quero ser louvado, como eu quero ser homenageado. Esses rituais, esses cerimônias divergem de um pra outro e por isso que criou diversas religiões.

It was not unusual then that the *terreiro* in which I carried out most of my fieldwork exhibited a self-styled assemblage of a number of "lines" or "nations" of religion, identified by their individual ritual practices and languages. Just as the contents of a house reflect the history, travels, and character of its owner, the unique structure of Pai's *terreiro* exhibits an inimitable accretion of traditions, artifacts, and influences that have marked his religious trajectory. Below, I present the specific circumstances of one person's encounters with spirit entities, possession, and the perceived power of the supernatural beings to intervene in his life and direct his affairs. One sees not only the figure of *pai-de-santo* that he is today, but also his experience as a client, a first-time host to possessing spirit entities, a *filho-de-santo*, an unbeliever, and a religious scholar. As such, Pai's story portrays some aspects of the experiences and circumstances of numerous *terreiro* members and frequenters that I got to know at different stages in their journey as *culto* participants.

Pai's Story

Pai was possessed for the first time at four years of age by a curing "master" of indigenous Amazonian origin, who made himself known as Mestre Juvenal, the river dolphin spirit (*boto encantado*). Shortly after the initial expressions of disbelief on the part of his traditionalist Catholic parents, he began his career in curing. As a child, Pai remembers being perturbed by the way people behaved toward him on "waking up" after such curing sessions. No one explained what was happening, what he did, or why he felt so tired and hoarse. "You'll find out when you are older," they used to say.

At fourteen years of age, a different kind of "manifestation" (*manifestação*) occurred, in which "he didn't sing and sing until he was tired of singing." It wasn't a *mestre*, associated with the indigenous line of curing, but a *caboclo*, or the spirit of an indigenous backwoodsman. The first spirit identified himself as Juremeiro. Then came Jose Tupinambá, in a memorably chaotic episode in which Pai describes himself as being thrown from side to side and beaten and shaken from the inside as he entered a state of possession.[3] Tupinambá announced that he had been sent by the curing *mestres*. Pai was now entering a new phase—"the phase of the Juremeiro people (*povo de Juremeiro*)." The Juremeiros constituted a larger group of spirit entities that was not limited to practicing healing alone. Pai recalls the anxiety that followed:

> It was terrible. I didn't have anyone to explain to me. I didn't understand what the Afro-Brazilian *culto* was, but even so, that entity took hold of me [*me apanhava*], ordered me to light candles, gave me messages, told me to buy images of the saints, images of *caboclos*, and I went slowly yielding, buying a thing or two, not much, but always hugely fearful. There was no one to explain to me what it was all about.

Distraught and bewildered, Pai sought the orientation of a local *mãe-de-santo* (female *terreiro* leader)[4] and personal relative under whom he would develop his mediumistic ability and eventually be initiated into the Afro-Brazilian tradition of Umbanda.[5]

Some years later, Pai was forced to abandon his undergraduate degree course in history due to serious health crises. In the Umbanda house he had been attending, it had taken some time for his *entidades* to grow accustomed to the drumming at the mediumistic development sessions and parties. It was only after his body had taken a considerable deal of rough treatment that the possession episodes started to stabilize and become calmer. On completing his first semester at university, however, he started to suffer from severe headaches. As his condition worsened, blood would stream out of his nose, and he would frequently fall over on the street and lose sense of his whereabouts, even at the corner of the street where he lived. He sought the counsel of various doctors and Umbandist and other religious leaders, but to no avail. Finally a private clinic verified that he had three tumors in his brain. Though these were subsequently removed, surgery failed to alleviate the pains. Pai recounts the story of his personal battle for physical and spiritual health, a story that is foundational to the formation, character, and composition of the religious *casa* he came to establish.

> I passed three months feeling really ill. I wanted to end my life because my mother was suffering so much—she was the one who accompanied me through everything.
> I thought, "Well, since I've got this incurable pain, I'd be better finishing myself off."

I went there to the Ver-o-Peso [*harbour market*] and sat under the image of Bom Jesus of the Navigators, looking out to sea. "Ok, I don't know how to swim. I throw myself off here and that's it."

Except that when I went to the edge, I thought, "If someone sees me jumping off here and saves me, just think about how annoying it would be to give that interview—'Why did you want to kill yourself?'" No, no way. So I went back and sat under the image.

At this point, a friend of mine appeared—I don't know who'd sent him—and said, "Hi [*Pai's name*]! How's it going? I heard that you weren't well and all. What about your mission [*religious activities*]—how's that going?"

So I said to him, "Everything's at a standstill."

"Look," he said, "let's go, you want to go to the house of a man I know."

I told him, "Look mate, my family already took me to various places and had no success whatsoever. To the contrary, they spent money and I continue in turmoil."

"No, let's go to this place. This person will definitely help you."

From there we took his car to the house of this man, a man from Maranhão called José da Trinidade, better known as Zé Baião. He used to have a *terreiro* near the port of Itaquí in Maranhão.

So I went to this man's house—this was around 1980—I arrived there and met him. The house was still in construction. The man came out from away in the back, a huge black guy, shirtless, with a cap on his head.

"Hi, my son, come in." And into myself I said, "It's the same rigmarole as always." I had no faith.

He called me and sat beside me, saying, "You've got this, you've got that, etc.," and I said that Maurício, my friend, had obviously told him about me, because sometimes people give information to him even without meaning to. His *chefe* [chief *caboclo* spirit] was in his head [*na cabeça dele*], the *caboclo* Baiano Grande, José Constantino, and said, "You don't believe me, but I'm going to tell you three things that will make you believe." And really, he touched on three things of great importance that had taken place in my life and that few people knew. And he had never met me.

"Ok," he said, "these are the three things I had to say. Now I want you to go to your house, and there in the back yard is a papaya tree. You will go behind the tree and dig down. There in the soil you will find a rock of yours, sacred, the rock of an Indian that you carry."

As he bid farewell, he said, "Listen, if you like, you can start to come to do your rites the day after tomorrow. There are three baths to take."

I went like crazy back home—I didn't even request a blessing, nothing. I ran, looked, got to my backyard, picked up a knife; and when I dug that knife in, it went *tchii*, and I went, "God Almighty! This man is the dog! He hit on it."

True enough, it was the stone of José Tupinambá, a large stone, and is buried right here today. When Jose Tupinambá started to manifest in me, he consecrated this stone for me.

Pai's treatments with Zé Baião eventually led to his initiation into the Tambor de Mina, an African-derived tradition that originated in the neighboring state of Maranhão. A year later, in 1982, at the recommendation of his dying *pai-de-santo*, Pai was initiated by a *pai-de-santo* of Candomblé Nago into this, the most African in the spectrum of Afro to Brazilian traditions. At the anniversary ceremony (*obrigação*), marking his seven years of initiation, and in which he was bestowed the right to initiate his own *filhos*, Pai swore a personalized, private oath in the presence of Oxalá, his chief *orixá*, that he was going to start to educate himself in the tradition of the *orixás*. He tells of how he started to study at the feet of the masters, traveling back and forth from Belém to São Luis in Maranhão, back along the trail that the famous Maranhense, Mãe Doca, took nearly one hundred years previously to bring Afro-Brazilian religion to Belém. Now, over two decades into his mission and a great deal more knowledgeable, he was frequently pleased to inform the anthropologist at various intervals during the research period that he was still waiting for her to ask him a question to which he did not know the answer.

Pai's multitrack trajectory to the worship of the one supreme God—Deus, Tupi, Olorun, Mawu-Lissa—is reflected today in the plurality of religious traditions practiced in his *casa*. Initiation into one tradition did not require that he renounce his initiated status within other traditions. Just as he simultaneously takes the title of shaman in *pajelança*, *pai-de-santo* in Umbanda and Mina, and *babalorixá* in Candomblé, so his *casa* carries several names (e.g., *Ilè Aşè Oşóguiã e Yemónja, Vodun-Kwê de Toy Lissá*). Until recently, in *terreiro* theology and practice, the frontiers between these nations were somewhat blurred. Certainly, at the time the Leacocks carried out their fieldwork in Belém, there was little evidence or record of any procedures and criteria whereby variations in *terreiro* practice were defined and labeled. Indeed, labels were more relevant to scholars, skeptics, and laypersons outside the religious community than to the people within the Afro-Brazilian religions. Now, however, extrapolating the line that traditionally traced one's source of authentic knowledge and practice to one's initiating *pai-de-santo*, many religious leaders are now more concerned to imitate as correctly and categorically as possible the sets of practices of the early forefathers of their alleged "nation," tribe, city, and *terreiro* lineage, as defined by their respective names.

Nations, Knowledge, and Learning

Although it is unanimously claimed that *fundamentos*—purported deep knowledge, secrets, and specialized ritual and ancestral knowledge—can only be learned "mouth-to-ear" (*boca ao ouvido*) from one's *pai-de-santo*, many afro-religionists are in a better position than ever before to acquire similar knowledge from other sources. In the past, high levels of secrecy surrounded cult wisdom and knowledge. A strict and wide-ranging code of silence, accompanied by gradual, staggered revelation according to hierarchical rank, produced a rule of censorship in which the answers to almost all questions were deep, secret *fundamentos*. Nowadays, through increased publication and circulation of historical and theological records, *pais* and *mães de santo*, and their *filhos*, are freely reading what was once considered guarded, specialist knowledge. The word "fundamento" has retained a high valence in cult practice and ideology, and still strictly refers to knowledge passed orally between *pai* and *filho* in private sessions. Nevertheless, although the notion of *fundamentos*, and the hierarchical component that they entail, is central to the formal sociopolitical character of the traditions, there is no doubt that book knowledge has created a booming new economy of knowledge that has undermined the influence of senior religious leaders, pushing the purported semantic content of existing *fundamentos* into even deeper (and more dubious) obscurity. For many participants, the *pai-de-santo* has been reduced to a symbolic, figurehead role, as they find that they are becoming more educated on the cults of their ancestors than their teachers are. Where leaders could once use the notion of secret knowledge as a device both to obscure their own lack of knowledge and to withhold knowledge from aspiring usurpers, they are now expected to deliver cogent, factual, and stimulating homilies on a wide variety of themes and issues.

These changing circumstances have exerted a subtle canonizing effect on *terreiro* practices, producing ideal models of authentic practice. Labels that are now commonplace in Belém, such as Candomblé Nagô, Candomblé Ketu, Candomblé Angola, Mina-Gege, Mina-Nagô, and so on, identify *terreiros*, sets of authentic practice and *fundamentos*. The widespread classification of practices and introduction of "nation" (*nação*) labels such as these have increasingly organized the miscellaneous "mixed salad" arrangement of generic African-derived traditions and practices (Johnson 2002:186) into standardized codes of practice. Where *terreiro* leaders diverge from or add to these core ideals, they frequently defend their actions according to the perceived, overriding authenticity of the source of their information—that is, a celebrated "great" *pai/mãe-de-santo*, past or present African religious leaders, and the *orixás* through divination techniques. Indeed, the nearer to Africa one can trace or claim a line of authentic transmission and knowledge acquisition, the truer one's pedigree, and the greater one's influence in the market for *filhos*. This, of course, produces a situation in which those leaders who fail to convince people of their authenticity and knowledgeableness are at risk of losing their followers to other more highly qualified or discursively competent *mães* and *pais-de-santo*. It is in this context that Pai accentuates the importance of his *boca ao ouvido* ("mouth-to-ear") learning with the great *mães* and *pais-de-santo* of Maranhão and mentions his personal library of books on the subject as an auxiliary source of "knowledge" (*conhecimento*), not *fundamento*. Whereas book knowledge is potentially everybody's and is therefore cheap, the knowledge of the late masters of the *culto* is exclusively his, gathered at great cost and only revealed with great caution to those *filhos* who are capable (*capaz / tem condições*) of receiving it.

Who, then, is capable? Although one's age of initiation is often invoked as an indication of experience and seniority in the *culto* for the allocation of religious *cargo*, or office, and general responsibilities within the *terreiro*, it is not the only criterion upon which Pai bases his judgment of the *filhos'* "preparation" (*preparação*) or capability to share in the deep knowledge that he is assumed to possess. Subjective considerations of quality of character—according to which he decides whether a person is capable not only of receiving knowledge in the academic sense, but also of meriting it through integrity, honesty, dedication, and sense of responsibility in daily *culto* affairs—are central to Pai's decisions to impart or withhold *fundamentos*.

Casa Structure and Social Organization

Although the physical seat of Pai's influence is confined to a humble, Belenense terraced dwelling, his extended family of hundreds of *filhos* and *filhas* stretches across Brazil and the rest of the world. His long mission has brought countless people of various backgrounds, statuses, and conditions across his path. Some don't return after their first encounter and he never sees them again. Others continue to attend his counseling sessions and other public *terreiro* activities and increasingly to support his mission with their time, favors, friendship, and financial support. A portion of these responds to the demands of initiation and subsequent full-time participation in the *ritualistica* (private and communal ritual practice) of the *casa*. Many from this group have set up their own *casas*, some of whom continue to visit, while others have dropped out of religious life altogether or have converted to another religious tradition (often any of the rapidly growing Pentecostal groups, e.g., *Igreja Universal do Reino de Deus*, *Assembléia de Deus*, and so on). Still others have immigrated to other countries as distant, both geographically and culturally, as Japan, North America, and England from which they continue to receive Pai's guidance. While more and less sporadic contact continues between Pai and many of his *filhos*, he is leader, counselor, ritual specialist, and spiritual father to a core of some twenty *filhos* (sons) and *filhas* (daughters), all of whom make up a community, or family, referred to as an *ilè*. The physical nucleus of the *ilè* is the *terreiro*, or *casa*, and these terms are often used interchangeably.

Just as Pai is distinguished by his "years of initiation" and position of responsibility (*cargo*) within the *casa*, so, too, are each of the initiated *filhos* within the *ilè*. Nagô-based hierarchy governs *terreiro* practice and the division of ritual functions. Pai's *casa* maintains a simplified version of the full Nagô hierarchical model, of Bahian origin, in which the clearest distinction is between the *pai-de-santo*, or *babalorixá*, and the *filhos*. Among the *filhos*, distinctions according to *cargo* (position of responsibility and hierarchical role) fall along lines of experience, or "years of initiation," and expertise. Nagô titles are derived from Yoruba terminology. An *abiã* touches the bottom rung of the ladder, defined as someone who is not yet initiated, but who has performed a minor *obrigação* (lit. *obligation*, or *ritual*) and frequents the *terreiro* to participate in certain ceremonies and rituals. Once an *abiã* passes through the series of rituals that constitute initiation, he or she becomes an *iyawo* and takes more active involvement in the daily and ritual activities of the cult and the *terreiro*. After seven years, a further ceremony marks the initiate's designation as a senior member of the *terreiro*, an *egbome*, meaning *my older brother*. In Pai's *casa*, a similar structure exists for those initiated into the Gege tradition, the main difference being the Dahomean Ewe language from which the title-names are derived.

There is a further significant classification that is not based on seniority, but on the distinction between those members who enter possession with their *orixás* and those who don't. Those who do not have the essential quality that facilitates possession, as is categorically determined for each individual by divination methods, generally fill the *cargos* of drummers (*atabazeiros*) and other percussionists, and *ogas* and *ekedis*. Although the extent of the responsibilities placed on *ogas* and *ekedis* varies from house to house, an *oga* is invariably male and is present at rituals and other religious activities as percussionist or general assistant to the ritual leader and participants, particularly when that leader is possessed by his or her spirit entities. The *ekedi* is always female, and it falls to her also to assist persons from the moment they first become possessed in a ceremony, through the various procedures that must accompany this transformation. If required, she also leads them in their movements between the dancing area and the *runkol,* the sacred "room of the *orixás.*" *Ogas* and *ekedis* are considered hierarchically equivalent and often work as a team, with each attending to various ritualistic and practical issues that arise throughout a ceremony, or *festa.*

In Pai's *casa,* the chief *oga* was resident in the *terreiro,* and so it also fell to him to attend to a great deal of administrative and care-taking tasks. The other three live-in initiates also assumed more day-to-day responsibilities than their fellow initiates of the same title assumed. Therefore, because of their constant involvement in cult activities, their actual experience was not merely quantifiable in terms of "years of initiation" and the narrow range of responsibilities that their cargo titles stipulated. These *filhos* clearly took pride in the unofficial superior status that this hands-on expertise bestowed, but they often expressed resentment at the heavy workload and lack of independence that their position demanded.

Another of the more observable *cargos* in the organizational structure of the *terreiro* was the *pegi-ga.* This position was held by one of the most senior members of the *terreiro* and entailed responsibilities directly connected to the maintenance and care of the *runkol* and its *orixá* inhabitants. One further senior *cargo* was represented in the hierarchical structure of the *casa.* This office is filled by the second in command to the *babalorixá.* Known as the *mãe pequena,* or "little mother," she is chosen by the *pai-de-santo* to serve as his immediate assistant. This person is selected on merits of age of initiation (i.e., seniority and experience), trust, and personal affinity with the leader of the *casa.*

An informal division of labor afforded by criteria that differentiates *filhos* and even laypersons according to variable levels of cult knowledge, experience, and expertise, and the flexibility demanded of the hierarchical structure by the pragmatic realities of everyday life, cut across and confounded the formal ranking criteria of the hierarchy. As was apparently the case with many other *terreiros* across the city, this frequently generated tensions that give rise to inter- and intra-*casa* conflicts. A prime example in the context of Pai's *casa* was his uneasy relationship with some of his hierarchical superiors. Even though they commanded separate *casas,* in theory, Pai was still hierarchically subordinate to his predecessors within the lineage, or *nação.* Publicly, Pai frequently referred to certain members as accomplished ambassadors for the *culto* throughout Brazil, but it was no secret that he felt that he had outgrown their levels of religious knowledge, commitment, maturity, sincerity, didactic skill, and leadership ability many years previously. He once described his search for *fundamentos* as being similar to a marriage that loses its passion. In the analogy he casts himself as the discontented husband who is always in pursuit of something better, leaving a trail of jealous ex-lovers to bicker over their deficiencies and insecurities.

Similar tensions exist within and between members lower down the *casa* ranks. Although open conflict between *filhos* occurred very infrequently, indirect forms of aggression and informal collaboration and cooperation between *filhos* was commonplace in the hard-fought competition for recognition within and beyond the *terreiro* walls. Gossip was a ubiquitous tool, readily accessible to every member of an extended group that included *filhos*, hangers-on, residents, fellow-cultists of other *casas*, other *terreiro* leaders, and so on. The amount of energy and time spent procuring and exchanging information about the lives of others was so considerable that Pai typically equated any casual chatting, of which he was not a participant, with "talking about the lives of others" (*falando da vida dos outros*), and soon dealt out tasks to occupy the time and minds of any guilty parties. Gossip *per se* was not met with disapproval and was often joked about as an identity marker of the *povo do santo*; but when the chatting distracted Pai from his work, or distracted the gossipers from their duties, it was swiftly cut short. Information on topics ranging from love interests to financial outgoings to ritual aberrations was widely available. As Johnson writes, in the market of rival leaders, "what weighs and fixes orthodoxy are the wobbly scales of reputation, gossip and relative status" (2002: 50). Strategic gossiping afforded immediate rewards in the form of self-elevation up through an informal hierarchy of evaluation that is premised on fleeting and opportunistic trust alliances. In playing people's reputations off one another, however, one was always conscious of the possibility of becoming the target of others' malevolent desires, and the critical potential for such rivalry and conflict to wind up in sorcery (*feitiço*). Unsurprisingly, the green-eyed monster and suspected *feitiço* has brought hundreds of clients to Pai's door for consultation and curing over the fourteen years since he opened his *casa* for public solicitation.

What's in It for the Clients and *Filhos*?

Given the potential for the occurrence of such a wide range of subversive social disruptions, Pai successfully captained a tight ship. The burden to maintain his public reputation and financial solvency required all hands on deck, and all ranks dedicated to the professional execution of their respective tasks. The demands of providing for the practical needs of a full household, and of sat-isfying the exigencies of clients and the high standards of watching peers, were so difficult to meet that Pai never quite felt that he was comfortably beyond all risk of falling into disrepute and insolvency. When Pai was under particular pressure from the demands of his office, he frequently expressed his disap-pointment at the *filhos'* lack of dedication, professionalism, and competence. Despite all his best efforts to transmit some of his religious wisdom and pas-sion for the *culto* to his *filhos*, he often shook his head in despair, saying, "They are ignorant and stupid because they just don't want to learn." It was certainly apparent from the many weeks and months of participation in cult activities that the majority of Pai's following was largely uninspired by his lectures on historical tradition and philosophy. So why did they volunteer to give up their free time, independence, and even limited financial resources to join this strict regime?

Answering the question of participant motivation is a central concern of this book. In the chapters that follow I review past and current attempts to address the issue of involvement in spirit-possession cults from a number of disciplinary perspectives. Over the last century, the vast literature amassed by anthropologists, psychiatrists, neuroscientists, sociologists, historians, com-parative religionists, and scholars in other neighboring disciplines has pre-sented numerous hypotheses that claim to identify widespread factors con-tributing to the appeal of spirit-possession practices in and across cultures. Recent work within anthropology has largely turned away from generalizing, reductive interests of earlier comparative studies, rejecting explanation in favor of fine-grained descriptive and phenomenological studies of possession and its variable, situated meaning for groups and individuals within their immediate cultural milieus. Starting and ending analyses with what people say about their reasons for participating, whether that has meant abandoning functionalist and sociological frameworks of explanation and interpretation or even embrac-ing the "reality" of spirits, has led to a proliferation of analytical perspectives and approaches.

In the *ilè*, the question of participant motivation for initial involvement is consistently answered on the surface level as a deliberate response to trouble-some, negative, and detrimental life circumstances. Essentially, first-time cli-ents suspect that there is something unnatural about their sudden or unabated, unhappy state of affairs, or at least suppose that their best hope of bettering their situation, having "tried everything else," is by methods that invoke su-pernatural powers. The client visits the *pai-de-santo* to discuss the nature of the problem, and the sacred divining cowry shells are thrown to determine if in-deed there is a spiritual cause and what the subsequent plan of action should be. Reading the casts of the shells (*quedas*), Pai draws on his long experience and the knowledge and wisdom he has accumulated from various traditions to suggest the most efficacious solution. A basic ritual "obligation," or *obrigação*, such as an offering or petitioning procedure, is often the first action of a potentially prolonged series of treatments (*tratamento*) and consultations (*consulta*), depending on the clients' circumstances. All client-related activity within the *terreiro* is collectively referred to as "work" (*trabalho*) or *atendimento*, with each work session corresponding to a *serviço*. Both *clientes* and *filhos* are dependent on Pai's specialist ritual knowledge and acumen for the resolution of problems.

The wide variety of offending issues that bring clients to the *terreiro* can be condensed into three main themes: love, money, and health. According to Pai, no one arrives at his consultation desk in search of a new philosophy, or having been informed or inspired by Afro-Brazilian theology. The rituals that a client may have to perform are relatively simple, means-to-ends procedures. From the client's point of view, when positive results are not achieved, the fault often lies with the so-called ritual specialist, and a trial-and-error selection of alternative rituals and specialists may continue until there is some closure to the problem. It falls to the specialist, therefore, to convince the client that he or she commands an impressive breadth of expertise to do with diagnoses, ritual procedures, and functions, for which brief and simple exegetical commentaries can be provided on demand. When a client or *filho* commits his or her well-being to Pai and his spirit entities, he or she must submit to their every instruction. Otherwise, ritual failure—an unfavorable outcome—will be justifiably claimed to be self-inflicted. Strict adherence to the instructions of the ritual specialist should ensure ritual efficacy. All ritual practice therefore exhibits an exaggerated concern with the fine points of ritual detail. Any negative effects are not traced, for example, to a lack of inward piety or credence, but to possible infractions of the rules that determine how a ritual should be performed.

Many ritual procedures closely resemble simple, everyday technical procedures. For example, before direct participation in any religious activity— *obrigações*, preparation of food offerings, possession, and so on—each participant must take a shower in which they must cleanse their body of any impurities with a special infusion. The efficacy of the model technical action, that is, showering for bodily cleansing, provides an implicit rationale for the ritual action of showering for spiritual cleansing. In an extension of the same theme, there are also infusions for revitalization and showers for exfoliation of excess negative energies acquired "on the street." It is perhaps not surprising then that close questioning among rank and file members and clients reveals little about *why* ritual procedures must be done according to a certain formula in a particular fashion—what matters for the end purpose of participation is correct practice and not an appreciation of the underlying theoretical correlations between means and ends. Actions matter more than belief—the anthropologist must take a shower with a special cleansing infusion before participating in a ritual immolation whether she believes it to be efficacious or not. By the same token, an initiate may go through all the prescribed steps of the initiation rituals with the best intentions and still suffer ill effects, believed to be traceable to the initiator's lack of competence. A person may request that a curing ritual be performed on an absent family member or friend without the patient's knowledge. What matters is that the procedure under such circumstances is performed correctly. This is the kind of knowledge that every aspiring leader wishes to acquire fast. Ultimately, a firm grasp of ritual procedures is an integral ingredient in the recipe for prestige and therefore enlarged clientele and profitable business. This is ideally supplemented with exegetical insights and historical narrative to further enhance the marketability of one's services.

The simple, basic rationale offered, if any, for almost every *terreiro* ritual activity, or *obrigação*, generally hinges on notions of cleansing, strengthening, and protection for the remedy of most bodily, social, and spiritual ills. Clients are often advised that their condition is caused by an inner *desequilíbrio*, or imbalance, a term for which I was rarely volunteered much elaboration— potentially any complaint was generically referred to as a *desequilíbrio*. Cleans- . Cleansing, strengthening, and protection are achieved through the ritual restoration of individual equilibrium, which is in turn contingent upon the equilibrium of the wider material and immaterial world. Central to all such religious activities is the concept of *axé*, another indefinite but oft-used term. A simple survey of definitions of *axé* elicited a variety of responses even among Pai's small, close-knit community, but most notions loosely converged on the idea of *axé* as a mystical force or energy, fundamental to all existence. It is said to be manipulated through ritual *obrigações* to the *orixás*, appointed as its ultimate owners and regulators by the supreme creator-god, Olorum. Each person has a direct spiritual connection to a particular *orixá*, of whom he or she is a *filho* (son) or *filha* (daughter). Individual *axé* is mediated and liberated between the orixás and their *filhos*, guaranteeing an exchange between *orun* (supernatural existence) and *aiye* (material existence) and the restoration of equilibrium.

Somewhere between *orun* and *aiye* is another dimension in which the *mestres, caboclos,* and *encantados* dwell. Families of spirits occupy their respective territories, or *encantarias*, in an unseen world that is parallel to the material earth inhabited by humans. These are the most accessible of all the spiritual entities to participate in *terreiro* practice. *Caboclos* and *encantados* are of extremely diverse origins and are organized into families or lines. Particularly influential in Pai's *casa* are the *Juremeiros*, the *Família da Bandeira* (Family of the Flag), and the *Família da Turquia* (Family of Turkey). Families and their members are "seated" (ritually established and identified as welcome members and authorities) in the *terreiro* and in the heads of their *filhos*. Their presence is most felt when they come and possess their *filhos*. In daily work this is commonplace, and Pai often "receives" numerous spirit entities in any one day. Clients and *filhos* develop bonds with particular entities and often seek them out for consultation. Of the many spirit entities that Pai has received throughout his life, only a fraction now comes regularly. Zé Pelintra, introduced in the previous chapter, is perhaps the most directly involved in the day-to-day business of the *terreiro*. He is the principle curing entity in Pai's present mission and is the director of a formal association of *filhos* and friends of the *terreiro*, the *Associação Afro-Brasileira de Oşoguiã* (ACAOÃ). Other prominent visitors to the *terreiro* are João das Matas (*Rei da Bandeira*), Mariana, Jarina, and the child spirit, Luizinho. Perhaps these *entidades'* most striking feature is their likeness to the people with whom they interacted, manifest through their relaxed sociability and what at times almost appears to be a zest for life. Countless times I found myself on the receiving end of Seu João's trustworthy advice, Zé Pelintra's pranks and affection, and Luizinho's cuddles and childish caprices.

These and other characters reappear throughout the following chapters as I seek to describe and account for people's participation in the *culto* at a deeper level of analysis. In this book, I aim to go beyond a superficial level of explanation for acceptance, transmission, and spread of this Afro-Brazilian spirit-possession cult. This does not incur a "betrayal" of the perspective of the research participants presented above. Indeed, the questions arise from deeper consideration of the local perspectives and individual stories and the issues they leave unresolved. For example, what leads these people to suspect that their misfortune is unnatural or nonrandom? Why do they suspect that supernatural, or superhuman, beings can help them? What makes these beings such good counselors?

These questions, too, are potentially answerable via direct interviewing techniques. Participants may present the evidence that convinces them of the presence and powers of supernatural beings. However, the possibility that the spirits are in fact real is extraneous to the explanatory approach I take in this book. This is chiefly because, whether or not spirits do in fact populate the research community, the widespread tendency for people to conceive of spirits in recognizably recurrent ways across cultures and the predictability with which people invoke supernatural beings under certain specifiable circumstances (e.g., when misfortune befalls) still begs explanation.

Indigenous and sociological, psychological and functionalist, and even anti-reductionist theories may take us part of the way in accounting for people's adherence to beliefs in spiritual beings, but they are, in the end, unsatisfying. They ignore the widely accepted claim that the material properties of our evolved mental architecture constrain and shape the generation of mental phenomena and their communication between people, giving rise to recognizably distributed patterns and regularities. From the perspective of the cognitive science of culture, causal accounts of the origin, persistence, transformation, and significance of cultural phenomena must take this as their point of departure. Part of the challenge of explanation, therefore, is to identify the mental mechanisms and processes that permit transmission of spirit concepts, enabling people to represent spirits in the ways they do and mobilizing the ready acquisition of such concepts in communication. Whether or not spirit entities exist "out there" is extraneous to this task.

4

Describing, Interpreting, and Explaining Spirit Possession

As a topic of enquiry in sociocultural anthropology, spirit possession has had a long-standing, magnetizing effect on researchers. The subject matter of numerous monographs, academic symposia, edited collections, documentary films, and cross-cultural surveys, its form and incidence across the world's continents have been extensively documented (e.g., Behrend and Luig 1999; Bourguignon 1968; Lewis 1971; Mageo and Howard 1996; Prince 1968). Scores of notable ethnographers have richly portrayed the diverse contexts in which spirits, their hosts, and other social actors coexist. In this chapter I review a small portion of this work in order to introduce the reader to the many and varied contexts in which spirit possession may be found.

There are at least two further reasons for reviewing the anthropological literature on spirit possession. First, this literature provides a rich resource for cross-cultural comparison and analysis. Second, it provides instructive insights into the contrasting challenges of describing and interpreting the facts of cultural phenomena and of explaining them. Anthropologists' long-term participation in the daily life of spirit mediums, cultists, shamans, and spirit hosts around the world, and their fine-grained, ethnographic descriptions of people's social activities and meanings, are indispensable for the identification and systematic comparison of globally widespread similarities. These records of the rich diversity of human life, when assembled together, constitute a rich and comprehensive database for the identification of cross-culturally regular ideas, artifacts, and practices. Such widespread or universal regularities and patterns are the focus of those who seek to explain why certain ideas and practices become widespread across cultures.

These concerns have been increasingly sidelined and even pointedly ignored by much of the anthropological literature on spirit possession. Much of the seemingly pertinent literature has departed from such explanatory interests in favor of interpretive aims. Increasingly, one observes across anthropological scholarship on possession that descriptions of events, upon which accurate, generalizable, causal accounts depend, are frequently indistinguishable from the interpretive efforts of the ethnographer. While all representation, understanding, and description of events, situations, and interactions experienced in the field necessarily presuppose a degree of interpretation, there are few checks, if any, on the legitimacy of the anthropologist's reading of the situation against local frames of understanding. The range of possibilities that could be entertained for the interpretation of novel or ambiguous situations, statements, or actions and the anthropologist's reasons for selecting any particular one are rarely articulated.[1] Without such evidential standards at the level of description, there is no clear boundary between basic, commonsensical interpretation and overinterpretation.

Overinterpretation is characterized by a high degree of speculation, roughly gaugeable by its remoteness from what the research participants themselves are likely to articulate or demonstrate as meanings for their behaviors. Judy Rosenthal, for example, makes such fabrication central to her interpretation of West African Vodu in which she writes, "I juxtapose ... northern (European and U.S.) texts with my interpretation of Gorovodu and Mama Tchamba." She continues: "My reason for doing this is not that the northern texts explain Ewe practices ... The two very different phenomena ... can play with each other in instructive ways ... I am stretching ethnographic and philosophical-critical texts to overlap with each other ... It is a fetishizing in the sense of bringing together very different sorts of ingredients in order to make something new—in this case a new translation, a made thing" (1998: 147).

In what follows, I review the work of scholars engaged in such "translation" and in description. This serves to highlight the distinctive aims and methods of a cognitive approach to human culture and to defend these against alternative approaches. In both this chapter and chapter 5, what becomes particularly apparent is the lack of precisely formulated, testable, causal accounts of recognizably recurrent and widespread features of spirit possession that have been so lucidly described in much of the vast literature accumulated over the last century. The distinctiveness of the present approach derives from its aim to combine a body of scientific theory and evidence that can explain, in part, universal features of human behavior, with ethnographic data collected over eighteen months of fieldwork with *culto afro* participants in Belém. Insofar as the descriptions of spirit possession and possession cults from other contexts are of reliable comparative utility, they are juxtaposed with this data. The overarching aim is to present generalizable accounts of the emergence, form, and spread of recurrent, widespread features of possession phenomena.

Experiencing Possession

The first fourteen pages of Paul Stoller's *Fusion of Worlds: An Ethnography of Possession among the Songhay of Niger* (1989) are filled with continuous textual, photographic, and diagrammatic description of one of the many possession ceremonies that he took part in during fieldwork. The remainder of the book presents the reader with a window into many more aspects of Songhay social life, with the result having been repeatedly appraised as being more like cinema than literature for its evocative portrayal of spirit-possession ceremonies and their actors' stories, including the fieldworker's place in them. Vivid images are portrayed throughout this presentation of personal life histories and other events as the "horrific comedy" (ibid.: 147) of Songhay experience is almost brought to life. Attention to wider historical and politico-economic detail is not eclipsed by this focus on rich description of the here and now but adds to the portrayal and the reader's experience of the world of Songhay possession and mediumship.

Nevertheless, a lack of substantive theoretical argument and comparative analysis also characterizes this ethnography. Stoller only briefly considers the question of why spirit mediumship in Songhay persists. Despite the modernizing influences of French culture and language and the popularity of Islam that were once seen as potential threats to the survival of mediumship and possession practices, he observes that there is still a "plethora" of mediums in Songhay. "The answer," he claims, "derives from kinship. Spirits search for mediums in certain families" (1989: 80). He describes the subset of social relations in Songhay society that binds people to both kin and kin's spirits, and the families of other mediums. This, he claims, creates obligations to the spirits that are met through attendance at ceremonies and support for the possession priests, mediums, singers, and musicians. The logic of Stoller's argument is left unelaborated, but a possible implication is that just as the roles of family members are pivotal in the system of kin relations and, therefore, in general

Songhay sociopolitical morphology, the social significance of the spirits, as the foundation of an important subset of social relations, is equally perdurable. Mediumship is "in the blood," as one member of the possession troupe told him.

Stoller hints at a functional role of mediumship and spirits: "Without mediums, there is no possession troupe. Without mediums, there is no rapport between the social and spirit worlds. Without mediums, the world becomes fully susceptible to the powerful forces of nature" (1989: 79). Even a modest glance at the comparative literature on spirit possession shows that the association between direct access to supernatural forces and special powers through spirits that become physically present in mediums' bodies, and the explanation, control, and improvement of life circumstances by appealing to those powers, arises with striking frequency in accounts of possession cross-culturally. This is a pattern that I explore later (see chapter 8) and one that Stoller's descriptions of possession practices richly depicts. We shall see that the social relevance of spirits who possess people is fundamental to the widespread persistence of the concept of spirits across cultures and that this is describable at a more fundamental, generalized level according to general principles of social interaction that operate in everyday contact with all agents, including spirits, humans, and animals. In that these principles are products of adaptive mental mechanisms selected in our evolutionary past, they help explain the social significance of spirits and their human hosts.

Stoller proceeded to coedit a series of contemporary ethnographic monographs at University of Pennsylvania Press, a number of which dealt with themes relating to spirits and spirit possession. One of the authors in this series, Edith Turner, branded her contribution as "a different kind of anthropology" (1992: xi), characterized by the recognition of her own experiences of religion as constitutive of "good anthropological material" (ibid.: xiii). Although this firmly positions it within the ethos of an already widespread "movement to bring the presence of the anthropologist into the ethnographic account" (ibid.: 15), the novelty lay in making her central focus the kind of "strange event" (ibid.: 4) that other researchers allegedly glossed over or ignored.

Turner describes the event as "the spirit experience," in which she claims to have actually seen a spirit manifestation at the climax of a healing ritual during fieldwork among the Ndembu of Zambia. This experience led her to form conclusions that diverged from most African scholars seeking to explain spirit phenomena. Rather than interpret indigenous exegetical commentaries about spirit rituals within functionalist, psychological, or sociological frameworks, she claimed that the spirits were in fact real. Therefore, she argued, "the Africans were right, there *is* spirit stuff, there *is* spirit affliction, it isn't

a matter of metaphor and symbol, or even psychology" (1993: 11). Her ethnography is a record of the events, her reactions, and the reactions of others,
and the complex social milieu in which both she and the Ndembu participated,
all laid out "as in a play, complete with social process and inner meaning"
(1992: 1). Description of the events she witnessed unfolds almost continuously, punctuated by discrete commentarial paragraphs, analyses, and deeply
probing personal reflections. She draws from her familiarity with Ndembu society and from comparative literature to explore the symbolic significance or
"inner meaning" of the event that she had not only witnessed but also experienced and seen "with the eyes of the body" (ibid.: 171).

Turner's concern was about the "spirit experience" as fact. The "seeing" of
the spirit, she maintains, was not a fabrication of the brain (ibid.: 160). It was
something seen "out there," "not as projected through the mind" (ibid.: 171).
Turner's experience of seeing provides the evidential substance upon which
she bases her evaluation of scientistic approaches to the facts of spirits and
spirit possession; "[James] Dow calls it hypnotism and suggestion," she writes.
"I cannot agree with Dow because his explanation does not fit with my experience" (ibid.: 177). Yet what Turner apparently fails to appreciate is that the
processes of "seeing" that she candidly describes at length from her own experience, Ndembu ritual, and other cases of shamanistic healing and clairvoyance cross-culturally are never external to human minds but are complex
series of embodied mental events and processes. Whether or not spirits are real,
perceptions and understandings of what they are, what they do, and what they
mean are only ever located in human minds. As such, these features can be
explained in terms of the general properties of our mental architecture.

The central premise of the arguments developed and claims forwarded in
this book is that insofar as recognizably recurrent patterns of sociocultural
phenomena exist and are widely distributed, even across cultures (e.g., spirits,
possession, healing, etc.), the existence and persistence of such phenomena,
as distributions of mental events, or representations, are partly explainable in
terms of the psychological mechanisms that permit and promote their selection (Sperber 1996). As the anthropological record demonstrates, certain ideas
about spirits are considerably widespread, if not universal, across cultures.
Turner claims that it is where "people are not locked into intensive Western
medicine" that other "sensitivities" (1992: 179), such as spirit medicine, can
develop. As we shall see, however, humans have the capacity readily to entertain and develop "odd and elusive causes of disease" (ibid.) even where scientific explanations are present. Indeed, scientific and supernatural causes and
remedies are often entertained simultaneously with little or no associated dissonance or perceived inconsistency.

Turner's choice to "come out" paved the way for the publication of similarly candid, writer-centered ethnographies of religious experience and conviction. In the introduction to his book, *Some Spirits Heal, Others Only Dance* (1999), Roy Willis makes numerous references to Turner's arguments for the reality of spirit entities against personal "strange events." Then, acknowledging himself to be a significant actor in the drama to be portrayed, he introduces himself to the reader, narrating a personal life history characterized by "strange events" such as near-death experience, healing gifts, shamanic encounters, and other paranormal experiences.

Again, he privileges indigenous worldview interpretations of spirit phenomena over scientific analyses in his account. Along with many others, Willis depreciates the "Enlightenment-derived cosmology" as "a product of a particular phase in the socio-economic history of Western civilization" (1999: 115), in which everything that could not be perceived by the senses or measured by scientific instruments was construed as illusionary. He also criticizes standard sociological explanations of spirit events in terms of societal forces on the grounds that they have also "had the effect of diverting attention from the subjective content or experience of 'spirit' agency" (ibid.: 116).

Yet, he appears to credit the findings of neuropsychology as relevant when he turns his attention to his own personal experience of trance, concluding that he didn't see spirits but did experience some form of altered state similar to that of his informant doctors and initiates. He maintains, however, that of all the causal elements involved in triggering durable trance states, the decisive factor is the quality of relations between the individuals involved (ibid.: 117). Describing this quality as "intangible," Willis claims that it creates a "specific atmosphere." When "positive," this atmosphere is one in which drummers "give of their best," thereby enhancing the mind-altering effects on the participants (ibid.). He describes the mechanism as follows: "What could be called the collective will, manifesting itself through the mental and physical actions of the musicians, effects the trance-inducing neurophysical changes in the nervous systems of the participants, including, presumably, the musicians themselves" (ibid.). Plausible as it appears against anecdotal evidence from his personal experience of "mild ecstasy" (that he presumes he shared with his fellows in the field), Willis nowhere suggests a reliable methodology whereby it could be tested. He argues that the neurophysiological evidence on ritual trance necessarily requires augmentation with considerations of the social, interactive context, or, the "atmosphere." "The atmosphere," he claims, "has a decisive effect on the nature of the neurophysiological activity in the brains of group members" (ibid.: 119), invoking Victor Turner's (1969) concept of "communitas" to elucidate more clearly the social component of trance states.

But his conclusions lack any indication as to how the social element could be rendered more precise for the purposes of such theoretical integration and for the evaluation of his hypothesis. Concluding the discussion with a return to a full description of his personal experience of being in the state of communitas (i.e., "intensely aware of myself in relation to my fellows"), it is apparent that once again the road from description to systematic, comparative analysis and precisely defined and testable theory is rarely carried through.

In *The Taste of Blood: Spirit Possession in Brazilian Candomblé* (1991), James Wafer similarly turns away from reductive explanations for possession trance. His evocative account takes as its focus a small community on the outskirts of the Bahian city of Salvador. Wafer maintains that the contradictory, ambiguous, and heterogeneous nature of human social life ultimately renders social phenomena pluricausal, and irreducible to the agent-patient distinction that is central to sociological and indigenous explanations for trance activity. Following Michel Maffesoli (1996), he claims that this multiplicity of causes forbids the strict separation of theory from description.

Throughout Wafer's various accounts of everyday life in the village of Jaraci, one not only acquires an increasing appreciation of the social setting of which trance and possession formed a part, but also gains an insight into the work and process of ethnographic research against the backdrop of Candomblé cosmology, custom, and ritual. Wafer adopts a strategy that typifies the combination of thick description, indigenous voice and interpretation, and reflexivity also demonstrated by the writers mentioned above. "My own approach," he writes, "has been to create an account of trance from the perspective of 'ordinary knowledge.' This entails locating particular instances of trance within the events of daily life, and attempting to reproduce the interaction of reason and imagination in the way trance was interpreted by those involved in the events, including myself" (ibid.: 106). He does not privilege either the insider or outsider understandings of trance behavior. Both, he claims, emphasize reason and fail to take into account the fantasy factor:

> For both the adherents of Candomblé and social scientists, trance
> is capable of being explained in terms of what counts for "rationality"
> in their respective milieux. But, like any social phenomenon, trance is
> embedded in an everyday world in which reason is suffused with
> fantasy. So, an explanation of trance that simply replaced the ratio-
> nality of Candomblé with the rationality of the social sciences would
> ignore a large part of what is interesting about the phenomenon. (Ibid.)

Wafer's work—as with each of these modern classics—is characterized by comprehensive description, interpretation, and straightforward and engaging presentation. Much richly documented ethnographic work has enhanced readers' understandings of mediumship and possession as it appears cross-culturally. When the emphasis is placed on content and experience, and less attention is given to broader thematic analysis, accounts remain largely descriptive in their orientation. As we shall see more markedly below, the interpretive approach to spirit possession goes beyond description, aiming to probe the content of possession practices and beliefs and how these may relate to generic themes of local cultural significance. The many potential ways of understanding the material preclude any single authoritative interpretation. Instead, the subtle nuances of everyday life and social interaction, as observed and experienced by the ethnographer, are laid out allowing a "Fusion of the Worlds"—reader, writer, spirits, and research community meet in a ongoing process of understanding as the text is read and reread.

In all these works, scientific explanation is thus largely rejected in favor of fine-grained, detailed description and analyses of particular places, people, and events and the researcher's place in them. Both hermeneutically and descriptively oriented approaches to culture and cultures-as-texts contribute little to the development of explanatory theories regarding the form and incidence of spirit possession. In a later book, Stoller self-critically remarks on this absence of theoretical analysis in *Fusion of the Worlds*: "In that book I proposed no solution to the theoretical quandaries of possession other than to suggest that it, like surrealism, is an attack on reality, an aesthetic reaction to the inadequacies of the world" (1995: 20). Turner also writes, "my theoretical underpinnings can be seen here and there in the web of the narrative" (1992: 16); and Rosenthal tells us that she has "not written much about theory as such" (1992: 32), clearly demonstrating the secondary status of cumulative theory-building for interpretivist anthropology.

Interpretivist "Explanations"

For those who continue to hold to the conviction that it is not the "reality" of the spirits and their activities that should be the focus of our investigation, but their functional role in the social organization and symbolic structure of society, appeal to sociological categories of analysis is frequent. This is particularly so in generalizing discussions of possession as an "ideology" (see Keller 2002: 45) of resistance. For example, Jean Comaroff, in *Body of Power*, describes how the Tshidi peasant-proletariat in South Africa articulates a separatist ideology through the idiom of Zionism (1985: 218). Tracing the processes by which the Tshidi became increasingly aware of the "structures of oppression" (ibid.: 194), she notes their responses and developing resistance in this "highly coded form" (ibid.: 195), the Zionist religious movement. In Zionist ritual, focal signs and symbols that have become objects of contest are graphically manipulated and resituated in a highly coded symbolic context. Comaroff describes the Tshidi as purposive actors in these processes of reconstruction, whose "intent is to deconstruct existing syntagmatic chains, to disrupt paradigmatic associations and therefore, to undermine the very coherence of the system they contest" (ibid.: 198).

In this ritual context, "filling with the Spirit" is the climax of spiritual, social, and physical healing; "the crucial act of innovative reconstruction" (ibid.: 219); and rejection of biomedicine, doctors, and the wider system from which they come. It is in this transformative moment of possession that the dissolution of boundaries among man, woman, and spirit occurs (ibid.: 231). Comaroff interprets this dissolution as

> a more intensified form of the condition that the whole movement
> seeks to produce in its daily practice, a condition not so much born of
> a universal quest for transcendence as of a particular attempt to re-
> verse the impact of colonization; to heal the immediate sense of
> estrangement, the loss of self-determination that the Tshidi experi-
> ence in their everyday world. (Comaroff 1985: 231)

By focusing on revolution on this humble scale, Comaroff concludes, we can begin to answer more fine-grained questions about the dynamics of sociocultural transformation.

Comaroff's study reflected a growing trend away from the exclusive study and analysis of possession, to the writing of finely situated ethnographies in which possession features as part of the broader picture.[2] David Lan's *Guns and Rain*, which also appeared in 1985, documents the role of spirit mediums in the guerrilla fight for Zimbabwean independence. Unlike Comaroff in the case of the Tshidi Zionists, Zimbabwean spirit mediums and their rituals were not in themselves considered effective forms of resistance by Lan's assessment, but their role in facilitating the participation of the ancestors in the struggle was believed by the combatants to be central to the liberation victory. Lan describes how rituals provided a space within which peasants could express resistance to their present situation, not through such explicit, purposive reconstruction of the meanings of potent symbols, but by reinstating traditional rituals that had fallen into decay, thereby experiencing, "if only for an instant at a time, the good life as they imagined it had been lived in the past" (1985: 228). Lan explains the deference of the guerrillas to the spirit mediums (and, by extension, pervasive belief in ancestor protection and assistance) exclusively in terms of the political authority bestowed on them as an effect of colonialism and the promise of practical gains (e.g., access to arms).

Returning to Brazil, and to the Umbanda cults of São Paulo in particular, Fernando Brumana and Elda Martinez further consider the role of possession in subaltern expressions of religion. Brumana and Martinez claim that Umbanda has an "anti-structural style" and it "uses every opportunity to suggest that its own wisdom and power surpass the wisdom and power of the official agencies" (1989: 48). Possession cults, they add, are a particularly suggestive instrument of subaltern expression through their emphasis on the body as the location of material affliction (e.g., illness, desire, economic survival) and the incorporation, expression, and communication of a new mystic code and religious order. In the Brazilian context, these cults provide something for the popular sectors that other manifestations of subaltern life do not. It is from this perspective that Brumana and Martinez interpret the immense popularity of Umbanda. Seeking to understand why so many people embrace this religion rather than another, or none at all, they find the answer in the semantic content of religion: "A religion tells them about the world; it discovers, establishes and/ or legitimates for them a sense of that world which may or may not correspond to the common sense of society. It says more: it speaks to the devotees about themselves; it gives them a place in a world whose sense has been articulated by it" (ibid.: 16). They claim to have abandoned the mechanicism of functionalist logic that they brought with them to the field and to have acquired the explanatory categories of the people they lived with. Thus, "initial chaos" was replaced by "interpretation schemes similar to those of the agents," affording them "glimpses of order" (ibid.: 19).

In her writings on Umbanda in Rio de Janeiro, however, Diana Brown (1979, 1986) challenges the continuing conceptualization of Umbanda as an expression exclusive to subaltern sectors of Brazilian society. Her data showed an exponential increase in Umbanda followers from both lower- and middle-class sectors. Participation of the middle sectors was crucial in effecting the politically motivated transformation of Umbanda as a religious heritage of the minorities to an expression of national culture. Yet Brown continues to account for middle-class participation in instrumentalist terms, maintaining class distinctions as the point of departure in her analysis. Reflecting on the contribution of her research to the understanding of Brazilian society, she writes,

> I think that its main importance for the field of Afro-Brazilian religions lies in its identification of the influence of the middle sectors, their shaping of Umbanda ritual and ideology in conformity with their own attitudes and values, utilizing of Umbanda as a source of

political clienteles and electoral support, and strengthening of
Umbanda's structural emphasis on vertical, hierarchical patronage
relations. (Brown 1986: 205)

Although Brown takes issue with mechanistic accounts of Umbanda
growth and development in broad terms of changing regional economic and
political conditions, her approach limits investigation to the same "shaping
factors" (ibid.: 213)—that is, socioeconomic, cultural, political—albeit with
increased sensitivity to their variable influence in different contexts.

Debates on the significance of class and gender divisions have remained a
central feature of anthropological analyses of possession-cult growth and popularity. Many anthropologists continue to focus their analyses on challenging
the assumptions of the pervasive model of resistance. Dolores Shapiro, for
instance, writes, "in contrast to the analysis of spirit-possession groups in other
areas, which emphasizes social change, resistance, or status enhancement . . .
my work indicates that Brazilian groups are agents not only of resistance or
rebellion but also of accommodation and status maintenance" (1995: 828).
Similarly, Janet McIntosh's data from the Giriama people of coastal Kenya
"does not seem to fit the paradigm of resistance. On the contrary . . ." (2004:
92). In another recent article on Tamil exorcisms, Isabelle Nabokov casts doubt
on the "widespread explanation that a major function of Hindu 'ghosts' . . . is to
express women's dissatisfaction with husbands, in-laws or female roles" (1997:
298), concluding that "it is hard to say what is fully or finally liberating for
women about Tamil exorcisms" (ibid.: 312). Jennifer Nourse questions the underlying assumptions regarding medium-agency, and asks, "What are the implications of regarding the spirits as the mediums do, of taking the loss of
human will seriously, and of believing that the spirit is the agent or force
speaking through the voice of the medium?" (1996: 425). Mary Keller also
maintains that "to remain within the parameters of the victim-agent dichot-
omy is to equate agency with an individual subject, which misses or dismisses
the radical agency of a person who has been overcome by an external agency"
(2002: 46). Keller, recognizing that she cannot make claims to knowledge of
the ancestors, deities, and spirits, focuses on the possessed body as doing work
instrumentally, coining the term *instrumental agency* to designate a "discursive
space in which the power of the possessing agencies is not explained away as
belief, idiom, guise, or psychosis" (ibid.: 75). Rather than elide the presence and
agency of the possessing deities and spirits, the concept of instrumental agency
emphasizes the "doubleness" of the possessed body (ibid.).

Keller's discussion of agency draws attention to its place as a concept underlying important assumptions upon which many sociological perspectives

are premised. Intentional agency is central to instrumentalist accounts of possession-cult participation and to the classic functionalist strategies that preceded them. The turn against master narratives was in effect a turn *en masse* toward interpretive trends that analyzed possession as an idiom for opposition. McIntosh comments, "The problem, then, is how to reconcile the current turn against so-called master narratives with the assumptions about resistance which seem to underpin so much of this work on possession" (2004: 92). While these sociological readings have increasingly merged with more symbolic interpretations (e.g., Maggie 2001), the theme of possession as a response to power, and therefore of agency, has remained dominant for the last three decades. Such accounts frequently present possession cults as institutions engendered or shaped by changing socioeconomic and political forces. Within anthropological scholarship, psychological and medical perspectives on possessed people[3] as passive patients have been replaced by situated analyses of intentional agencies—individual and collective—engaged in meaningful social action.

Nevertheless, in this approach, an implicit language of explanation is often apparent. Scholars arbitrarily select mechanisms and factors that they claim contribute to the transmission and persistence of spirit possession as it appears in specific contexts. Starting with this context, they generalize their accounts to all comparative contexts that appear to provide confirming evidence, producing highly speculative, interpretive generalizations (see Sperber 1996). Lambek, for example, couches his claims regarding the form and incidence of possession trance in the language of explanation. His argument, however, accompanies the widespread abandonment of true explanatory theorizing, replacing it with a different set of challenges that accompanies the tasks of description and "understanding," or interpretation.

Explaining Culture

In a paper entitled *From Disease to Discourse* (1989), Lambek criticizes naturalizing approaches to possession trance, arguing that "the institutionalized appearance of trance—its form, meaning, incidence, etc.—is cultural . . . [T]he appearance of trance is mediated by the cultural model, by its social reality; the collective representations of trance precede its incidence" (1989: 38). He affirms that "it is this social reality of trance in which most cross-cultural investigators are interested" (ibid.). Hence, it is the variability and complexity of cultural phenomena that should be given central place in our comparative investigations. Since these "interesting" aspects are constrained by variable and complex cultural models, there is little reason to investigate factors outside of these models. "In cultural matters," Lambek writes, "the lowest common denominator cannot tell us very much" (ibid.: 37). Lambek's line of reasoning has been used to warn against the careless imposition of interpretive categories upon trance behavior, such as pathology as a diagnosis for possession-trance phenomena, and the futile application of monothetic definitions of spirit possession to a category of wide-ranging and diverse phenomena. Nevertheless, the reasoning by which he seeks to demonstrate a lack of fit between decontextualized, theoretical categories and the diverse phenomena encountered on the ground contains some over-hasty assumptions that stand in the way of truly explanatory projects.

In their critique of what they call the standard social science model (SSSM), John Tooby and Leda Cosmides lay bare the faulty logic upon which the dogmas of relativity and particularism are based. In what sounds like an echo of Lambek's understanding of culture, they write:

> If the psyche is general-purpose, then all organized content comes from the outside, from culture. Therefore if something is contentful, then it must be cultural—it is plastically variable; if it is plastically variable, then there can be no firm general laws about it. Ergo, there can be no general principles about the content of human life (only the contentless laws of learning). (Tooby and Cosmides 1992: 42)

In this view, again as Lambek explicitly instructed, the emphasis of the anthropological contribution to the social sciences should be on careful and close description of human variability. Not only would this serve to "disprove" theories premised on patterns and regularities, but also understandings of the practices of distinct and unique communities would alone provide the material for the generation of particularistic accounts of the variable incidence, form, and meaning of sociocultural behavior. Such "accounts," however, account for very little. Often using the language of explanation, they misrepresent the meaning of a behavior, tradition, event, and so on, as its cause. Yet, even where a particular practice could be shown to hold broadly similar meanings across a population, it is not with reference to these recognizably recurrent meanings that its incidence is explained. As Dan Sperber writes, "A meaning is not a cause; and the attribution of a meaning is not a causal explanation" (1996: 43). The meaning is simply one more feature of the phenomenon that needs to be explained.

Faithful to Tooby et al.'s description of the collective approach embodied in the standard social science model, Lambek frequently contrasts the "cultural" and the "social" on the one hand, with the "natural" and the "biological" on the other hand. For Lambek, culture is infinitely complex (1989: 47), is something that constrains and shapes human activity and experience (ibid.: 40), and is primarily collective and social (ibid.: 38). Taking trance to be "fully human" (and therefore cultural) (ibid.: 47), according to these criteria, he claims to avoid reductive, naturalizing theories that ignore variability. But as Tooby, et al. observe of this approach, "it leads anthropologists to actively reject conceptual frameworks that identify meaningful dimensions of cross-cultural uniformity in favor of alternative vantage points from which cultures appear maximally differentiated. Distinctions can be easily found and endlessly multiplied..." (1992: 44). It seems that many anthropologists are content to make endless documentation of these distinctions the focus and endpoint of their ethnographic contribution. Ultimately, however, clear, candid, descriptive, and rich ethnographic scholarship can potentially provide high-quality data for the construction of empirically grounded, generalizable hypotheses about the recurring, cross-cultural features of spirit possession. It is to past and continuing endeavors to investigate the causes of these recurrences and regularities that I turn in the following chapter.

While I agree with Lambek that "it is our conceptualization of the relationship between human thought and practice and human experience that must serve as a guide for how we view trance and possession" (1989: 40–41), I believe that this conceptualization is not only to be articulated and investigated through a consideration of sociocultural and historical details, but also through the cognitive and neural mechanisms employed in any possession-trance episode. The "social reality" of trance and possession is fundamentally a psychological reality—for our research participants, possession and trance are mentally represented (and interpreted, understood, passed on, and so on) according to universal principles of cognition. By paying attention to what is known about cognitive processes activated in the representation and the flow of ideas, beliefs and behaviors between individuals, we can begin to explain recurring features of their organization on the ground. Let us briefly consider the methodological implications of such a research program.

How Do We Know What Is Interesting?

What matters to scientific theories is not that they describe and explain every feature of a given phenomenon, but that the specific factors that are predicted to be causally significant to the aspects of the phenomenon being investigated can be empirically evaluated and that what counts as counterevidence to the claims advanced is clearly specified (Popper 1959). According to this rule, claims can only be considered propositional if it is possible to conceive of evidence that would prove them false (Lett 1997: 107). The data relevant to the testing of the propositions are therefore the *interesting* data, to use Wafer's term. This guides us as we look at the descriptive content of historical and ethnographic data and accounts, providing a clear idea of what counts as relevant information and what is superfluous to our hypotheses' claims (though perhaps "interesting" on other levels). Hence, we can adopt a cumulative approach to the construction of reliable knowledge and valid theory.

This contrasts alarmingly with the dominant agenda of anthropological scholarship, in which the sole mandate of epistemological relativism produces a situation in which anything goes, provided that it is suitably presented. Satisfactory ethnographic presentation may now privilege ambiguity over precision, erudition over substance, overdramatic vivification over faithful narration, and obscurity over clarity. Extreme critical originality is valued over the incremental construction of increasingly precise and penetrative theoretical hypotheses. This is reflected in anthropologists' highlighting of the particularistic distinctions in their field locations, which, if considered against a body of theory, are often presented as yet one more instance of the indefinite variability of human behavior and the futility of comparative generalizations. Tooby, et al. compare the situation to some nightmarish story in which "scientists are condemned by their unexamined assumptions to study the nature of mirrors only by cataloguing and investigating everything that mirrors can reflect" (1992: 42). The story drags on, becoming "an endless process that never makes progress, that never reaches closure, that generates endless debate between those who have seen different reflected images, and whose enduring product is voluminous descriptions of particular phenomena" (ibid.).

For others, the situation is further removed from the ideals of valid explanatory theory, sound ontology, and even solid description, not only because of overinterpretation of ethnographic material presented, but through an exaggerated appeal to shifting stylistic fashions. Harvey Whitehouse, who shares Tooby et al.'s objection to the supremacy of the hermeneutic agenda, writes, "We need approaches that are willing to salvage old materials, where appropriate, and that are based on wide cooperation among neighbouring building projects rather than on the kind of competitive aesthetics popular in many humanities disciplines today, which so often privileges critical originality over theoretical precision and empirical productivity" (Whitehouse 2004: 173).

On the one hand, good stories, evocative images, and fluent discourse surely make for effective prose, but may hide a lack of theoretical substance. On the other hand, deliberately obscure rhetorical techniques employed in the production of some ethnographic analyses can hide a lack of ethnographic evidence. Such methods are incongruous with the precise and determinate evidential standards demanded by scientific explanatory strategies.

The antiscientific premises and praxis of overindulgent interpretivism[4] are incommensurate with an anthropology that seeks scientifically to study human nature and social life. Nevertheless, nonscientific and antiscientific ethnographic research has generated vast amounts of data and innumerable tentative conclusions on the diversity of human social existence across the world for over a century. Many of these data are of indeterminate quality due to the lack of direction and systematicity in their collection and the journalistic, unrepresentative, and piecemeal manner in which they are presented. Theoretical constructs are frequently untestable and are therefore of negligible or unknowable value. Some work, however, can be salvaged, augmented with findings and records from other social research disciplines, and appropriated for use in the construction of far-reaching hypotheses with increasingly greater explanatory power. Whitehouse encourages us to regard the appreciation for empirical enquiry that continues to exist in most ethnographic research, even where the agenda necessarily imposes a very slippery conception of reality:[5] "Even the methodological sloppiness of interpretivism and, more generally, of the postmodern autocritique have not managed to destroy the traditional empiricism of much ethnographic enquiry. To dismiss all the findings of anthropologists simply because of the vagueness or pretentious obfuscation of some scholars (some of the time) would be an overreaction" (Whitehouse 2004: 25). So, by what standards can we judge materials to be not only relevant or *interesting*, but also valid?

The high degree of theoretical precision and evidential accountability in natural and social scientific inquiry is achieved by heeding some common principles in the organization and classification of knowledge acquired. Principally, knowledge is judged to be reliable on the basis of a set of guidelines known as scientific objectivity. As James Lett clearly spells out, this implies "first, that the truth or falsity of a given factual claim is independent of the claimant's hopes, fears, desires, or goals; and second, that no two conflicting accounts of a given phenomenon can both be correct" (1997: 105). He further explicates these guidelines in the light of common misconceptions from opponents of scientific methods, observing that the claim to objectivity is not equivalent to the positivistic claim to absolute certainty:

> Scientific objectivity does not deny that perception is a process of active interpretation rather than passive reception, nor does it deny that the acquisition of reliable knowledge is a highly problematic undertaking. Instead, scientific objectivity merely denies that all

claims to knowledge are equally valid, and it provides a set of standards by which to evaluate competing claims. (Lett 1997: 106).

The scientific method, therefore, articulates a set of procedures by which we can evaluate evidence relevant to any propositional statement. Objectivity simply demands that knowledge or evidence acquired can be submitted to tests of public verifiability that could be performed by others. The truth or falsity of any proposition must therefore be testable against empirical reality in a systematic, replicable, and nonpartisan way. This does not deny the existence of nonempirical reality (reality that is not amenable to the five senses) but requires that as long as our data collection procedures allow us to present only empirical facts in a publicly ascertainable way, nonempirical data (gained through faith, inspiration, revelation, etc.) cannot be incorporated into the scientific method (ibid.). Scientific objectivity, in this sense, when applied to the methodology of participant observation, denies neither the human, personal side of social research nor the presence of researchers' cultural background in interpreting the "reality" they perceive. Richard Feynman once put it as follows:

> If a thing is not scientific, if it cannot be subjected to the test of observation, this does not mean that it is dead or wrong or stupid. We are not trying to argue that science is somehow good and other things are somehow not good. Scientists take all those things that *can* be analyzed by observation, and thus the things called science are found out. But there are some things left out, for which the method does not work. (1998: 16–17)

Few ethnographers accept the idea of a single objective reality. This is not at odds, however, with scientific principles, and, as Feynman explains, such doubt is essential to the progression of precise, explanatory reasoning:

> It is of paramount importance, in order to make progress, that we recognize this ignorance and this doubt. Because we have the doubt, we then propose looking in new directions for new ideas. . . . If we were not able or did not desire to look in any new direction, if we did not have a doubt or recognize ignorance, we would not get any new ideas. . . . What we call scientific knowledge today is a body of statements of varying degrees of certainty. Some of them are most unsure; some of them are nearly sure; but none is absolutely certain. (1998: 27)

Ethnographers and scientists deal with this philosophy of uncertainty in very different ways. Whereas in science, doubt remains something to be welcomed and incorporated into truly progressive and cumulative empirical frameworks, many hermeneutically oriented ethnographers award uncertainty such high status that all scientific aspirations should be abandoned. However, in excising claims to a single objective reality, those skeptical of the verisimilitude of science and its methods have proposed little by way of plausible alternatives that match its evidential standards—and the resultant progression and accumulation of knowledge.

One widely held view within the relativist, phenomenological perspective is that in order to acquire knowledge of the categories and rules by which native informants organize and interpret their world, the observer must share in their lived experience. Supporting this idea is the assumption that, through participation in similar actions, one's own subjective experiences are similar to others'; and hence the participant observer's motivations, goals, and intentions are analogous to native thought strategies. For example, Jeanne Favret-Saada claims that in order to understand the meaning of witchcraft experiences and discourse, she had to practice it herself, thereby becoming her own informant (1980: 22). Ethnographic authority therefore pertains to both the observer and the observed, and consensus among both parties is the closest one can get to "understanding" the people. The test of adequacy of one's data and understanding is to produce an account that the native informant accepts as real and meaningful. For many anthropologists, such insight does not inspire the generation of generalizable, explanatory hypotheses, but only permits that theories reflect the "system of intelligibility" (Silverman 1975: 77) of the communities being studied. However, by ignoring the explanatory potential and even the existence of causes that fall outside the actor's meaning and purpose in everyday lived experience, this approach harbors grave risks for misrepresenting the causes of sociocultural behavior.

It is helpful to revisit the original concepts of "emic" and "etic" when considering these distinctions drawn between the native as insider and the anthropologist as alien observer. Noting the many divergent meanings ascribed to these terms since they were originally coined by Kenneth Pike, Francisco Gil-White (2001) returns our attention to the value of their original conceptualization. Gil-White argues that the Pikean concern was not an insider/outsider or native/scientist distinction. This is a misrepresentation of the original conceptualization of the distinction that has led to erroneous and prejudicial claims both to the special epistemic status of outsider knowledge, on one hand, and for the doomed inevitability, on the other hand, for cultural facts to be misconstrued at their very perception by the outsider. Rather, Pike used the terms "to distinguish the variation in any given domain—*etic* phenomena—that are parsed by people in a given culture into the same categorical slot—or *emic* unit"

(Gil-White 2001: 239). Therefore, within the category capable of being glossed as "possession," as in all cultural domains, there may be many different kinds of events and experiences that are lumped together. The boundaries of the *emic* category can be determined by the *etic* variation—the objects, events, people, interactions, performances, and so on—that it encloses. Where the insider/ outsider distinction becomes relevant is that often natives, as insiders, may not be aware of or able to explain their own categorization processes. The outsider, Pike observes, may often find these category systems strange, demanding an explanation. Gil-White observes, for instance, that just as Japanese speakers of English include the sounds 'l' and 'r' in the same phonemic category (sound group), similarly "one should expect that people from different cultures will often parse the world of objects, events and performances in different ways that will surprise and confound the ethnographer" (ibid.: 240). Recognizing the potential for our analyses to be flawed when we superimpose our own categories on the cultures we observe, anthropologists endeavor to learn the culture in a similar way that children do—by observation, participation, and imitation.

But it is important to remember here that divergence between insider/ outsider *emic* categorization schemas is not automatic or inevitable. Insofar as people have broadly similar experiences of the world around them, mediated by the highly structured, species-typical, information-processing mechanisms of the mind, *emic* schemas are consistently more likely to display high degrees of similarity, even across cultures. The mental mechanisms that inform and constrain processes of perception, learning, knowledge, and procedural competence do not comprise a contentless, general-purpose, information-processing machine. There is now extensive evidence from the field of developmental psychology that even the infant's mind is not a blank slate upon which "culture" is inscribed (e.g., Gopnik, et al. 2001). All learning and mental processing from birth through to adulthood is contingent on the highly specialized operations of our evolved mental architecture and its universal development schedules. Much of this architecture emerges naturally, giving rise to panhuman "understandings" of the world of objects and people (e.g., distinguishing between inanimate and animate objects, functional and nonfunctional properties of tools, etc.) without any need for explicit instruction. Some of these abilities emerge at a very early age. For example, from as young as ten weeks, infants have a concept of objects as bounded and moving as a unit by which the infants may infer fundamental principles of physical causality, e.g., two solid, physical objects cannot occupy the same space simultaneously (Spelke 1988, 1990, 1991).

Such discoveries show that the way we parse the world around us is not exclusively or primarily informed by the *emic* units of culture. All perception, learning, interpretation, representation, and evaluation is constrained by the universal properties of the evolved human mind. From the perspective of the cognitive science of culture, a scientific approach is not satisfied with the discovery of *emic* truths alone, by which people categorize and make sense of their surroundings. The *etic* details of who, when, where, and what of different kinds of events, objects, and performances may disclose comparable patterns and trends amenable to causal investigation of universal value. The explanatory power of resultant taxonomic categories and methods of parsing the world of sociocultural action cannot be denied or simply dismissed as alien and insensitive.

Conclusion

Explanation is necessarily achieved by understanding a complex thing in terms of its parts and the interactions between those parts. Endless interpretation and reinterpretation of the thing may produce interesting stories about the *emic* structures of other people's worlds, how they may perceive, appreciate, and understand that thing, much as endless discussion of the beauty of a flower could give rise to many and varied narratives. But such pursuits are insufficient for—some would say irrelevant to—scientific explanation. Continuing the analogy, it is only when we look at the constellation of the features that comprise the flower that we can then *explain* color, texture, smell, growth processes, and so on. Explanatory hypotheses are evaluated not by their faithfulness to *emic* categories alone, but by their ability to identify generalizable, causally significant features in the etic details of the phenomena that we seek to understand. Although it may suit the agenda of some approaches to ignore the presence of universal components in sociocultural systems in their particularistic accounts and interpretations of field events, it is against such observations that scientific ideas, or predictions, are generated. Let us turn to some theorists' attempts to generate causal accounts of particular aspects of spirit-possession phenomena.

5

Medicalist, Physiological, and Sociological Explanations

To follow a review of descriptive and interpretivist literature on spirit possession with a chapter on explanatory accounts is to reverse, as it were, the developmental course of scholarly analysis of the subject. As with anthropological scholarship on many other domains of culture, grand master narratives and explanatory theses invariably gave way to context-sensitive, particularistic descriptions of complex, variable phenomena. By defending the importance of explanatory over interpretive approaches, I am not advocating a simple return to the past, however. As will become apparent, early attempts to describe and explain possession-related phenomena were fraught with difficulties. These included imprecise concepts, overemphasis on spurious behavioral and biological factors, and varieties of functionalist analysis that confused effects with causes. Yet, by recognizing the concerns, strengths, and weaknesses of early accounts, and by paying attention to relevant knowledge from recent and contemporary scientific research, it is possible to make considerable progress toward explaining the forms and incidence of spirit possession.

Medicalist Accounts of Possession

The challenge for anthropologists seeking to *explain* spirit possession has been to map out the key points of intersection between possession phenomena and other cultural and biological domains. Early explanations for possession behavior focused primarily on its hysteria-like qualities (e.g., seizure, motor and sensory disabilities, disturbed mental states).[1] Trance was best explained in clinical terms as a form of psychopathology, and the point of intersection between possession trance and psychopathological illness was therefore believed to be the crucial one for explaining its incidence.

In 1930, the English translation of T. K. Oesterreich's work on possession was published, bearing the title *Possession, Demoniacal and Other, among Primitive Races, in Antiquity, the Middle Ages, and Modern Times*. Oesterreich's conclusions are illustrative of the unilineal evolutionist bias that was standard in many early interpretations of spirit-possession phenomena. This permitted him to carry a section on possession in the "higher civilizations" as distinct from the "primitive races," though those included in the former category were largely considered to be on the same level as the "primitives" anyway: "the psychic state of the lower strata of the population [*of higher civilizations*] amongst which possession generally manifests itself is not essentially higher than that of the primitive world" (1930: 145).

Oesterreich describes most cases that have been identified as possession as "no more than physical maladies, considered . . . by primitive peoples as due to the entry of a demon into a human body" (ibid.: 131). This interpretation is largely explainable from the standpoint of what he calls religious and racial psychology (ibid.). Describing primitive personality as unstable and easily overcome by autosuggestion, "which never exercises the same influence on civilized man" (ibid.: 241), he accounts for the disappearance of possession beliefs as owing to the loss of belief in the spirits (in turn, a "fruit" of the "Age of Enlightenment" [ibid.: 76]). Therefore, "from the moment they cease to entertain seriously the possibility of being possessed, the necessary autosuggestion is lacking" (ibid.: 378).

The fundamental assumptions of Oesterreich's account, many of which were shared with contemporaneous theories about cultural evolutionary progression, have long since been repudiated and discarded by all scholarship on human social life. The explanatory power suggested by terms such as *racial psychology* was scientifically unfounded. Alleged variation in psychological makeup could not be reduced to categories of race. Primitiveness, categorically defined according to the unilineal evolutionary assumptions inherent in the prevalent theories, is not a determinant of mental instability. Other terms, such as "autosuggestion," "primitive personality," and "civilized man" lacked precision. "Necessary" degrees of autosuggestion and civilization were therefore nonquantifiable. Nevertheless, medicalist aspects of the theory's claims were not wholly discarded by subsequent approaches to possession.

The relationship between possession trance and psychiatric health remained a major focus of academic interest. A trend emerged toward the development of specialist areas of expertise along traditional disciplinary divides. While anthropologists continued to add to a growing body of ethnographic description on the subject, they relied largely on the insights of psychiatrists for characterization, classification, and identification of the underlying psychological causes of trance behavior. Colleen Ward, one of the foremost writers on altered states of consciousness (ASC) and mental health, describes the division of labor between the two camps: "For psychiatrists the focal concern has been mental health and illness, with ASCs either contributing to or detracting from psychological well-being. For anthropologists, a primary objective has been the collection of rich ethnographic data, of which ASCs may be a part" (1989: 24).

Universal features identified in the wide range of spirit-related experiences documented by anthropologists were potentially definable in terms of recognized psychobiological idioms and categories. As records of these experiences identified clear-cut patterns and the precise elements that defined and differentiated them, parallel psychological and neuroscientific discoveries within the field of pathology studies were contributing to the development of a refined system of categorization by which such groups of "family resemblances" could be labeled. Details of "visitor experiences" (characterized by such behavioral and perceptual alterations as a sense of presence, swirling or vortical sensations, internal vibrations, floating sensations, detection of auras and glows around the edges of objects, profound meaningfulness, subsequent depression, etc.) were attributable to temporal lobe processes (Persinger 1989).[2] Creeds about gods and possession, it was argued, are "brought into being by playing on emotional arousal, increased suggestibility and abnormal phases of brain activity" that accompany "hypnoid" states (Sargant 1973: 198). Widespread auditory, visual, and kinetic experiences both at the onset of sleep and on waking up, in which reports commonly described feelings of the presence of other beings in the room, were diagnosable as hypnagogic and hypnopompic[3] hallucinations respectively (Ohayan, et al. 1996). Temporal lobe epilepsy, it was claimed, correlated with sudden religious conversion (Dewhurst and Beard 1970); catatonia with creative, religious interpretation (Fischer 1971);[4] and hysteria and hypnosis with hallucinatory and dissociative states (see Neher 1962: 157). Broad varieties of mediumship, trance, ecstasy, and religious and mystical experiences were thus comprehended within taxonomic systems that parsed the varieties of human experience and personality according to the definitional criteria of psychiatric categories.

Certain antagonistic differences of disciplinary emphasis, however, eventually put considerable strain on this arrangement. Anthropologists' analyses

emphasized the definitional problems inherent in comparative projects, leading them to question the validity of identified "causes." To what degree were
the western standards of normalcy capable of being more widely applied?
Could these standards be used to produce generalizable theories of possession trance incidence? Should the numerous "disorders" witnessed, in all
their unusual and varied forms, be classified according to standard psychiatric classification systems alone?

It was some time before psychiatric literature paid heed to anthropologists'
reservations. Ward contrasts Ronald Simons's (1985) conclusions from a
medicalist perspective with Anthony Colson's (1971) ethnographic data in the
case of *latah*, a temporary dissociative state frequently found among Malay
women. While Colson's data showed that *latah* behavior was considered unusual but harmless and "correct," Simons characterized it according to standard hysteria terminology. Another example given is Julian Silverman's (1979)
analysis of shamans, who are described as "instrumental medicine men who
communicate directly with the spirits who exhibit the most blatant forms of
psychotic-like behavior" (1971: 120). Ward continues, "Although Silverman
notes the prestige accorded to the shamans in their indigenous environments,
he regards their ceremonial ASC's as hysterical and argues that the route to
shamanism parallels that of acute schizophrenia" (1989: 25).

The growing body of ethnographic data increasingly confirmed doubts
about the assumption that the unusual states under investigation were intrin-
sically pathological. Surveys of the extent of ASC activities (Bourguignon 1973)
and investigations of indigenous defining criteria for mental illness reported
significant statistical evidence to the contrary (Edgerton 1966; Westernmeyer
and Wintrob 1979). Ward lists a number of psychiatric analyses from the late
seventies and eighties that reflect these findings and commends analyses that
recognized the importance of sensitivity to cultural meaning and context.
Characterized by a rejection of pathological labels and a shift of attention to
potential therapeutic aspects of ASCs, studies such as these widened the scope
for explanation of individual participation in trance activities to include
neurophysiological, psychological, and sociocultural factors.

The transition from medicalist to context-sensitive and sociological perspectives on possession, however, was marked by a lingering attachment to
definitions of possession as mental illness. Dichotomous models continued to
use "abnormal" and "pathological" as labels for some possession-cult participants, describing other participants as normal and nonpathological. Perhaps the most influential example of this is Lewis's cross-cultural study (1971),
in which he proposed the classification of possession cults according to a
"central"/"peripheral" taxonomy. Boddy observes,

Lewis's cross-cultural account lent sociological support to the medical tack by distinguishing central possession cults, where possession is a positive experience involving spirits who uphold the moral order (ancestors, culture heroes) and typically speak through men, from peripheral ones, where possession by amoral spirits is locally regarded as a form of illness that typically affects women and other individuals of marginal or subordinate status. (Boddy 1994:410)

Lewis's classification of demonic and undesirable possession as instances of peripheral cult behavior supposedly differentiated pathological cases of possession from the nonpathological, now that a method of parsing the two was deemed necessary for meaningful comparison (see Klass 2003). Felicitas Goodman reiterates some aspects of the model's distinction almost two decades later. She classifies "institutionalized trance," or "religious trance," as normal (1988: 38). This is on account of it being "a *ritualized action*, capable of being called forth and terminated on a given cue or signal" (ibid.). When brain disease and biochemical disturbances are manifested in losses of consciousness, hallucinations, and convulsions, this, she claimed, can be defined as an illness.

To relate uncontrolled behavior to a lack of institutionalization and even illness led to further definitional problems, however. As Klass argued, there could be no room for pronouncements of "illness" in the two modes if they were to retain widespread relevance and consistent analytic value:

As Lewis notes, the anthropological literature is replete with accounts of religious leaders (particularly the ones usually labeled *shamans*) who customarily enter into their profession by first experiencing seemingly "uncontrolled" and "undesirable" altered states of consciousness. It is clear that Lewis believes that such an occurrence of "unsolicited" or "demoniacal" possession, even when found in societies in which there is belief in such things, still implies the presence of mental disorder of some kind. But then, he points out . . . the "unsolicited" possession may somehow become transformed into "solicited" or "ecstatic" possession, something that in Lewis's view does not reflect *any* degree of mental disorder! (Klass 2003: 65)

Klass criticizes Lewis's failure to reveal the path by which a state of mental disorder becomes a state of mental health, and the ambiguity that surrounds his definition of illness.[5] Attempting to avoid the ambiguities and inconsistencies of Lewis's model, he re-parses the whole domain of what he has termed "Dissociative Identity Phenomena" (2003). He distinguishes two

categories of behavior that fall within this domain: "Dissociative Identity Disorder" (DID) and "Patterned Dissociative Identity" (PDI) (ibid.: 119). In DID,
individuals assume alter identities that are highly idiosyncratic and varied
against their will. In PDI, the alter identities are familiar entities within a
society's belief system and act in recognized ways.

Arguably, this method of categorization avoids some of the ambiguities
and inconsistencies apparent in Lewis's account. But these may potentially be
more accurately clarified and corrected through reference to recent discoveries
and hypotheses in neuropsychology and behavioral psychology. Dissociative
phenomena cover a broad continuum of symptoms, from common, temporary
disruptions in memory and consciousness through to conditions, such as DID,
in which an individual appears to have more than one identity. This suggests
that the conditions defined as "normal" and "pathological" may be better understood as occupying a place on a continuum of disruptions in consciousness,
from those that are rare and fleeting through to more frequent, intense, and long-
lasting discontinuities of memory and identity. Dissociative Identity Phenomena, at the more intense end of the scale, may result from minor tweaking of
the normal psychological mechanisms that enable people to behave in different
ways depending on the social context and circumstances (e.g., quiet in a library,
boisterous at a party). This "tweaking" may be caused by situational (e.g., emotional) factors, such as stress (see Hacking 1995; Ross, Joshi, and Currie 1990;
Spanos 1994, 1996; and Speigel 1994). That all humans have the capacity to
experience disruptions in consciousness, and that the intensity of such disruptions increases according to certain external conditions and situational factors,
suggests that the distinction between normal and abnormal, where it need be
applied, may be more usefully understood as a describer of the episode, not of
the individual (as Klass's criticism suggests) nor of the cult (as Lewis claimed).

Parting with "Pathology"

Psychological hypotheses can build upon scientific investigation into the universal biological mechanisms that underlie consciousness and permit trance
behavior. The classification of the behavioral outputs of certain kinds of neurological activities as "disorders" or "abnormalities" is useful for some disciplines and professional practices. Psychiatrists have employed the data for the
definition of pathologies and the development of treatments. Anthropologists,
in turn, have traditionally received and appropriated it via the interpretive filter
of psychiatric analysis. These psychiatric characterizations, however, are of
limited comparative and explanatory utility to anthropologists seeking to explain the incidence and form of possession trance. The explanatory aims of

anthropologists may be better informed through a clearer, unmediated appreciation of the scientific findings.

Anthropologists objected to the "explanation" of possession-trance phenomena in terms of standard psychiatric systems of classification chiefly due to their categorical diagnosis of the phenomena as a "disorder." Possession-trance phenomena were considerably widespread, if not universal, and this cast doubt on allegations of participants' abnormality. Also, these so-called mentally ill individuals were often highly respected leaders, counselors and physicians in their own societies. Western claims regarding their abnormality, therefore, implicated whole populations who entrusted their well-being and even their lives to these people. Furthermore, as Lambek argued most clearly, typologies of ASC-related experience and phenomena could not provide a causal account for cross-culturally recurrent spirit-possession beliefs. Possession was not an epiphenomenon of trance, nor was it secondary or reducible to trance.

Nevertheless, while possession trance is not wholly reducible to the neurophysiological dimensions of trance states, such descriptions remain "interesting" for the investigation of certain features that are integral to the whole phenomenon. Questions, for example, surrounding the conscious awareness of the participants, recall for trance episodes, temporal lobe activity, and so on, are of value to understanding aspects of motivation, intention, and meaning for any possession-trance participant. Recent technological advances have increased our knowledge of the neurological processes that underpin consciousness and behavior. As we will observe below, evidence from neuroscience and biology may be employed in the generation of hypotheses that are relevant to research problems in the study of culture.

What matters to those seeking to describe the mechanisms responsible for a particular behavior is not the (often ambiguous, subjective, and multivalent) name tag attached to that behavior, for example, "trance" or "mental illness." These are convenient labels, or interpretations, for complex neurological processes that produce fundamentally similar behavioral outputs across populations. These behaviors may be awarded different interpretations in Belém than in Belfast. But an explanation of the behavior is achieved by identifying its *causes*–biological and otherwise. Interpretations, whether local, medicalist, sociological, or psychoanalytical, neither reveal causes nor constitute explanations. Recognizing the misconceptions that lurk in the conflation of biological processes with their exegeses, anthropologists and others seeking to describe, compare, and explain human behavior must exercise caution when employing interpretive labels such as "illness" and "pathology."

As noted above, a second objection to biologically reductionist explanations was raised. What many anthropologists were (rightly) dissatisfied with were those accounts that "explained" possession exclusively in terms of trance, specifically in terms of the necessary biological substratum that facilitated the trance state. Throwing the baby (causal mechanisms) out with the bathwater (ethnocentric interpretative labels), however, many anthropologists attempted to account for the incidence of possession with reference to the reported religious belief systems and social contexts within which spirits and spirit possession hold specific meanings and value. Had there been any attempt to rewrite a meaning-informed typology of spirit-possession phenomena for the purposes of comparative analysis, however, it too would have been of limited explanatory utility. A typology of human experience and thought that is informed solely by reference to participants' self-report–the kind of data collected by anthropologists–ignores out-of-awareness features of those thoughts and experiences. As observed in the previous chapter, mental processes that operate beneath the surface of conscious awareness are of unmistakable causal significance to the incidence, form, and meaning of cultural phenomena. The universality of these processes and the mechanisms that underpin them afford us a means of comparing like with like and of identifying foundational causal mechanisms. A cognitive approach potentially mediates between and connects neurological and particularistic accounts of the form, meaning, incidence, and spread of possession.

Typologies of possession trance have spawned some overambitious claims with regard to their explanatory potential and scope. A typology of possession trance that removes unpalatable terms such as *disorder, syndrome,* and *illness,* that clarifies distinctions through increasingly precise itemization and sorting criteria, and that integrates possession beliefs and trance behavior in a way that reflects their compound unity in practice, nevertheless remains a typology—a device for sorting and categorizing. Insofar as this permits the identification of like phenomena at some level of abstraction, it is potentially a useful tool for comparative research. But typological categorization *per se* is not explanation. Categorization *assists* us in drawing inferences and making predictions about particular phenomena, but in order to contribute to explanatory projects, our categorisation systems must parse the phenomena according to causally significant criteria. Then we can know that any similarities identified are not superficial or arbitrary and that we are comparing phenomena that are alike according to scientifically established causes and conditions.

Explaining Neurological and Social Correlates of Possession

The identification of potentially causally significant correlates between possession incidence and any other material category requires meticulous, widespread, ethnographic, and statistical research (Bourguinon 1968; Kehoe and Giletti 1981; Shaara and Strathern 1992). One can then begin to formulate a description of the general principles that may govern the recurrent, widespread correlations discovered. Explanatory approaches to possession within the anthropological literature tend to stumble at the first step, often veering into the terrain of interpretive generalization (see chapter 4).

A notable exception is Michael Winkelman's cross-cultural analyses of magico-religious healing and ASCs (Winkelman 1986; Winkelman and White 1987). These analyses built upon the findings of Bourguignon's cross-cultural survey (Bourguignon 1968), which indicated that the occurrence of possession trance correlates with societal complexity. Winkelman's research defined more precisely the societal markers that strongly correlate with possession-trance incidence. Societies were coded using Murdock and Provost's cultural complexity scales (Murdock and Provost 1973). These scales distinguish between stages of societal development according to characteristics such as types of agriculture, degree of technological specialization, economic organization, political organization and levels of political jurisdiction, and numbers of graded status distinctions (social stratification). Statistical analyses of possession incidence and measures of societal complexity revealed that high possession incidence is specifically associated with complex political organization, that is, societies with levels of political administration above that of the local community. Societies with higher population density and multilevel status distinctions also showed strong positive correlations with the societal incidence of possession.

Winkelman also tested for neurophysiological factors associated with possession trance. He found that physiological variables reflecting temporal lobe syndrome (e.g., amnesia, seizures, tremors, or convulsions) also "contribute to the phenomena of possession" (1997: 413). Although both the political integration and temporal lobe variables were so strongly associated with possession as to powerfully suggest the presence of a predictive, or causal, mechanism, the physiological variable was the more significant of the two.

Winkelman suggests explanations for these patterns. First, he proposes an evolutionary model that accounts for the strong positive correlation between possession incidence and complex political organization. This is premised upon the hypothesis that transformations in ASC characteristics (e.g., from shaman to healer and then to medium) are a function of increases in social complexity (as measured by the Murdock and Provost scales). The transformation of shamans into other types of magico-religious healers, such as mediums, is brought about by increases in societal complexity. More specifically, data analyses suggest "a systematic change in the shaman, such that agriculture and the resultant fixity of residence leads to the development of the shaman/healer, which is in turn differentiated into the medium and healer as a result of the process of political integration" (1990: 332).[6] The "social trans- formation" (ibid.: 325) of the shaman, he observes, is characterized by an in- creasing degree of role specialization and a decrease in the social status of the shaman/healers. Winkelman claims that the increased role specialization "is consistent with the demands of an organized practitioner group in a complex society, since specialization can be expected to reduce competition within the practitioner group" (ibid.: 338). The decrease in the social status of the shaman/ healers, he suggests, reflects "the leadership role of shamans in their societies and the general presence of other types of practitioners with higher [socio- political] status (priests) in societies with shaman/healers" (ibid.). Synchronic data collected across a broad spectrum of societies have provided a firm basis for these hypotheses. Diachronic data is still required to evaluate more compre- hensively Winkelman's transformation hypothesis and to disconfirm alterna- tive hypotheses (e.g., the hypothesis that the shaman's role ceases to exist and is replaced, or that the allegedly emergent magico-religious healer forms are the result of cultural diffusion).[7]

Second, because "possession ASC traditions that are associated with tem- poral lobe symptomology occur in the lower classes of stratified societies," Winkelman claims that this "indicates that their deprived status and resultant experiences may contribute directly to the physiological conditions" (1997: 414). A possible chain of causation, he suggests, derives from changes in the central nervous system and behavior caused by dietary and nutritional defi- ciencies common to lower-class sectors of societies. These may also be common to women who are restricted from adequate nutrition by cultural rules. This is commensurate with the calcium deficiency hypothesis, presented by Kehoe and Giletti (1981, considered below). Again, further evidence is required from other sources for the assumption—based largely on ethnographic and phenomeno- logical evidence—that all trance states (i.e., in shamans, mediums, etc.) are basically similar because of the fundamentally similar changes in temporal lobe activity. Winkelman draws attention to the need for "pscyhophysiological re- search" on "trance practitioners who are monitored for EEG patterns and changes" (1986: 186).

Since then, technological barriers have been surmounted to allow the first recording of multichannel electroencephalographic (EEG) measurements from a possessed person under natural conditions. In 2002, *Clinical Neuropsychology* published EEG measurements of possession-trance participants in a Balinese ritual ceremony (Oohashi, et al. 2002). Although few anthropologists have heeded Klass's admonitions to discover what really is happening on the psychophysiological level,[8] this interdisciplinary project, and others like it, has made exciting inroads into the investigation of fundamental neurological and psychological mechanisms underpinning possession-trance behavior. The Balinese pilot study reported an enhancement of alpha bands of spontaneous EEG activity, a finding also reported by EEG measurements during meditation or Zen. Further breakdown of the variability of alpha rhythm with different activities during trance (e.g., eyes-closed phases and eyes-open phases) suggested an association between depth of trance and alpha EEG. The study also reported that the EEG findings differed from those of neurological and psychological disorders, including epilepsy. This area of research is ripe for further investigation, and the advances thus far hold the prospect of yielding data that can inform and refine our understandings of the characteristics of possession trance in different settings, and of ultimately contributing to the investigation of factors influencing its emergence and spread.

The Calcium Deficiency Hypothesis

Kehoe and Giletti's calcium deficiency hypothesis appeared in *American Anthropologist* in 1981. They claimed to have struck on something novel and causally significant in the question of women's preponderance in possession-cult activity. Though not an immediately obvious correlation to most anthropologists investigating possession trance comparatively, it was incredulously simple by virtue of its reduction, not to sociological "forces," but to nutritional deficiency and the psychochemical mechanisms of the human body. While Lewis, Bourguignon, and others cast their net widely, producing answers that, by their generality and myriad possible mechanistic links (often unelaborated), appeared to speak to many cases, Kehoe and Giletti sank their line into one potentially fruitful, yet untested, spot. They write: "Our suggested explanation for women's preponderance in spirit-possession groups derives from demonstrable relationships between diet and behavior. There is a strong correlation between populations subsisting upon diets poor in calcium, magnesium, niacin, tryptophan, thiamins, and vitamin D, and those practicing spirit possession" (1981: 550).

Kehoe and Giletti, convinced by the data available that this was no red herring, presented their lay readers with an intricate account of the mechanisms by which the correlation was proposed to be causally significant:

Free [calcium] ions circulate in the blood plasma; calcium is stored as fixed ions in bone. If plasma calcium decreases below a critical concentration, synapse nerve-end potentials can depolarize, releasing

quanta of transmitter substance across the synapse, producing
spontaneous (cortically uncontrolled) neural impulse transmission.
Muscle contraction is initiated by calcium ion release from the
sarcoplasmic reticulum, where ions are bound to the protein tro-
ponin. (Ibid.: 551)

With "cultural sensitivity" as the watchword of the day, this was a particularly daring thesis–novel, yet unfashionable and anachronistic, comparative
and generalizable, yet deemed unrepresentative. Kehoe and Giletti's formulation barely acknowledged any relevance for religious and cultural contexts,
meanings, and motives; and on this count in particular it subsequently came
in for a great deal of criticism. Lewis declared them to be "cavalier," "confused," and "mistaken" (1983: 412), taunting that if they wanted to take this
already well-trodden reductionist path, they might at least have taken the
trouble to get their facts straight: "It is a pity that they ignore Leiris' subtle
account of the cult in Gondar, Ethiopia. Leiris records that the incidence of
possession is higher in times of plenty than in times of scarcity" (ibid.). Rejecting the challenge of systematically testing the hypothesis in order to assess
accurately its explanatory power, he went on to list further counterexamples, a
list that was to be extended by fellow skeptics to follow.

Concerns about apparent lack of fit with the data aside, it was again argued
that explanations of trance could not in themselves account for possession.
Possession as a belief could not be reduced to trance as its behavioral element.
Indeed, the two did not always coincide–trance is not always interpreted as
possession, nor does trance always accompany possession. Yet, even if Kehoe
and Giletti had tidied up their definitional criteria, clearly they could not reduce the issue of the preponderance of women in possession cults to a mono-
causal, biological hypothesis. This was despite appeals to their critics that their
paper was presented not as an "exhaustive treatise on possession, trance, and
cults" (Kehoe 1983: 416), but as a suggested additional explanation that could
potentially stimulate empirical research into the precise links between human
diet and behavior. They presented their hypothesis as additional and complementary to other possible explanations and clarified that the causal factors
identified were not necessarily associated with all possession cults. Later the
hypothesis was recognized for its potential to explain the cross-cultural patterns of possession-trance incidence discovered by Winkelman (1990,1997).
Yet, despite having done so much to arrive at a possible (partial) explanation,
reactions were so hostile that no further systematic, empirical testing of the
hypothesis was attempted.[9] Unelaborated theoretical constructs based on notions of flawed mental functioning that were described by vague terminology

for pathological conditions had been given more attention. Yet these medicalist perspectives, as we have observed, got little beyond description for classification purposes.

Sociological Theories

Offering an alternative to particularistic interpretation of possession and reductionist, biological and neurological investigations of trance, are the generalizing aims of sociological analysis. Sociological approaches offer explanations for the emergence and spread of forms of human behavior with reference to shaping "forces" of the wider societal context. According to this perspective, class, race, state, and economic structures, for example, are viewed as the pillars that bolster the social system and determine and control the form and incidence of elements within the society (including human behavior and thought). Religious participation, to take an example, may be explained with reference to the class-ordered composition of the society. In the sociological study of possession, a crucial bread-and-butter question, says Lewis, is "How does the incidence of ecstasy relate to the social order?" (1971: 27).

Roger Bastide describes ordered ecstatic trance in the African religions of Brazil as a "sociological creation—control of the individual by the group" (1978: 191). In those African religions of the New World that maintained the collective (i.e., group-wide) values and status quo of African society, group control was manifest in the orderliness of the trance. Those in trance danced in harmony, bound by the strict rigidity of rank and hierarchy and "communal censure" (ibid.: 186). Because of the shifts from slavery to free labor, however, and from free labor to proletarianism, personal misfortune and class tensions gave rise to individual interest, instincts, hopes and desires, or drives, which potentially threatened the control and order of the organized African religion. The degree of control, he claimed, was inversely correlated with the degree of "hysterical violence" in the trance (ibid.). The explanation offered is sociological: "The susceptibility of this trance to infiltration by personal drives seems to me to be associated with the individualization of the black in the industrialized big cities as he has been proletarianized through contact with whites" (ibid.: 381). Sacred values of African religion, he claims, which were once shared by everyone irrespective of social position, are distorted into ideologies of a colored proletarian class.

The collective-individual distinction was premised upon the putative dialectic between values (subsuming habits, attitudes, meanings, etc.) and structures (e.g., family, class, race, etc.). Individualist values expressed in the chaotic, violent, disorderly, and unorthodox ecstatic trance resulted from the overthrow of existing political and economic structures that had hitherto maintained the system of shared, collective values. The emergence of inequality, expressed in "tensions between social groups" and "racial frustrations" (ibid.: 403), was identified as the pivotal factor explaining the incidence of disorderly, hysteric trance.

The dichotomous center/periphery model of trance types offered by Lewis (noted above) is premised upon strikingly similar assumptions. Lewis asserts that peripheral cults, characterized as involving possession with amoral spirits, "play no direct part in upholding the moral code of the societies" (1971: 32). Like central cults, their incidence implies the existence of acute social pressures. Unlike central cults, however, in which the pressures are external to the society and are felt by the society as a whole, these pressures arise from oppression to which only subordinate members of the societies are subject (ibid.: 176). Possession in peripheral cults is "a form of mystical attack," ecstatic and uncontrolled, an illness that requires treatment (ibid.: 32–33).

Despite failing to pay much attention to wider social, cultural, aesthetic, and psychological factors, Lewis's model resonated with many anthropologists' observations, particularly regarding the widespread occurrence of overwhelmingly female participation in "uncontrolled" and "ecstatic" forms of possession. That this could correspond to an index of their marginal or subordinate status seemed reasonable. Eliminating assumptions of mental illness from Lewis's model, anthropologists positively assessed the value of its sociological insight, particularly in questions relating to social inequality and conflict, and the perceived instrumentality of possession in achieving social redress. Lewis's model seemed to account for certain ethnographic facts—possession *did* seem to appear most frequently among the disadvantaged and marginalized sectors of any society, and, in the peripheral cult, it often *did* appear to be an expression of rebellion, a chance to achieve limited redress, and a means of coping. It seemed that confirmatory cases were abundant.

For example, in Lucie Wood Saunders's case studies (1977) of two women involved in the Ethiopian *zar* cult, she presents two very different stories that she claims are consonant with Lewis's hypotheses. One of these women was married to a rich husband, with little in her domestic and family life that would appear to generate stress. The other was married to a landless laborer following a failed first marriage, and she had suffered difficulties throughout her adult life. Saunders describes both cases as substantiating Lewis's hypotheses concerning the function of peripheral possession cults: *zar* participation, she claimed, ultimately enabled both women to manipulate their husbands through its multiple social functions. In another example, Cynthia Nelson (1971) describes the Egyptian *zar* ceremony as an opportunity for women to express themselves in ways that are otherwise not possible or acceptable in the society. She recounts how one woman repeatedly carried out ceremonies in order to impoverish her husband, thereby withholding from him the means by which he could take a second wife. Patricia Lerch suggests a similar account for the predominance of women in the Umbanda cults of Porto Alegre, Brazil, in terms of relative powerlessness afforded by typical (marginal) female socioeconomic roles in the modern Brazilian economy. Although Lewis is not cited in Lerch's paper, there are conspicuous parallels between the two explanations; spirit mediumship offers women "access to 'power' and thus offsets the relative powerlessness typical of comparable socio-economic roles available to them in the modern economy" (Lerch 1982: 238).

Of course, one could probably build a good case for characterizing almost anybody as relatively disadvantaged, distressed, or oppressed in some way, particularly women in traditional marriage partnerships. In Lewis's quest to discover whether certain categories of people are more or less likely to be possessed, he had centered on power asymmetries connected with gender and class. However, it was, in part, by failing to define more precisely the parameters and potentially measurable psychological effects of "personal affliction" (such as stress), and by failing to elaborate the mechanisms by which such broad categories came to bear on possession, that his model was ensured widespread—but superficial—applicability to so many possession incidences worldwide. Lewis's model was highly seductive to many anthropologists whose ethnographic data appeared to substantiate the general claims. The broad appeal of his interpretation, however, may have blinded many to other equally plausible interpretations for possession-cult activity.[10]

Yet even with so much evidence apparently supporting Lewis's characterization of peripheral cult activity, some classical and modern studies have attempted to demonstrate that possession activity is not only the province of the powerless (e.g., Brown 1979; McIntosh 2004; Nourse 1996). More significant, where possession appears to coincide with powerlessness, scholars argue that any causal link between the two may not be as inevitable or as straightforward as suggested by Lewis's functionalist sociology (Nabokov 1997). Boddy objects that "the idea that possession is a sex-war salvo implies that the genders are homogeneous groups" (1994: 415; see also Sanders 2000) and mentions a number of analyses that retain a focus on gender and power while rejecting the assumptions of an androcentric anthropology.

With others (Keller 2002; Boddy 1994), I further maintain that sociological perspectives on possession often misrepresent the perceived key axes of power—class and gender—as central causal forces exerted on possessed persons, ignoring other equally if not more pertinent factors (see Sperber 1996). Rarely, if ever, are these "forces," their direct effects, and the mechanisms that bring about these effects described. Bastide, for example, does not consider how one might test his claims about the dialectics of superstructures and values in order to confirm that the factors he singles out are not arbitrary and hollow, but causal.

Accounts of possession and inherent concepts are rarely refined in order to establish precisely mechanisms and patterns whereby their correlation with social or other factors are demonstrably causally significant. They lack clear definition of causal factors and independent and dependent variables, sufficient and necessary conditions, predictions of how these may coalesce, methodologies for testing, guidelines as to what counts as refutation of the hypotheses, and so on, that are demanded by the standards of scientific explanation. Sociological interpretations also divide the world of those most likely to "succumb" to possession—or a particular form of possession—from those least likely to succumb, according to a scheme that is premised largely upon the intentional agency of the possessed person. From this perspective, possession is essentially a tool that is voluntarily used to vent anxieties (catharsis and therapy), and to forward aims (protest and rebellion). Again, Lewis and his supporters did not offer a sufficiently elaborated account of the mechanisms giving rise to these processes, much less a reliable methodology for testing and describing how these mechanisms operate in various contexts. Had this been accomplished, subsequent investigation could have proceeded in a systematic and prescribed way, rather than through impressionistic speculation of both supporters and opponents of the model's claims.

Functionalist approaches and more nuanced, interpretive utilitarian accounts that succeeded them have dominated the field of possession studies. Volumes of writing from and against these perspectives, however, have demonstrated over the decades that the devil is in the detail. Apparent support—and refutation—hinges on data that are as vague and superficial as the wide-ranging hypotheses offered. Suggested correlations and their causes are dismissed in a cavalier manner, often based on single cases, anecdotal stories, and even personal distaste for (necessarily) reductive explanations. Although it is possible that ad hoc reasoning about the possible function that possession may fulfill in society can be a potentially useful means of investigation for the generation of explanatory hypotheses, hypotheses were often presented as conclusions before they had been rendered precise, testable, and substantiated accordingly. Were one to begin these tasks, one would need to expend considerable resources initially identifying and assessing the theories' first principles and basic arguments. The few who have sought to detail the mechanisms on which their hypotheses are based have met with heavy opposition despite no evidence of systematic testing.

Progressing toward Explanation

Nevertheless, the concern to explain the incidence of possession has persisted in some sectors of scholarly analysis on the subject. A number of scholars have presented various hypotheses and theories, generated from a growing body of data from across the world and across disciplines. Exploration of the necessary and precipitating conditions for the multifaceted phenomenon of spirit possession has advanced on many levels of analysis. Neurological, biological, and sociological analyses are distinguished by their particular questions, aims, and methodologies. Some questions necessitate the invention of new scientific technologies, such as the purpose-built EEG telemetry system used in the Balinese study mentioned above. Other lines of enquiry require the probing interview techniques of the trained anthropologist. Collaborative projects can build on and refine their hypotheses against novel findings in a collective, cumulative way.

Unfortunately, however, there have been notably few interdisciplinary projects on this multifaceted cultural expression. Anthropologists, for example, are continually refining their definitions and descriptions of agency, consciousness, resistance, motivation, and so on, with little recourse to interdisciplinary expertise. The investigation of issues such as these, and concomitant consideration of the emergence, spread and meaning of cultural practices and concepts, must necessarily employ a many-pronged approach, gathering data through multiple methodologies. Academic boundaries that have formally separated particular domains of interest, such as "biology" and "belief," are potentially interpenetrable through dialogue and collaboration for the production of an interconnected and coherent corpus of knowledge on the complex phenomenon of spirit possession.

Some principles guide such scientifically grounded, collaborative investigation. The particular aspect of possession that one seeks to explain and the precise claims made determine the issues that need to be explored. The questions that arise, in turn, determine appropriate methods for acquiring the relevant data. If one seeks to establish the significant correlates between brain changes and subjective possession-trance experience, participant self-report through direct interviewing, though potentially relevant to the hypotheses' claims, will not enable measurement of the physiological variables hypothesized. By the same token, the discoveries permitted by EEG measurements, enabling us to describe, compare, and explain conscious, semiconscious, and unconscious states, do not provide sufficient data from which to generate interesting hypotheses concerning the spread of certain kinds of ideas and patterns of thinking about spirits. In this sense, as Lambek and many others have stated, trance, as a biological capacity, does not explain belief.

Nevertheless, whatever the aims and level of our investigations into human behavior, a crucial first principle is that humans are biological organisms that exist in interaction with their surrounding environment. Hence the necessity for collaborative research that connects disciplines that deal with the social, the cultural, the biological, and the psychological. Tooby, et al. write,

> The rich complexity of each individual is produced by a cognitive
> architecture, embodied in a physiological system, which interacts
> with the social and non-social world that surrounds it. Thus humans,
> like every other natural system, are embedded in the contingencies
> of a larger principled history, and explaining any particular fact
> about them requires the joint analysis of all the principles and con-
> tingencies involved. (1992: 21)

The "joint analysis" of possession behavior and ideas must integrate scientifically grounded bodies of knowledge from a wide variety of sources on account of their mutual relevance to the subject matter. The ultimate objective is to provide a *synthesized* explanatory account (not a collection of overambitious reductionist postulates) of spirit possession and mediumship. This book, in which ethnographic methods and data are woven together with investigation and evidence from the cognitive sciences, is a small contribution to this endeavor.

Conclusion

I have argued that modern social scientific analyses of spirit possession have retained many of the problematic assumptions and conceptual tools upon which earlier sociological theories were premised. "Instrumental agency," for example, is often taken to be fundamental to the reconstruction of meaning in times of oppression, social change, and upheaval. The instrumentalist implications inherent in this assumption filtered through to symbolist and hermeneutic approaches.[11] Yet this assumption of collective or individual utility underlying generations of explanatory and interpretive approaches to possession begs a number of crucial questions. Are cultural meanings infinitely malleable and fluid? What, if any, are the nonsocial constraints on the creative limits of agency? Does intentional agency alone account for participant motivation? What makes certain ideas, such as those surrounding possession, propagate so widely, regardless of (our characterization of) them being forms of resistance or not? Can ideas be "collective"? Do "culture" and socioeconomic "forces" really *explain* the popularity and form of possession-cult activity? Can the mechanisms by which these "forces" shape cultural expression and meaning be articulated? And, in light of the physiological evidence, why is it that concepts of spirits and healing so often accompany the documented changes in brain physiology? In short, what is the appeal of these concepts? Why spirits?

This book returns our attention to the universal features of people's ideas concerning spirit possession and to the sets of conditions that are necessary for their emergence and spread. Klass's comparative research and interdisciplinary explorations bear out the notion of the apparent presence of an *identity* during possession. He claims that this identity is as real as any other. In subsequent chapters we will see how these identities and the ways in which they may be constructed and used are contingent upon sets of mechanisms that have not yet been considered by sociological, medicalist, and neurophysiological theories of possession. We shall observe that there is much more to explain about "what really is going on" when someone is possessed than Klass offers in his description of possession as a form of *dissociative identity phenomena*.

In the following chapters, I will describe certain mechanisms of cognition that are of particular value in the investigation of causes contributing to the particular form and incidence of possession among a group of Afro-Brazilian cult participants in Belém. The identification of these general mechanisms has considerable potential to explain aspects of possession as it appears cross-culturally. I do not wish to underrate or dismiss the analytical value of sociological, interpretivist, and descriptive projects. The explanatory factors that I propose are not exhaustive and may prove to complement—and provide some basis for—the unsubstantiated, imprecise, unelaborated, and often cavalier claims of some of this scholarship.[12] In their disclaimer for failing to consider psychological aspects of their subject of study, Brumana and Martinez remark, "Explanation at the psychological level gives the uncomfortable feeling of pulling a rabbit out of a magician's hat or, as in a bad detective novel, of discovering that the murderer is someone who has not yet been introduced" (1989: 298). They continue, "This is no excuse, however, for not describing how these phenomena intervene in our subject of study" (ibid.). My aim is to redress the imbalance, to request a retrial, as it were, by introducing some historically elusive, guilty characters.

6

Spirits as Concepts

Desejo ao Seu Zé muitos anos de vida! Muita saúde e felicidade!

I wish Seu Zé a long life! Much health and happiness!
>—A filha addresses the spirit entity Zé
(possessing Pai) at a "birthday" ceremony
marking the date he first possessed Pai

The apparent variability in the way in which spirits are represented cross-culturally is widely documented in anthropological literature. Spirit concepts populate diverse cultural landscapes, and the broad range of people whom spirits are believed to possess appears to defy reduction to any generalizable, typological category conjectured by social and medical sciences. Anthropological and native accounts portray seemingly countless varieties of spirit beings with many variations in the way in which spirits manifest themselves. Some episodes are controlled, others chaotic; some are collective and others individual; some are accompanied by rousing rhythms, extravagant costume, and ceremony and other spirit possession incidents go almost undetected. Some bodies are possessed by divine or ancestral beings, while cacodemons and evil spirits possess others. Some possessed persons remain fully or partly awake thereby forming memories of the episode, and others enter a state of semiconscious or unconscious trance with little or no recollection of the events that took place. Some spirit-possession beliefs and practices form part of a systematic ritual or religious tradition, while others appear to be only loosely convergent among a population, even idiosyncratic, yet normal and continuous with the profane or everyday domain. One need not carry out widespread surveys of the literature to recognize such contrasts and variability—the whole gamut of spirit-possession phenomena may often be demonstrated in a single religious tradition, or population, or even in one individual over the course of their development as a medium.

Could it be that somewhere in the midst of this apparent randomness and variation there are some principles that govern and constrain the kinds of spirit concepts and possession practices that have pervaded human civilizations since culture's beginnings? Why do some ideas enjoy relative success, becoming widespread and stable over time, while others fall by the wayside or remain localized? Why is it that some ideas survive and spread, even across cultures, while others do not? In *Explaining Culture*, Sperber offers a pertinent model for the investigation and explanation of cultural transmission. He claims that to explain culture is to explain how certain ideas "happen to be contagious" (1996: 1). Sperber maintains that causal explanations for the incidence and popularity of certain cultural facts should start with one key question: why are some cultural representations more successful in a human population than others (ibid.: 58)? Cultural representations here refer to mental outputs (e.g., ideas, beliefs, etc.) that are widely distributed throughout a population. As such, they may include everything from descriptions of a piece of music as "classical" and of a behavior as "typically English," to recognizably recurrent ideas about gender, concepts of gods, notions about beauty, and schemas for appropriate social interaction.

Investigations that seek to identify factors contributing to the incidence, form, and transmission of representations concern both anthropologists and psychologists. Sperber makes clear that these questions are not answerable by reduction to psychological processes alone. From an epidemiological perspective, "psychology is necessary but not sufficient for the characterization and explanation of cultural phenomena" (ibid.: 60). Sperber argues, however, that the selection of representations can be explained in part in terms of micromechanisms at work in the material processes of the brain. He claims that this "is a materialism with theoretical implications: mental processes are attributed causal powers in virtue of their material properties" (ibid.: 14). His epidemiological model of cultural contagion is therefore different from holistic, sociological explanations in that it explains population-scale macroprocesses as the cumulative effect of microprocesses, not as the effect of other macrophenomena (e.g., political and economic institutions).

Within the epidemiological approach, Sperber explains, there is no grand unitary theory in store for those looking for a simple, systematic explanation of human social life. There is, however, the potential to identify numerous conceptual tools that are fundamental to explaining the existence and fate of various sets of cultural representations. The mental tools that facilitate the generation and spread of representations are the product of our species' evolutionary past. As such, they constitute a relatively fixed, generic cognitive architecture across human populations. The regularities of the structures of the human mind potentially provide instructive insights for the explanation of the distributional patterns of recognizably recurrent cultural representations across modern societies. Questions surrounding the character of a cultural representation—its emergence, development, transmission and persistence in a population—are answerable at the level of individual mental mechanisms and inter-individual communicative mechanisms (ibid.: 54). This, Sperber adds, is true materialism.

I take this "true materialism" as a way forward in the identification of general mechanisms and processes that underlie the extremely complex and multifaceted phenomena of possession. The pervasiveness of ideas about spirits and spirit-possession phenomena throughout cultures and across time suggests that widespread factors are responsible for driving the selection and transmission—the acquisition, memory, and communication—of these ideas. While the names, characters, and preferences of spirit concepts and entities may vary widely across cultures, there are some fundamental continuities in the ways that spirits are represented in human minds. Whether they are gods or goblins, divinities or demons, ancestors or still unborn spirit beings, I will argue, following recent theories in the cognitive science of religion (e.g., Atran 2002; Boyer 2001; Barrett 2004; Whitehouse 2004) that all such concepts are subject to similar sets of cognitive constraints. Scott Atran, Pascal Boyer, Justin Barrett, Harvey Whitehouse, and others have developed and begun testing specific hypotheses based on the assumption that the successful transmission or otherwise of particular kinds of representations of supernatural beings is contingent upon these constraints, many of which operate below the level of conscious awareness. Comprehensive explanation of the incidence and spread of representations requires consideration of causes that fall outside of the scope of "local" explanations and interpretations offered by research participants and social theorists. This chapter shows how explanations of spirit possession can benefit from recent advances in the scientific investigation of the processes of cognition.

Encountering Spirits

Imagine that someone tells you that the friend who is sitting chatting in front of you is not the person you know her to be. In fact, you are informed that the person is not actually "here" but is currently being animated by a spirit being who normally lives an incorporeal existence on another dimension. While this revelation may explain puzzling changes in the person's voice and conversation, there is no obvious or compelling reason to believe it. Indeed, it might seem much more plausible to you that the person is acting. Nevertheless, the person telling you this information certainly appears to think that it is true. Yet, before you can even think about accepting what the person says, you want some proof. You might wonder if this being has any special powers or qualities that allow it to exceed normal human capabilities. Perhaps he or she knows something about you that you have revealed to few people. Against the odds, it seems, the being speaks through your friend to reveal some hidden thought you may have had at that moment, or some tragedy you have passed through recently, with impressive accuracy. You relate the incident to your friend at a later point, but your story apparently triggers no recollection in her mind. It really is just as if she had not been there. You tell other people and find to your surprise that your experience is not isolated, and that these people seem to be quite content with the explanation that had been offered to you previously. The notion that a spirit being really possessed the person starts to seem more plausible, even if it seems as though you need to suspend all rational thought to accept it.

Regardless of whether or not you have read this story and thought, "Not me!" you were readily able to comprehend the story (i.e., you are *not* now feeling lost in a sea of bizarre and unfathomable concepts), and you might also accept that it could potentially describe, albeit simplistically, a real-life scenario. After all, people would believe anything, or so it would seem, especially when it comes to the bizarre and unpredictable world of religious and supernatural concepts and convictions. Indeed, surprisingly or not, this story portrays a situation that occurs frequently in spirit-possession traditions and distils the essence of numerous personal accounts related to me throughout research in Belém.

Now consider the following scenario:

You hear of another spirit that possesses a person. Information about the spirit is limited to a few characteristic features and behaviors. First, the spirit lives in a dimension within which he has no awareness of activities on earth. Second, the spirit is a thinking being but forgets his thoughts the moment they occur. Third, the spirit only has these thoughts in dreams as he always sleeps, even when in possession. However, the person can only be possessed with the spirit while engaged in strenuous exercise. Fourth, when in possession, the spirit can perceive all musical sounds everywhere on earth but cannot comprehend, or have, any verbal communication. Finally, the spirit only exists—in any dimension—for the first half of any month.

The combination of conditions attached to this possession scenario may demand much more of our imaginative capabilities than the previous scenario and may even appear tortuously incomprehensible at first glance. Perhaps it just seems odd or bizarre. It certainly does not look like anything ever reported by any anthropologist. We know that ideas and beliefs about spirit possession are hugely variable and frequently become widespread across cultures. Yet, something suggests to us that *this* set of ideas is not likely to enjoy widespread credibility and transmissive success. We are not denying the possibility that such concepts could exist somewhere in the world—after all, since I just thought them up, perhaps anyone could come up with something similar— nor are we passing judgment on whether or not such ideas could be believed or accepted as true. It just seems unlikely that both these scenarios would be equally successful in cultural transmission, an intuition that is in fact supported by anthropological descriptions of spirit-possession phenomena crossculturally.

The question, then, is: why do some notions of spirits and spirit possession, of which there are many variants, enjoy particularly widespread and accurate transmission, while others might only be momentarily entertained and rapidly eliminated from our thoughts? One method of investigation could be to catalogue all variants of notions relating to supernatural beings in all cultures. We could use this to see if any common theme or recurrent features can be detected. Yet, as Boyer has observed, no matter how we might attempt to label such features (e.g., as "strange," "bizarre," "sacred," and so on) we would still be no nearer an explanation as to why such features are so recurrent (2001). Catalogues and lists do not reveal causal mechanisms.

A more productive approach is to identify the universal psychological constraints that operate both consciously and unconsciously when people acquire new concepts, whether from other people or by individual, spontaneous thought. Contrary to popular opinion, people do not just believe anything, nor do they easily imagine absolutely anything, successfully freeing their imagination from known facts they hold about the world and causal links between them. This is partly because imagining is not something that people engage in on a wholly explicit, conscious, or reflective level. Cognitive scientists and social psychologists have begun to show how many of our nonreflective (or implicit) intuitions and expectations—and "minitheories"—about the world are anchored in our mental structures and tools, most of which operate automatically and outside conscious awareness (see Tooby, et al. 1992; Gilovich, Griffin, and Kahneman 2002). These tools enable efficient and rapid mental processing of countless perceptions, thoughts, and problems without concentration or conscious calculation. They also powerfully constrain the ways in which we imagine, speculate, and theorize about the world. Scholars working within the rapidly developing field of the cognitive science of religion have applied these findings and methodologies to theories and predictions about the incidence and spread of particular kinds of belief and practices. To date, however, no ethnographer has considered in depth these experimental findings and hypotheses against a real empirical case. Before we consider some of the cognitive tools that may be operative in the representation of spirit entities and spirit possession, then, let us take a closer look at the organization and content of spirit concepts in the *culto afro*.

The Spirit Pantheon and Its Organization

Within the *culto*, several categories of supernatural entities can be distinguished on the basis of divergent origin, ritual tradition, character, and hierarchy. For example, most people hold to some belief in a supreme God. When asked about the supreme God, research participants indicated little variation from the ubiquitous view of Catholicism. In fact, some participants recited the catechism response that they had memorized for their first communion. God and the Yoruban supreme God, Olodumaré/Olorum, were considered to be one in the same entity. The two terms were used interchangeably in the liturgical prayers that often accompanied curing ceremonies. As was characteristic of wider Brazilian society, people often casually referred to God in conversation (*Graças a Deus!* [Thank God!] and *Deus me livre!* [God forbid!] being common exclamations). Nevertheless, the Catholic notion of a supreme God or Yoruban Olorun/Olodumaré was largely absent from the ritual and ceremonial practices of the *culto*.

Of all the spirit beings that are invoked in ritual and everyday life, the *orixás* were considered to be the most powerful, exerting the most influence on human affairs generally. These were the entities who, for example, "ruled over" (*reger*) certain months of the year and phenomena, such as war, political struggle, and so on. Another *nação* (nation) represented in the *terreiro*, identified as Dahomean-derived, is characterized by worship of the *orixá*-like *voduns*. These correspond, in character and hierarchical position, to the Yoruban *orixás*, differing by name and African place of origin. Spirits known as *vo-*

dunsus, (or *brancos, gentis*) are described as "almost *voduns*" (or *orixás*). They
are believed to have lived on earth as great legislators, soldiers, rulers, prin-
cesses, and so on and to have passed through a "portal" into another dimension without having died. They comprise various "families," or named groups
of aggregates, many of whom are believed to have historical origins in Europe
and the Middle East. Lower down the hierarchy are the groups of spirits commonly referred to as *caboclos.* A widespread definition used outside the religion identifies *caboclos* as indigenous backwoodsmen. In everyday *culto* discourse, this term is extended to include a collective of spirits, such as "Old
Blacks" (sprits of black slaves), spirit guides, and other spirit entities more
strictly referred to as *"encantados"*—spirits who are believed to have lived as
humans but who, like the *vodunsus,* passed into the spiritual dimension, the
"encantaria," without having physically died. *Guia* is a generic term that is
frequently used to refer collectively to named and unnamed spirit beings who
accompany and guide one through life. Child spirits complete the hierarchy of
regular visitors to the *terreiro.* Like the *caboclos,* certain child spirits are associated more closely with the widespread Afro-Brazilian tradition of Umbanda
and are not considered to be part of the African pantheon. The child spirits
of Candomblé are known as *erês,* and in the Gege "nation" they are called
toquêms. Represented as children, they are "born" as such at initiation and
comprise a mixture of the initiate's and the *orixa's* personalities. These are
unique to each initiate and cease to exist on his or her death.

 This hierarchical system constitutes a relatively abstract schema, allowing
for the organization and accommodation of spirits and deities from many
origins and religious traditions within one *casa* structure. In practice, ritual
activities that directly concern the *orixás* are kept separate from activities that
concern the *caboclos.* A strict rule of segregation is enforced in all cult practice.
Although the *orixás* are said to be superior to the *caboclos,* what this really
meant was not clear. Observation and interview data reveals that *orixás* are
considered to be wiser and nearer to the supreme god, and they exist on a
higher plane than the other entities. Nevertheless, these descriptions remain
vague and abstract even when interviewees are probed to elucidate further
(e.g., "they have superior vision," *eles têm uma visão além*). The criteria according to which hierarchical position is bestowed were therefore difficult to
determine. An outsider's description of the most powerful and most relevant
gods based upon observation of the contexts and situations in which they are
invoked would have looked very different from the above official *casa* account.
Caboclos and *encantados* were the most involved in casa affairs—both ritual
and nonritual—and despite their representation as less-than-perfect beings,
their special supernatural qualities and powers were rarely construed as being

relative to, or less than, the powers of the *orixás*. The way in which this hierarchy is commonly represented is perhaps best portrayed metaphorically, as in the following statement from Pai:

> You often see that a person has a great devotion for a *Preto Velho*
> ["Old Black"], or with a *cabocla*, *cabocla* Mariana, or an *entidade*. Why?
> Because that *entidade* is right near him, listens to his problems,
> knows his wrongs, his failings and also affirms that it can't do everything. So, this relationship between the adept, the beggar, and the
> one who can do something, is much stronger than that of the beggar
> with the one who can do everything . . . it's the same, for example,
> if you take a person there from Tucunduba, a humble/poor person
> and get him to talk to the governor. He's going to become really
> shy, and is going to say, "No, I'll talk to you and afterwards you
> talk with him." It's the same thing with the divine being. We don't
> have this perspective to put African theology in the heads of the
> *filhos-de-santo*, or be it, the presence of Olorum because, for us, if
> that *filho* cultivates well his *orixá*, if that *filho* cultivates well his *entidade*, he is indirectly cultivating well Olorum. This is the idea
> we have and it's because of this that you don't see one speaking
> about Olorum in rituals; few *doutrinas* [songs] have the word
> "Olorum." Generally one refers to the intermediary gods, that's to
> say, *orixás*.

> *Tu vê muitas vezes, a pessoa tem uma devoçao muito grande com o preto*
> *velho, ou com uma cabocla, cabocla Mariana ou uma entidade. Por quê?*
> *Porque aquela entidade está alí perto dele, ela escuta os problemas, ela*
> *sabe dos erros, dos defeitos e ela também afirma que ela não pode tudo.*
> *Então, esse relacionamento entre o adepto, o pedinte, e aquele que pode*
> *fazer alguma coisa é muito mais forte do que do pedinte pra aquele que*
> *tudo pode fazer . . . é mesmo que por exemplo você pegar uma pessoa lá do*
> *Tucunduba, uma pessoa humilde e colocar pra conversar com o govern-*
> *ador. Ele vai ficar muito acanhado, vai dizer que não, ele vai conversar:*
> *"eu converso contigo, depois tu fala com ele." Mesma coisa é o ser*
> *divino . . . Nós não temos essa perspectiva de colocar na cabeça dos filhos-*
> *de-santo a teologia Africana, ou seja, a presença de Olorum, porque pra*
> *nós, se aquele filho cultiva bem o seu orixá, se aquele filho cultiva bem*
> *a sua entidade, ele está indiretamente cultivando bem Olorum. É essa*
> *que é a visão que tem, é por isso que você não vê num ritual se falar em*
> *Olorum. Poucas doutrinas que falam a palavra 'Olorum'. Geralmente*
> *se refere aos deuses intermediários, vamos dizer assim, orixás.*

The everyday relevance of the *entidades* to the rank and file of cult practitioners was not to be found in elaborate descriptions of their powers, in fairytale legends, or even in historical record and conjecture, but in how they could exercise their powers to influence people's immediate circumstances, life situations, and even their character. As this statement by Pai suggests, "cultivating well" (*cultivar bem*), the *entidades* is clearly motivated by material concerns and issues. While these practices are also believed indirectly to convey adulation of the Supreme God, a common phrase to be heard within the *terreiro* perhaps indicates which of the two effects carries more motivational weight; participants would frequently state that it is "through pain, not through love" (*pela dor, não pelo amor*) that people come to participate in *culto* activities. In other words, it is pain and misfortune, and not love for the *orixás* or the *culto*, that bring people to the *terreiro*. As we shall see, the relevance of the spirits to people's everyday lives is a significant factor in the transmissive success of notions about spirits. The form that the notions take, however, is also important. Regardless of where these spirits may be located in the *culto* hierarchical structure, and the salience they possess for participants, there are features of their descriptions that they all share and that make them easy to remember and pass on. This will become clearer as we consider the cognitive mechanisms that underpin them. First, let us consider in more depth some of the descriptions that surround some of the most powerful spirit entities in the *terreiro*.

Orixá Concepts

Complex, theological descriptions of highly counterintuitive gods with special, supernatural qualities do not feature in explicit discourse and instruction in the *terreiro*. In the place of theological sermonizing on the nature of the gods, for example, are stories and legends, passed down from ancient Yoruban culture. These stories are the chief narrative reference that members possess for the group of African deities known as *orixás*. The gods that feature in these stories display very humanlike demeanors in their social dealings with one another, acting on the basis of their desires and whims. Jealousy, vengeance, bad blood, and trickery color the conniving between the characters of this elysian soap opera. The following description of the *orixá* family ties (offered by Pai) and the story about the *orixá*, Ossain (the lord of the leaves (*senhor das folhas*), below, illustrate these features.[1]

Oxalá had a wife called Nanã, and with this wife he had several sons and daughters. He had Oxumaré, Obaluaiê/Omolú (taken to be

the same person), yes—Oxumaré, Ewá and Babá Iroko. These are
taken to be sons and daughters of Oxalá and Nanã. Because Nanã
was already very old, Oxalá married Yemanjá and with Yemanjá he
had the rest of his sons and daughters (which are from the Nagô
nation and the sons and daughters of Nanã are from the Gege nation). OK. Ogun—he was initially married to Yansã. Xango took a
liking to her, stole Yansã, and Yansã became Xango's wife and Oxum
too. . . . They say that . . . before Oxum was the wife of Xango, she was
Oxossi's wife. With her, Oxossi had a son called Logun. . . .

Oxalá teve uma mulher chamada Nanã e com esta mulher teve vários
filhos. Teve Oxumaré, Obaluaê/Omolu, é visto como a mesma pessoa,
é— Oxumaré, Ewá, e Baba Iroco. Eles são tidos como sendo filhos de
Oxalá com Nanã. Como Nanã já tava muito velha, Oxalá desposou
Yemanjá e com Yemanjá ele teve o restante dos filhos que são da nação
Nagô e os filhos de Nanã que são da na nação Jeje. Bem, Ogun, ele
primeiramente foi casado com Yansã. Xangô simpatizou com ela, roubou
Yansã, Yansã passou a ser mulher de Xangô. Além de Yansã,
Oxum . . . contam também . . . antes de Oxum ser mulher de Xangô foi
mulher de Oxossi e com ela, ele teve um filho chamado Logun. . . .

Ossain, the lord of the leaves (Verger and Carybé 1997: 24, my
translation):
    Ossain received the secret of the leaves from Olodumaré.
    He knew that some of them brought peace and might.
    Others brought luck, glory, and honour, or misery, sickness, and
accident.
    The other *orixás* did not have any power over any plants.
    They depended on Ossain to maintain their health and for the
success of their initiatives.

Xango, who had an impatient, pugnacious and imperious tempera-
ment, was irritated by this disadvantage and used a trick to try to
usurp ownership of the leaves from Ossain.
    He told his wife, Iansa, the lady of the winds, his plan.
    He explained to her than on certain days Ossain suspended a
gourd containing the most powerful leaves from a branch of *Iroko*
[a tree].
    "Unleash a severe storm on one of these days," said Xango.
    Iansa accepted the mission with great pleasure.

The wind blew in great gusts, removing the roof tiles from
the houses, uprooting trees, breaking everything in its path and—the
desired end—releasing the gourd from the branch where it hung.

The gourd rolled a long way and all the leaves flew around.

The *orixás* took possession of all of them.

Each one became owner of some of them, but Ossain remained
lord over the secret of their potency and of the words that must be
pronounced to cause their action. In this way he continued to reign
over the plants as absolute lord.

Iansa, Xango, Ossain, and various other *orixás* that have survived into
Brazil's modern era continue to be represented in such stories, invoked through
divination methods, and manifested in possession episodes. They bring their
emotions, preferences, conflicts, and dislikes to the dance circles and possession ceremonies of their human "sons" and "daughters" in Brazilian *terreiros*.
Their behaviors and the steps of the dances that they perform are subtle
reminders of their stories, histories and their "humanity." Nanã's languid
dance speaks of her senior years, as the oldest goddess of the waters. Oxossi,
the god of the hunt and the forest, carries his bow and arrow, as well as a
flywhisk made from a bull's tail—the insignia of royal dignity and reminder of
his reign as king of the African nation of Keto. Iemanjá, goddess of the waters,
imitates the movements of the waves with her arms. Oxumaré points to the
heavens and the earth, demonstrating his/her duality as both male and female
at the same time. (Note that this potentially hard to conceptualize notion of
dual sexuality was made more manageable as he/she was actually considered
to be male for six months of the year and female for the other six months.)
Overall, narratives, whether they are retold through possession mimicry and
costume or prose, take the form of relatively simple, easily transmittable
stories. Each story is a hub of inferences that can potentially link to analogous situations in daily life (Whitehouse 2004; Turner 1996). As we will observe, interpretive license allows the events and their outcomes to be projected
almost unlimitedly onto the everyday contexts in which they continue to be
invoked.

People are free, nonetheless, to engage in more profound philosophical
musing about the nature of the *orixás*. The absence of explicit instruction and
of any official, orthodox line permits a certain poetic license on this matter.
Nevertheless, such musings are confined to the writings of a minority of
well-educated individuals whose influence largely fails to penetrate the wider
terreiro membership. Arguably, such writings are intended for the prestige
marketplace that extends outside the immediate community of practicing

Candomblecistas[2] to the influential political and academic sectors of society. The following is an extract from the work of one of these *pais-de-santo*. Sales writes of Oxumaré:

> Oxumaré, the *orixá* of motion and activity, is a large mythical serpent that left the depths of the earth and ascended in the direction of the sky, girding it about with its long tail-end that was shaded with various colors, becoming a rainbow, and then returning to the earth from where it came. He/She[3] originates in Dahomey, in a place called Dan. He/she comes from the territory of Mahi, as does his/her brother Obaluaiê and mother, Nanã.
>
> Oxumaré is the symbol of continuity, of the forces that generate motion, assuring the unity of the world and its eternal renovation. He/she extends his/her power over the world, at the dawn of the day, spreading it with strength, accompanying the break of day. He/she is the multiplier, the mystery of eternal rebirth, the great force that possesses and transmits energy; he/she dries away the rain, is the seer of the skies and the curer of the gods. (Sales 2001: 100; my translation)

Within the community I researched, such elaborate descriptions were absent from all discourse about the gods. Even the legends were recounted only in piecemeal fashion on extremely rare occasions. The *pai-de-santo* did not consider them to be important to the *filhos'* education within the cult, turning instead to what is known and spoken about the *orixás* as historical figures, about how they were worshipped according to the traditions of the African peoples, and about the practices that have surrounded their subsequent cultivation in Brazil. Most members of the *terreiro*, however, displayed little interest in such details. Their knowledge about the *orixás*—both mythical and historical—was gleaned from casual conversation with members of this and other *terreiros*, from popular culture (e.g., in paintings and other craftwork depicting the *orixás* with their characteristic traits, costume, and symbols accentuated, and in the lyrics of popular rap, pop, and samba songs), from magazines and the media, as well as from divination responses, explanations given for ritual taboos associated with individual *orixás*, and personal experiences of the *orixás* in their everyday affairs. It is unsurprising, then, that a survey of what some of the *filhos* understand by "*orixá*" revealed diverse perspectives:

> José: For me the *orixás* are like God for our religion. We cultivate and respect them—for me, it is as if the *orixá* was a person, a god, because we really respect the *orixás*. We never say no to them, because I

feel that the *orixá*, my *orixás*, they protect me . . . they really help me, at the moment in which I meet with difficulty.

Pra mim, os orixás são tipo um, duma forma de Deus pra nossa religião. Nós cultuamos muito, respeitamos—pra mim, os orixás são como se fosse uma pessoa, um deus, porque a gente respeita muito e a gente nunca diz não a ele né porque eu sinto pra mim eu sinto que o orixá, os meus orixás, ele nos protege. Eles me ajudam muito no momento em que eu encontro dificuldade.

Marcus: *Orixá*, for me—I think they are our divinities, ancestors that were in Africa . . . and now we have the opportunity to cultivate and receive them in Brazil. Of course, lots of *orixás* didn't come, just some, but for me the ancestors are the *orixás*.

Orixá pra mim—eu acho que são divindades nossas, antepassadas que ficaram na África . . . e que agora a gente tem a oportunidade de cultuar e receber aqui no Brasil. Claro que muitos orixás não vieram né, alguns só, mas pra mim é os antepassados, os orixás.

Maria: I used to think that *orixás* were figures that brought us strength in our spiritual life . . . and that they had a form, according to the illustrations that we see, and all that. But I saw the form of the *orixás* to be very black human beings . . . some strong and others thin, some bodies were model-like and others not. In some research that I did recently, I discovered that the *orixás* are also forces of nature, and they are also present with us at all times. I discovered that there are *orixás* that participated in the creation of the world, and for having done heroic feats, they had the privilege of becoming *orixás*—kings, queens, founders of cities. So, really the *orixá* is everything that we can see and that we can feel. . . . I also discovered that they have qualities and flaws—some are very similar to human beings in that they both get things right and commit errors.

Eu pensava que orixá eram formas, né, que traziam pra gente uma força a mais na nossa vida espiritual . . . e que tinha formato, de acordo com os desenhos que nós vemos, essa coisa toda. Mas eu via os formato dos orixás muito - seres humanos negros . . . uns fortes e outros magros, corpos modelados e outros não. E na pesquisa que eu fiz agora recente, eu descobri que orixá são também forças da natureza, só que eles estão também presentes com a gente em todos os momentos. Eu descobri que existem orixás que não particparam da criação do mundo, e por ter tido feitos heróicos, eles tiveram o privilégio de se tornarem orixás, né, no caso de reis, rainhas, alguns que fundaram cidades. Então, realmente, orixá é tudo que a gente vê, que a gente sente também. . . . Também descobri que tem seus defeitos e qualidades, ou seja, alguns têm uma proximidade muito grande com os seres-humanos no ato de errar e de acertar.

Marcelo: Orixá is a life, a past life, it is a being of nature.
Orixá é uma vida, uma vida passada, é um ser da natureza.

Ivone: Orixá, in my way of thinking, is—*orixá* was a person like us, that suffered just like us, but the power of God had that, that, how would you say it, that chance to turn around and come back, in order to counsel those people who needed it, to give a little attention to those people, to bring light to that person.
Orixá na minha maneira também de acreditar, é, orixá foi uma pessoa como a gente, que sofreu como a gente, só que o poder de Deus teve aquela, aquela, como é que se diz, aquela chance de tornar a voltar mas pra aconselhar aquelas pessoas que precissasem, pra dar um pouco de atenção àquelas pessoas, pra trazer luz pra aquela pessoa.

Rosa: There were *orixás* that lived and afterwards, they passed to a spiritual existence [in another dimension—"*se-encantaram*"] and came to be cultivated. The *orixás* are manifestations of nature, the *orixás* are present in everything—in the air, the leaves, the day-to-day, in technology, even in the kitchen. They are present in everything. *Orixá*, for me, is this, especially for me as I live in the *culto* twenty-four hours a day.
Existiram orixás que viveram né, e depois se encantaram, passaram a ser cultuados. Os orixás são manifestações da natureza. Os orixás estão presentes em tudo, no ar, nas folhas, no dia-a-dia, na tecnologia, até na cozinha, tudo, os orixás estão presentes. Orixá, pra mim, é isso, principalmente pra mim que vivo no culto 24 horas.

Márlia: I understand that *orixás* are divinities, African gods, some of whom lived here like us, and others that didn't.
Eu entendo como orixá, divindades, deuses africanos que alguns viveram como nós e outros não.

Andrea: What I understand by *orixá* is a divinity, superior, that they say were blacks who lived a long time ago in Africa. Afterwards some *se-encantaram* [passed to a spiritual existence], others died. They were brought here to Brazil.
O que eu entendo de orixá é uma divindade, né, superior que contam né, que foram negros que já viveram há muito tempo antes na África, depois uns se-encantaram, outros morreram né, e foi trazido pra cá, pro Brasil.

Eduardo: *Orixá* is the messenger—let's say that God is a boss and needs workers. He is the boss who distributes the tasks to the servants, the messenger between God and the earth.
Orixá é o mensageiro, digamos, deus e os orixá, digamos assim que deus é um patrão e precise de empregado, então, é o chefe que distribui as tarefa pros servos. [Ele é o mensageiro] entre deus e a terra.

Augusto: *Orixá* is a divinity, a human being of nature, brought by the ancestors, by the slaves.
Orixá pra mim é um divindade, um ser-humano da natureza trazido pelos antigos ancestrais pelo escravo, é isso.

Daniela: *Orixá*—within our *culto* we think of God as a president who has his ministers. I think it works more or less like that. God left them to be responsible for everything on earth, the sea, the forest.
Orixá—dentro de nosso culto a gente tem o conhecimento de Deus como se fosse o presidente e Deus tem os seus ministros. Eu acho que é mais ou menos isso aqui que funciona. Deus deixou eles pra tomar conta a cada passo da terra, do mar, da mata.

Lucas: *Orixá* is the same as, for example, John the Baptist. To say that [*the orixá*] Xango is God is wrong. God is unique—all the rest came after him. So, he created a group of his descendants, the disciples, people that lived on earth I think, that evolved, that reached a level that's not the heavens, but a superior level. For me, that's what the *orixás* are. What I don't say is that Xango is Saint Jerome, in the case of syncretism. They aren't equal. They are just equivalent— Xango for us would be, for example, Saint John the Baptist for the Catholics. . . . *Orixá* translated means saint.
O orixá seria o mesmo que, por exemplo, João Batista—dizer que Xangô é Deus, não, Deus é único. Todos os demais vieram após ele. Então, ele criou o grupo de descendentes dele, os discipulos. Acho que as pessoas que viveram na terra, que evoluiram, que chegaram numa nível, não no céu, mas um nível superior. Assim pra mim são os orixás, eles também fazem parte desse. O que eu não digo é que Xangó é São Jerônimo, no caso no sincretismo. Não é igual. So que eles são equivalentes e eles—Xangô pra nós, o que seriam, um exemplo, São João Batista pros católicos. . . . Orixá traduzido significa santo.

Fábio: What I learned up until now is that *orixás* . . . are *entidades* that came to help people with whatever they needed . . . that they are spirits of light who are ready to help us at the time we need them.

*O que eu aprendi até hoje é que orixá são, são entidades que vieram pra
ajudar as pessoas no que elas necessitarem, no que elas tiverem precisando,
que são espiritos de luz que estão prontos para nos ajudar na hora que
estamos precisando.*

Taíssa: *Orixá* is similar to God. . . . I won't say he's greater than him, but
is similar to him. Because you can also make requests and be thankful
to them. If you are deserving, he will help you, just the same as God.
*Orixá é semelhante a Deus. . . . Não vou dizer que é maior do que ele,
mas é semelhante a ele. Porque voce, também com eles você pode pedir
e agradecer. Se você merecer, ele vai te ajudar, igualmente a Deus.*

These statements demonstrate the diversity of explicit representations of
the *orixás* even within this small community. For some members, *orixás* are
analogous with other culturally widespread superhuman agents, such as saints,
and with ordinary human functional roles, such as messengers, servants, and
ministers. They are represented as forces and manifestations of nature and
as divinities. They are ancestors, human beings, persons, and counselors. Yet,
despite the lack of consensus, all of these responses differ qualitatively from
the kind of elaborate description given by Sales above. Highly abstract concepts are exchanged for familiar metaphors and simple interpretations that—
for example, in the case of Ivone, Fábio, and Taíssa—produce clear inferences
for making sense of everyday situations. People's actual representations of *orixás*, if not their explicit descriptions, are consistently anthropomorphic. Even
when the *orixá* is said to be a force of nature, one observes that in practice, this
apparently nonhuman metaphor is differently conceptualized, particularly when
inferences and explanations must be drawn from it. Frequently, intuitive and
basic notions of agency underlie the solution of relevant real-time problems.
These "forces of nature" are attributed motivational states, desires, and intentions that result in certain recognizable forms of action; for example, a rough
sea may be attributed to the supernatural intervention of an angry *orixá* of the
oceans. In the rapid mental quest to make sense of a situation such as a rough
sea or a poor harvest, the abstract, nonagentive idea of an ethereal "force"
simply does not generate inferences, predictions, and explanations as swiftly
as the more intuitive, simple notion of an agency that causes that force. These
tendencies are the natural consequences of the workings of our cognitive machinery. Before we continue our description of people's concepts of spirits,
and particularly of spirit possession, let us pause to consider how some of the
general characteristics and content of the above statements are informed by
the tools and processes of the mind.

Necessary Cognitive Mechanisms

Research in the cognitive sciences is increasingly providing a clearer picture of the possibilities and limitations of the devices of human cognition. A subset of these mental devices has been termed "inference systems" (see Boyer 2001; Barrett 2004). These specialized systems, of which there are many, automatically generate multiple chains of inferences from perceptions of events. For example, the group of inference systems activated by physical objects is often referred to as "naïve physics" (by which we may intuitively represent, for instance, the push and pull of mechanical forces). Biological features are handled by our "naïve biology" system (allowing an intuitive understanding of processes of growth, reproduction, etc.), and goal-directed motion and intentional actions by our "naïve psychology" (permitting social interaction). Identification of a physical object with goal-directed motion, for example, activates inference systems for the handling of physical beings, such as persons or animals.

Inference systems organize information according to sets of principles for abstract categories of concrete concepts. Pascal Boyer (2001) describes these intermediary products of our mental systems as templates, or "domain concepts" (2003). Templates denote abstract categories, such as ANIMAL, PERSON, TOOL, and so on, which minds use to organize concrete concepts such as CAT, MAN, and HAMMER. They help organize like-kind concepts according to a set of principles or generalizations that specifically characterize the relevant template. If a person identifies a particular concept, "X," as belonging to the ontological category ANIMAL, much information can be inferred about X without any explicit instruction or further input. One can reasonably infer that X was born and will die and that it breathes, eats, grows, and gives birth to like species and so on. When a cat runs in front of you, mental tools operate automatically and below the level of conscious awareness in detecting, identifying, and nonreflectively describing the cat's biological properties according to the ANIMAL template. One also intuitively expects the cat to have all the properties of a normal, bounded physical object. The idea of a cat that levitates violates our intuitive assumption that physical objects fall to the ground when left unsupported. We also expect the cat to act on the basis of its motivations and intentions; we might presume that it eats because it wants to eat and that it has its reasons for fighting another cat.

Casting our minds back to the first hypothetical possession scenario presented at the beginning of this chapter, we can now grasp how much nonreflective, rapid mental processing must occur to allow for ready comprehension of the situation portrayed. In telling this story, it is not necessary to state explicitly that the friend in the story was born, has only one body, eats to survive, talks through her mouth, operates according to her own intentions when not possessed, and that the spirit possessing her has thoughts and acts and talks according to those thoughts, for all this information to be inferred. The efficiency of our mental tools allows us to recount the salient parts of the story without reducing the ease with which many unacknowledged details can be inferred and the whole situation comprehended. The concept of a person possessed by a spirit being may raise an interesting set of questions, or re- flective considerations, however. There are some things about such an idea that do not fit with our expectations about normal human psychology and our understandings of the laws of physics. Yet, it is not particularly cognitively cumbersome to imagine and comprehend that a person's body could be tem- porarily used by another thinking being that has no body. (Of course, this does not necessarily lead to ready acceptance of the *truth* of such a claim.) As Boyer has shown, this is because we are dealing with a special kind of concept, one that lends itself to rapid comprehension and is particularly interesting and easily remembered.

Counterintuitive Concepts

Spirit beings are one example of a class of attention-grabbing concepts that have been called Minimally Counterintuitive Concepts (MCIs) (Barrett 2000). MCI is a technical term that specifically denotes a concept, such as STONE, that meets most of our intuitive assumptions concerning its categorization (e.g., physical object, nonagentive, etc.) and description (e.g., solid, subject to gravity, etc.) but violates a property or a small number of properties that may normally be inferred for that concept (Boyer 1994, 2001). An example may be a smiling stone or a breathing stone or a happy stone. Note that saying that a concept is counterintuitive is not the same as saying that it is untrue. A growing stone is an MCI concept, but stones are known to expand under certain thermal conditions. Similarly, a plant that grows before your very eyes would not conform to the expectations we typically have for plants, yet we know that some bamboo grasses grow by up to four feet daily. To specify a concept as counterintuitive, therefore, does not necessarily imply a reference to its bizarreness or unusualness. Rather, the counterintuiveness of a concept is a qualitative classification based on and determined by naturally occurring assumptions that are generated by the inference systems activated by the concept and the domain that organizes information about that concept. As Barrett points out, this is precisely why MCI concepts in one culture will be

MCI concepts in another: mental "categorizers and describers operate essentially in the same way in all people everywhere. . . . A person who walks through walls is MCI anywhere. A rock that talks is MCI anywhere." He continues, "This independence from cultural relativism enables identification as an MCI to be a valuable tool in making pan-cultural predictions and explanations" (2004: 22).

Why should this be such a valuable tool for explaining features of spirit possession? Let us return to the idea of spirits. The concept of spirit may be created by taking an ordinary concept, such as man, and adding one or two counterintuitive features, such as intangibility and invisibility. Take, for example, the notion of *encantado* as described in the *culto*. Pai offers a description of what happens when a person becomes an *encantado*, as related to him by one of the *encantados* who regularly possesses him: "That's what Seu Bandeira told me. . . . When he went there [to the dwelling place of the *encantados*, the '*encantaria*'], he was no longer a person (*gente*). He became an *encantado*—he lost his physical nature, but he didn't die. His body wasn't buried. He passed from one dimension into another." *Foi isso que o Seu Bandeira me contou. . . . ele quando passou por lá, ele deixou de ser gente, ele passou a ser encantado, ele perdeu a natureza dele física, mas ele não morreu. O corpo dele não foi enterrado, ele passou de uma dimensão para outra.*

The *encantado* concept, as with many spirit concepts, is only *minimally* CI, in that it is still continuous with much of what we take for granted about people, such as the assumption that they think, have desires, and are motivated to behave on the basis of their desires.[4] Across cultures, many concepts about supernatural beings follow this pattern. MCI gods, ghosts, spirits, angels, and demons populate the world's religions. Although it seems that they may come in all shapes and sizes, our mental tools—inference systems, templates, categorizers, and describers—exert powerful constraints on the possibilities that our minds are likely to entertain and comprehend. The kind of highly counterintuitive spirit described in the second spirit-possession scenario at the beginning of this chapter has little potential to become a cross-culturally widespread concept. Although much more empirical testing is required, preliminary findings from cross-cultural studies that tested recall for similarly complex—or maximally counterintuitive—concepts support this claim (Boyer 2001: 85). The reason that recall is so poor is that too many of the inferences and assumptions that our mental tools generate are violated to allow ready conceptualization and memorization. As in the first hypothetical possession scenario above, the person being possessed by the spirit takes on counterintuitive qualities, insofar as his/her mind is no longer here but is replaced by another mind. However, unlike the first scenario, this spirit concept exhibits violation after violation of the physical, biological, and psychological expectations that normally define the ontological category of PERSON—it does not have its own body, it does not grow or age, it can hear all music everywhere when in the body of a person, it exists discontinuously, and so on. To this description is added a number of odd qualities (not *ontological* violations, but violations of *kind* expectations) that further violate people's normal expectations about a person—the spirit always sleeps, forgets its thoughts immediately, cannot communicate verbally, and so on. Although it is not impossible to acquire, accurately remember, and make some sense of the full description of such a spirit-possession episode, our mental categorizers and describers are so confused that we end up with a highly cumbersome brainteaser. Consequently, maximally counterintuitive concepts such as these do not spread well. Experimental and cross-cultural evidence suggests that concepts that achieve an optimal balance between the amount of intuitive and counterintuitive features—i.e. MCIs—are more likely to be faithfully passed on, all else being equal, than maximally counterintuitive or merely odd concepts (Barrett and Nyhof 2001; Boyer and Ramble 2001).

MCI Agents

There is another important factor relevant to the spread of the particular kind of MCI concept that concerns us here. As stated above, gods and spirits are construed very much like people. People across all cultures create gods and spirits in their own image, demonstrating an anthropomorphic tendency in the representation of supernatural beings (Guthrie 1993). Indeed, the fact that supernatural beings exhibit only minimal "tweaking" of the properties of normal persons allows our mental tools easily to generate inferences in much the same way as in normal interpersonal communication. The most important property here is the mind. Of all the human features that could potentially be projected onto supernatural beings, the one that is universally recurrent is the mind. Spirits and gods are agents with mental states, desires, motivations, and dispositions that drive their behavior. In this important regard, they are just like ordinary humans and animals. These are beings that, as Barrett observes, "do not merely respond mechanistically to the world around them but also act on the world because of internal (mental) states" (2004: 26). It is precisely for this reason that, of all the MCI concepts that could potentially gain attention, spirit and god concepts are the ones that are the most culturally widespread. Barrett continues,

Agents have tremendous inferential potential. Agents can cause
things to happen. . . . We can explain why things are so by appealing
to agents. We can anticipate what an agent might do. We can't anticipate what a rock might do, only what might be done to it. Not
surprisingly, then . . . intentional agents are the MCIs that people tell
stories about, remember, and tell to others.[5] (Barrett 2004: 26)

Spirit concepts trigger richer inferences in a wider range of situations
than nonagent MCI concepts do. The range of inferences afforded by the
presence of an agent that thinks, influences, and acts in any situation makes it
highly relevant to the things that happen around us (Sperber 1996; Sperber
and Wilson 1986; Boyer 2001). This relevance is tremendously increased
when that agent has special access to relevant information that mere humans
may not be privy to. Returning to our two scenarios at the beginning of the
chapter, even if both kinds of spirits only minimally violated our intuitive
expectations regarding normal persons, allowing for ready conceptualization
and recall, the spirit in the second of our two hypothetical scenarios would still
have significantly less potential to be transmitted between people. As stated
above, cultural transmission is relevance-driven. A spirit being that has no
access to knowledge of what goes on around and between humans, that cannot communicate, and that is always in an unconscious state will generate
very few inferences of any personal or social relevance. Compare this with
spirits like the *orixás* who may know my thoughts; my past; whether my
marriage will be a success; whether or not my partner is cheating; what the
cause of my misfortune is; and whether someone lied, stole, or cheated or
knows that I lied, stole, or cheated. Such facts, and the inferences and plans of
action that can be generated as a result of knowing them, matter to social
interaction. And, as Boyer points out, "what is 'important' to human beings,
because of their evolutionary history, are the conditions of social interaction:
who knows what, who is not aware of what, who did what with whom, when
and what for" (2001: 167).

In the early stages of our species' evolutionary history, accessing or in-
ferring particular kinds of information that could increase our advantages, as
potential prey, was crucially important in ensuring survival. Such evolutionary
pressures and complex social exchange were responsible for the selection of
specialized mental capacities that enable cooperative social interaction in fully
modern humans. Information we can gather about those around us still holds
strategic value in many social situations. In some cases, the knowledge may be
relatively inconsequential and unimportant, providing only fleeting rewards,

for example, as an item of gossip. Sometimes it is crucial for our own prospects in life that we have access to certain kinds of information about the activities of our enemies, potential rivals, friends, and kin. The shape and success of our plans in marriage and work, for example, may depend on the knowledge we can acquire about what our partners, bosses, and workmates are doing and planning also. Boyer has labeled these kinds of knowledge "strategic information" (2001)—on the basis of knowledge acquired about other people's moves, one can make educated decisions and maneuvers for personal gain. This information, however, is not always available to us. Much of what other people do that influences and affects our chances in life remains hidden from our view. This is where spirits come in. Spirits typically enjoy privileged access to strategic knowledge. They can observe the wider network of interconnecting relationships—and actions and their consequences—in the past, present, and often in the future. They are therefore potentially powerful allies in the individual struggles and competition of everyday life. It is significant then that the result of millennia of cultural selection is that gods and spirits across the world most recurrently appear as agents who know more than we do (see chapter 8).

This brief account postulates and describes some of the fundamental mechanisms by which certain kinds of spirit concepts become cross-culturally recognizable, recurrent, and relevant. The idea of person-like beings that have unlimited access to socially strategic information is a readily comprehensible and inferentially powerful idea. All else being equal, such ideas enjoy a selective advantage in cultural transmission. Conceptually "heavier" ideas of supernatural agents do get transmitted, but these require costly cognitive resources to ensure faithful representation and transmission (Whitehouse 2004). This may explain why *culto* participants rarely, if ever, seem to represent their *orixás* as nonagentive "manifestations of nature" outside of theological and analytical reflections. This requires instruction, study, and time to reflect. In fact, studies by Barrett (1998, 1999) suggest that even in those religious traditions that possess deities that are maximally counterintuitive (e.g., all-seeing, all-knowing, omnipresent, etc.), as described in explicit report and theological teachings, people's implicit representations of these same gods diverge from such stated beliefs. Cognitive constraints are such that real-time processing of such agents' qualities demonstrated divergence away from cognitively cumbersome representations of the gods toward more intuitive MCI representations. For example, a god that is explicitly stated to be in all places at all times was often represented by participants, when their cognitive systems were under pressure,[6] as being subject to normal human, physical limitations (Barrett 1998).

This suggests that the very same tools that *facilitate* the conceptualization and transmission of god and spirit concepts also *constrain* the particular ways in which our minds can represent the properties and actions of gods and spirits. Conceptually heavy notions of supernatural agents are more demanding on our ordinary mental tools and therefore require additional instruction, mental rehearsal, and deep reflection to ensure faithful representation over time and between people. In such cases, certain transmissive dynamics may come into play that simply are not required for the acquisition, memory, and communication of MCI concepts (Whitehouse 2004). MCI concepts, contrastingly, so capitalize on the ordinary structures and tools of the mind, diverging only so slightly in any significant cognitive respect from the intuitions that those structures afford, that their rapid spread is quite natural (all else being equal). It is the spirits' proximity to the ontological category of person that makes them so easy to conceptualize even without much explicit instruction—the fact that they do not have bodies does not interfere significantly with the way in which we can intuitively reason about their nonphysical properties. Knowing that they have minds is enough for us to infer that they have beliefs and desires that motivate behavior, they can see and hear and communicate, and so on.

The specific descriptive content and meaning of MCI spirit concepts, and the ecological and cultural contexts and situations in which they occur, though important elements in the whole complex, cannot in themselves explain why such sets of concepts tend to be universally widespread. Minimal counterintuitiveness, agency, and access to strategic knowledge are widespread properties of spirits that are not only "interesting" for descriptive purposes. The proposed cognitive mechanisms that underlie their transmission across cultures are potentially crucial for explaining the form and incidence of globally widespread spirit concepts. They are therefore pertinent to explaining the form and relevance of spirit concepts among *culto afro* participants in Belém. We have observed how *orixá* and other *entidade* concepts may be characterized as MCI. We can now appreciate that the kinds of *orixá* concepts held by members of the *terreiro* community are fundamentally different from complex versions that may appear in the texts of *culto* scholars. The spirit beings that feature in the stories and legends are agents that are sufficiently counterintuitive to be catchy, memorable, and rich in potential inferences. Yet their actions and behaviors exhibit little distinction from the social dynamics and expectations that characterize interaction between humans. For example, wrong behavior may incur the *orixás'* punishment. Good behavior may curry the *orixas'* favour (see Taíssa's statement above). We shall see in chapter 7 how the representation of the *entidades* as social beings with feelings, beliefs, principles, and moral intuitions contributes to their everyday salience.

There is another way, however, by which *entidades* become relevant to everyday life and meaning that does not depend upon notions of spirits as social actors. *Orixás*, in particular, are believed formatively to shape *filhos'* personality, character, and attitudes. The nature of this influence is represented as analogous to similarities between parents and children or to the determining influence of birth signs. Each individual exudes certain features of personality and even appearance that are characteristic of being a *filho* (son) or *filha* (daughter) of a particular *orixá*. This generates enormous potential for people to perceive the influences of the *orixás* in the mundane features of personality and character and to predict and interpret how these influences cause people to act in certain ways. Every individual is said to "be of" a particular *orixá* (e.g., *Ele é de Oxum*, "He is of Oxum"). One's chief *orixá* is discovered through the simplified, *ifá*-derived, Yoruban divination method of tossing the cowry shells. A secondary *orixá* is also identified, revealing the male-female *orixá* couple of which one "is," or to which one belongs. The moment one's chief *orixá* is discovered is often preceded by much speculation on the basis of physical characteristics, such as appearance, health, physical defects, beauty, strength, and agility, as well as psychological profile, assessing such attributes as vanity, ambition, confidence, generosity, selfishness, intelligence, and so on. On confirming the identity of the *orixá*, a common sentiment to be heard throughout the community is, *Mas ela é a cara de Iemanjá, uma verdadeira filha de Iemanjá*, "Well, she's just the image of Iemanja, a true daughter of Iemanjá," on account of the matching character traits. It is particularly gratifying, then, to be identified as "of Oxum," the *orixá* of beauty. Oxumaré, often associated with riches, is another reassuring result, although this *orixá*'s double nature may be reflected in one's tendency to vacillate. Indeed, the *filho* of Oxumaré often exhibits, or is suspected of, bisexual inclinations.

But who is the image of whom here? I have argued that, because of the intuitive expectations that we have for agents in general, our minds are constrained to process and represent divine beings in certain ways. The resemblance, therefore, fundamentally operates in the reverse direction. Our intuitive notions about agency are so bound up with our expectations about human psychological properties that we are predisposed automatically and easily to make gods in our own image. Klass has referred to this process more generally as the "constructive capacity" by which spirits and divinities emerge. He encourages those attempting to explain the emergence of spirit concepts to return to and consider a remark allegedly made by Voltaire: "God created Man in His own image—and man returned the compliment" (Klass 2003: 125). Perhaps

this is best achieved by considering people's representations of spirit possession. It is in possession that the tendency to represent spirits as humans is
particularly apparent. Spirits who possess people, as obvious as the point may
be, are invariably and inescapably incarnate in human form.

Spirit Possession in the *Culto*

Numerous theories of *incorporação* ("possession") circulate in Afro-Brazilian
traditions. Even within the *terreiro*, people offer divergent descriptions of what
occurs when a person is possessed. Depending on whom one asks, on entering
a state of possession, one's own spirit is said to "lie down" (*deitar*), "journey
to the other world" (*viajar pro outro mundo*), "dream" (*sonhar*), "sleep" (*dor-
mir*), or "remain watching" (*ficar vendo*). Some people hold to the view that
there is an exchange of energies, while others have more elaborate theories
that appear to carry little explicit reference to agentive beings. However, on
closer observation of behavior and even informal chat about possession, a
number of clear points of convergence emerge.

First, spirits are normally represented as entering the person's body. Some
members describe possession as the moment in which a spirit or energy of a
spirit "leans against" (*encostar*) the person, but acknowledge that this notion
had been explicitly taught to them by certain religious leaders who regarded
notions about spirits entering bodies as erroneous. Nevertheless, among the
majority, the locus of control is not commonly represented as existing outside
the body or the person, but within the body, and specifically in the head.[7]
People refer to possessing spirits in particular episodes as "Spirit X in the
head of Person A." Spirits are said to "throw themselves into the body" (*se
jogar no corpo da pessoa*), to "come in the head" (*vir na cabeça*) of the medium,
and "to descend in a person" (*descer na pessoa*). People are said to "catch"
(*pegar*) or "receive" (*receber*) spirits. When in doubt about whether a person is
possessed, one can check by asking, "Who is it?" "Who's speaking?" or "Who's
there?" The underlying assumption is that, in terms of psychological faculties,
one is interacting with either the person or the spirit. The confirming answer
invariably identifies either one or the other, and conversation will proceed
accordingly. If the person is possessed, the interlocutor may pick up conversation from where he left off the last time he chatted to that particular spirit.
He may recount secrets that he wouldn't otherwise disclose, or he may ask for
advice. Whatever they talk about, there appears to be a clear assumption that
because a person is possessed, that person is no longer present as a conscious,
thinking, acting agent; that consciousness, or mind, has been displaced by

another. The possessing spirit entity refers to the host-medium in the third-person singular. For example, when Pai was possessed once, the possessing *entidade* offered his opinion about some issue, swiftly adding, "I don't know if Pai would agree" (*Nao sei se o pai-de-santo vai achar a mesma coisa*), indicating that the words were those of the *entidade*, and not of Pai. Whether the host's (i.e., the person who is possessed) spirit is said to be sleeping, to be off on a journey to another dimension, to have taken flight, or to have remained wherever it was at the moment in which the host became possessed, there is a clear demarcation drawn between the two agents. One medium describes the changeover as follows when she is possessed by her *erê* (child spirit):

> I don't know where my spirit goes, I don't know. I only know that I switch off. I don't remain in me. When the *erê* is close to me, I feel like eating sweet things, I feel like being mischievous . . . you can be sure that the *erê* is coming.
>
> *Não sei te dizer pra onde o meu espirito vai, eu não sei te dizer. Eu só sei que eu apago, não fico em mim. Quando a erê tá perto de mim eu sinto vontade de comer doce, eu sinto contade de fazer traquinajem . . . Aí, pode contar que a erê vem.*

Another described how one's own spirit withdraws and another spirit comes and throws itself in the body. (*Incorporação é o seguinte, é aquele espirito, afasta, e vem um outro espirito e joga no teu corpo.*). On a number of occasions, people recounted how, when they had mistaken a spirit for the medium, or not realized that the medium was possessed, they would be firmly told, "I am not [medium's name], I am [spirit's name] (*Eu não sou . . . eu sou . . .*)."

Second, one observes that the most significant and consistently believed effect is the transfer of control from the person to the spirit. The spirit is said to "take control," "dominate the mind," or "command the body and the mind." Evidence, if required, can often be found in behavioral changes, in the particular performances of possession. Striking transformations certainly increase the credibility of the episode. However, this is not always a necessary part of possession behavior. In fact, in the *culto afro*, mediumistic ability is often judged by the control with which people enter possession. When an observer can barely detect that the medium is possessed, the medium is accredited with an advanced degree of mediumistic development. What is important here is that *any* action performed is not attributable to the intentions of the host but rather to the intentions, motivations, and dispositions of the spirit that is now in control. As one of my informants once stated, "Possession for me is a state of unconsciousness . . . in which we are not answerable for our actions, our bodily movements....We don't have control of our bodies anymore. It's the total loss of control of the body and the mind. Something else controls—it is the spiritual being" (*Incorporação pra mim é um estado de inconsciência . . . A gente não responde mais pelos nossos atos, os movimentos corporais. . . . A gente não têm mais commando sobre o nosso corpo, e é isso, é perda total do commando do corpo e da mente . . . Algo comanda, é o ser espiritual*).

Some of the behaviors and actions that ensue from this proposition produce amusing spectacles. For example, on one of the occasions that the *pai-de-santo* was possessed by an indigenous, *índio* spirit, he initially rubbed his beard and scratched his face for some time, appearing to suffer some discomfort. This behavior was attributed to the fact that the Indian was perplexed by the presence of facial hair. *Índios* were known to be a clean-shaven people, and, according to some *filhos*, it was possible that he may have thought that there was some kind of creature on his face. Other behaviors and preferences are acknowledged as integral to the spirit's character and should be recognized and entertained. Mariana's love of fine jewelry, robes, and perfumes is attributed to her life on earth as a Turkish princess. Making gifts and providing her with such items when she possesses Pai is an important gesture of welcome and respect. This appeals to her goodwill for assistance in the accomplishment of everyday events and ensures return visits.

The Significance of Possession

The very presence of the spirits through possession is interpreted as something significant, or, as one member of the community said, as "a message." Depending on the spirit and the context, something positive or negative is communicated simply by the spirit's arrival. In everyday activities, such as in the daily "work" (e.g., counseling, healing, and so on) the same spirits reappeared almost daily. Their function as counselors, guides, and curers was widely recognized, and their presence was taken for granted. Zé Pelintra, for example, presided over an association that was responsible for the organization of various events in the *terreiro* and regularly came to chair meetings. Some spirits, such as the *orixás*, visited the *terreiro* to possess their *filhos* only on set occasions stipulated by the annual calendar of ceremonial activities. In these episodes, they rarely conversed and actually did little other than perform their dance and bestow blessings on *filhos* with a simple physical gesture. They are believed, however, to communicate a certain message by making their very presence visible amongst the mortals. For example, a ceremony for the female *orixás* was judged as a success on account of the number of *orixás* that saw fit to come and possess their *filhos*. In another ceremony, the appearance of the *vodun* Acossi was interpreted as an omen of bad fortune.

Similarly, the failure of the spirits to "manifest themselves" at a ceremony may be reflected upon at length. Pai tells the story of a ceremony at one *terreiro* in which participants sang, danced, and beat the drums "the whole night, waiting for the *entidade* to manifest herself and she didn't. It was the *festa* for her and she didn't want to come, and didn't come. Later, we discovered that she didn't come because she didn't like the clothing that was made for her" (*Houve casos de bater uma noite toda esperando tal entiddade se manifestar e ela não se manifestou. Era dia de festa dela e ela não quis vir e não veio. Depois nós fomos saber que ela não veio porquê ela não gostou da roupa que foi feito pra ela*). A rather different kind of situation also illustrates this point aptly; one *culto* participant who had previously attended another *terreiro* in the city started to frequent activities at Pai's *terreiro*. He had been identified as an *oga* in the previous *terreiro*, or as someone who does not have the inherent mediumistic quality that enables possession by spirits. In Pai's house, however, he began to sense the approximations of spirits and started to develop his mediumship (*mediunidade*). The approximations and anticipated possession by the spirits signaled that he had come to the right place for his spiritual development.

In all such possession contexts—counseling, curing, homage ceremonies, and *casa* administration—the outward behavior of the possessed person is potentially attributable to the intentions of the possessing entity. There are many variations in the performances of possessed individuals. Nevertheless, in episodes in which the person is acknowledged to be truly possessed, all behaviors and communicative interaction (whether verbal or otherwise) are explicitly represented as being ultimately governed by the minds of the spirits, as distinct, autonomous persons. This is intimately connected to the appeal that possessing spirits hold for individuals soliciting supernatural (superhuman) guidance.

As we have observed, *culto* participants enjoy the counsel and assistance of the spirits in everyday affairs. While these spirits' personalities often display such a high degree of resemblance to human hosts that the observer is often incapable of distinguishing between a possessed and a nonpossessed individual, it is the characteristic nonhuman—or the superhuman—properties of the spirits that makes them appealing. Incorporeity, for example, grants them freedom of access to knowledge that normal humans may not easily acquire. It also permits the very possession of the medium. This potentially grants the interlocutor direct access to a rich reserve of strategic knowledge. The belief that an individual can become a supernatural agent (in terms of personhood) provides a powerful resource for the negotiation of the everyday situations that one confronts. As noted above, because supernatural agents have desires, beliefs, intentions, and the ability to act and to cause things to happen, they have tremendous inferential potential for the interpretation and explanation of events. Barrett writes, "Contrast agent concepts with vanishing rocks. . . . The vanishing rock cannot begin to support inferences regarding morality in social interaction, why trouble befalls people, how the rains come, why the crops succeed or fail, or what happens to the dead. MCI agents can" (2004: 28). Couple the inferential potential of supernatural agents with the facility that we have easily to reason about the intentions, beliefs, and desires of other social beings, and we have a powerful tool for reasoning about the causes of fortune and misfortune in everyday life. Being able to confirm one's suspicions through prayer, divination, and other means is a desirable prospect. Direct communication with the gods in consultation with a possessed medium is a particularly attractive option. Despite risking mockery by individuals who trick observers and clients by faking possession states, the payoffs of a "real" possession can be highly rewarding. These issues will be discussed more fully in chapter 8.

Conclusion

In this chapter, we have considered the cognitive processes that underpin cross-culturally recurrent features of the form of spirits and possession. It has been suggested that the mechanisms that enable people to make inferences about other agents, particularly humans, are employed in the representation of spirits. That the properties of spirits only minimally diverge from those of humans in specifiable ways makes such concepts easy to grasp. That they are agents specifically with properties that allow them increased access to strategic knowledge and that enable them to cause things to happen (e.g., to influence one's personality, answer requests, heal, etc.) makes them particularly relevant to explaining everyday situations and to efforts to improve one's life circumstances generally. Their appeal is enhanced by their increased accessibility through possession. *Culto* participants can converse, plead, joke, and cry with the spirits; directly question them about their personal concerns; and potentially receive concrete, unambiguous answers to their requests and queries. We have also observed how notions of possession are constrained by the capacities of the inference systems employed in the representation of people and spirits. Participants' descriptions of possession emphasize the displacement of *minds*. Because the host's mind has departed, all actions are now attributable to the possessing agent. Interaction with the spirit—and appeal to his/her powers—is direct and immediate, providing a rich source of counsel, guidance, and assistance in everyday life.

Observations from the field, however, indicate that the above account of possession presents a more simplistic, or ideal, description of possession than is the case on the ground. It appears that not all behaviors of the hosts are attributable to the possessing agencies. Intervening social factors appear to influence people's perceptions of the controlling agency of possessed hosts. Morally charged aspects of social perception are inevitably activated when one represents the incorporation of a novel agency "into the head" of another person. These aspects are relevant to anthropological writings on the inconsistency and ambiguity that surrounds possession episodes and worlds that are inhabited by spirits. In the following chapter, we shall consider in more depth the ways in which possession is mentally represented and possession behavior is interpreted in practice (e.g., by the host's friends and enemies). The illustrations, observations, and claims I shall make help us begin to think about how processes of cognition and social perception constrain the real-time processing of actual possession episodes. The ethnographic data and analysis suggest ways in which real-world workability of an idea—even those ideas that largely fit with intuitive assumptions—is potentially constrained by a wider complex of social-cognitive factors.

7

Observing Possession

Quando eu desincorporava, eu via aquelas pessoas, estranhas para
mim, mas elas se sentiam íntimas minhas porque conviviam com minha
entidade.

When I came out of possession, I used to see those people, unknown
to me, but they felt themselves to be close friends because they
were on intimate terms with (*lit. lived alongside*) my spirit entity.
                                  —Pai describes his experiences as a medium
                                  during early childhood

Studies of spirit possession from across the world tend to present
observers' perceptions of possession as straightforward and unambiguous. Witnesses of possession performances are reported to be
captivated and compelled by the spectacle of the spirits taking control
of their human hosts. The character of host fades into the background as the embodied spirit becomes manifest. The transformation
is total—all actions performed by the host are now attributable to
the agency of the possessing spirit. Stoller, for example, writes of a
successful performance among the Songhay, "In possession, the
sounds of the Songhay possession ceremonies *are* the voices of the
ancestors. These distant voices are heard in the godji's cries, the gasi's
clacks, the sorko's words, and the spirit's screams" (1989: 209). In
his account of Haitian spirit possession, Ari Kiev affirms that "possession occurs when a loa selects to 'mount' or 'enter the head' of his

cheval (person possessed), thereby replacing his soul. . . . All thoughts and behavior are then attributed to the loa" (1966: 143). In his ethnography of "*orisha* work" in Trinidad, Kenneth Lum writes, "Since it was the spirit (the 'actual you') which animated the physical body, after an orisha had manifested on a person, it was that orisha who was now animating that person's body. . . . The displaced spirit only returned when the orisha had left" (2000: 156). Lewis also makes explicit the association between displacement of control and the apportioning of blame, claiming that in the Trinidadian Shango cult, as elsewhere, "whatever the possessed person does is done with impunity since he is considered to act as the unconscious and involuntary vehicle of the gods" (1971: 105).

Some anthropologists, however, have noted the contradiction, inconsistency, and ambiguity that characterize the worlds of spirits they have attempted to understand. For example, Niko Besnier's account of discourses on spirits on Nukulaelae Island, Tuvalu demonstrates the heteroglossia that so often accompanies spirit phenomena: "Vagueness and uncertainty suffuse Nukulaelae spirit discourse across many contexts. . . . [T]hese characteristics are indicative of the multivocal texture of spirit discourse, a multivocality that sometimes results in several seemingly conflicting voices being heard at once, or in rapid succession to one another within the same speech event" (1996: 87). Besnier claims that heteroglossia defines mediumship: "Mediumship is a competition between the voice of a spirit and the voice of a medium, since the two have only one mouth to speak through" (ibid.: 85). Similarly, Lambek writes, "Possession contains the central paradox that an actor both is and is not who she claims to be" (1989: 53); and Boddy observes that possession by the *zar* spirits, "however social they may be, creates a paradox in and for those involved, as the possessed are simultaneously themselves and alien beings" (1989: 9). Bloch comments, "It seems probable that the spectator at a séance never imagines a direct relation with the spirit but always a relation via the medium" (2004: 62).

These observations beg crucial questions of those approaching this situation from a cognitive perspective: How does the observer cognize the transference of agency in practice? Is this largely intuitively grasped? Or does it demand additional cognitive resources at the conscious level? Does the possession context alter everyday concepts of intentional action? Does the potential for incongruence between statement and intent (of the possessed host) raise observers' sensitivity to particular kinds of behavioral cues (e.g., behaviors that are perceived to be out of character for either the host or the spirit)? Do contextual factors, such as relational situations between hosts and observers, impact on perception processes? If so, do they inform implicit representations, drive explicit responses, or influence behavior toward the possessed person?

How do these factors potentially constrain the forms and transmission of possession concepts and practices?

In this chapter I suggest possible causes for the apparent ambiguities that often arise in the conceptualization of actual possession episodes. I present ethnographic data from possession episodes in the *culto afro* that suggest that observers do not consistently perceive the behaviors of a host (who is believed to be possessed) to be attributable to the intentions (or intentional agency) of the spirit. I claim that this inconsistency is due to factors other than the perceived success of the performance. The incongruity between what people *say* happens in possession (i.e., the spirit comes into the head, the person's spirit leaves—what may be termed the "principle of displacement") and what they *do* (i.e., behave as though the person was still present) is often apparent even when the observer is certain that the possession is genuine. This suggests that observers' perceptions and interpretations of possessed hosts' behaviors are influenced by factors of which they are not necessarily aware. On the basis of scientific evidence on processes of social interaction, I argue that subtle contextual cues and psychological biases come into play in any possession episode. These biases generate inferences that may not be explicit or accessible to conscious reflection, but can (sometimes observably) influence the nature of the observer's behavior toward the host. These factors may explain the apparent difficulties that observers of possession episodes have to represent implicitly the transference of agency and the transformation of the host into a new person. A basic appreciation of how humans perceive, interpret, and explain the behaviors of other humans, of how contextual and relational factors may influence such perceptions, and of the ways in which neurological, cognitive, and psychological factors lead to biased judgments of other people's behaviors in everyday social interaction, helps us begin to appreciate the complex processes entailed in representing the act of possession.[1]

"Possession Communication"

Stoller's ethnography on Songhay spirit possession closes with the following reflection: "Possession is more than a domain of philosophical reflection and academic exegesis; it is also an arena of human passion in which individuals of diverse social standing have been thrown together" (1989: 211). The notion of an arena of passion, in which acts, actors, and their audiences meet, evokes a theatrical aspect of possession that has been widely employed in anthropological interpretations of spirit possession phenomena and of ritual more broadly (e.g., Leiris 1958; Turner 1982). Boddy, for example, describes possession rites and individual experiences of zar spirits as "public matters," in which "the zar, as a corpus of beliefs and their ritual dramatization, is viewed as an aesthetic form" (1989: 9). Viewing possession as a form of theatre invokes a useful metaphor for the appreciation of the fundamental social units in performance and observation of the possession episode. At a basic level, it highlights aspects of possession that are necessary or conducive to its successful transmission.

Possession episodes are generally composed of hosts, spirits, and observers. Hosts and observers are as essential to the enactment of possession as actors and audiences are to the activities carried out on theatre stages and film sets. Spirit hosts are the necessary medium of the possessing entity, the performers of the script, so to speak. The audience is also a vital element of the possession arena. Possession is widely associated with medium-centered séances, healing practices, counseling sessions, the delivery of oracles, communal possession ceremonies, and many other social activities. Furthermore, if, as anthropologists have suggested, possession is about resituating identity, and if it is often used as a medium of resistance, a social critique, a theatrical parody, a political act, moral statement, mimetic compulsion, embodied aesthetic, and for the "rendering of embodied knowledge graspable by others through performance and conversation" (Boddy 1994: 426), an audience is desirable for the delivery of the message. These views of possession are reminiscent of traditional functionalist and symbolist interpretations of ritual as, respectively, instrumental and expressive. To put it crudely, rituals *do* something social (i.e., they have effects upon the world), as well as *mean* something (Bloch 1986). As Turner observes, "participants . . . try to show others what they are doing or have done; actions take on a performed-for-an-audience aspect" (1986: 76). The performance metaphor enables one to focus both on what possession does, that is, on possession as an action, and on what it means to the participants and observers. It also helps one consider the crucial role of the spirits, the complex partnership between spirit and host, and how this affects observers' perceptions of what is "done" and "said" in possession episodes.

It has long been debated among anthropologists, however, whether ritual acts actually mean anything (Bloch 1974; Staal 1979). Many anthropologists have observed that participants and observers in rituals often cannot express what their rituals mean. Yet they also deny that they are meaningless. Although the continuing challenge for some anthropologists has been personally to reflect on what the rituals could mean to the participants, and on their wider social effects, others have entertained doubts about whether anything is really communicated through ritual. Ritual, on this view, is simply a repeat performance of a series of actions and statements that no longer carry meaning for the participants.

Maurice Bloch has suggested that rituals, in fact, lie "somewhere between an action and a statement" (1986: 10). They are neither only about doing (in the sense of "merely repeating") nor only about saying, but lie somewhere between the poles of simple imitation of others' acts and meaningful communication of a message. Bloch observes that "ritual communication" differs from everyday communication in that the origin of the actions and their meanings do not lie in the intentionality of the actor, but in the minds of historically "remote authorities" (2004: 74). Participants in the ritual defer to these authorities, accepting the truth of what is being said and done without necessarily understanding it and without clearly identifying to whom they are deferring. As Whitehouse states, "The intentional states behind ritual actions...are assumed to be located at least partly outside the mind of the actor" (2004: 4). What rituals do, express, and say is therefore ambiguous and fuzzy, permitting different and potentially conflicting understandings among participants in the same ritual.

Bloch characterizes spirit possession as an "act of deference," in which mediums and spectators "abandon their intentionality" (i.e., the effort to understand what the spirit is saying), deferring to the supernatural source of the words the medium is "quoting" (2004: 62). In the possession episode, as in ritual, it is not relevant whether the medium or the spectators understand the utterances coming out of his or her mouth. The supernatural source of the words demands "compulsory deference." Utterances are held to be true, even though they are not fully understood. Bloch claims that in spirit possession "the effort in being transparent, that is, in deferring totally, is the real focus of the action" (ibid.). In contrast to ritual, however, the identity of the spirit, as the originating mind behind the utterances, is known to both hosts and observers.

This final observation may seem obvious and incontestable. Indeed, many times during fieldwork, research participants informed me with confidence about the identity of possessing spirits. For the duration of possession episodes hosts' names were replaced by spirits' when talking with or about them. All behaviors and statements were said to be unambiguously attributable to the possessing agent. On the surface, it often appeared that once the possession had occurred (i.e., the host's agency had been displaced by the spirit's), there was little difference between what could be called "possession communication" with an embodied spirit and everyday communication with other (deference-deserving) humans.

"Possession communication," however, as with Bloch's "ritual communication," differs fundamentally from everyday communication in ways other than heightened deference. In everyday situations, an "actor" does something—the act—which the audience observes. The actor is the agent performing the behavioral event, and the observer is the agent perceiving the behavioral event. Take a simple gesture, for example; *Mauro kissed Flávia's hand.* Mauro, in this case, is the agent performing the action, and Flávia is an observer of the action. Assuming that Flávia perceives Mauro's behavior not as inadvertent, but as intentional, something is communicated via the act by Mauro to Flávia. In possession, however, the body and agency of the host are separated and a new agent animates the host's body. The host loses his mind, so to speak, and the spirit gains a body. In the case of possession, then, Mauro, as the medium of the spirit, is the physical performer of the act, but he is not the agent. "Possession communication," therefore, differs from everyday communication in that, although there is only one body involved, there are potentially two, or more, candidate agents.

Bloch has stated that spirit possession differs from ritual in that the originating mind of the actions is known. I suggest, however, that this misses a significant point of divergence between "possession communication" and "ritual communication." In ritual, actions are performed according to a standardized procedural script, or at least they are perceived to be. Possession, unless it occurs within a stylized, ceremonial context, has no such prescribed formularity. Although elements of the possession episode are standardized, or fixed, they are no more so than in everyday communication. For example, just as there are expectations and "rules" that may govern one's social behavior in general (e.g., do not hold a conversation with your eyes shut, face the person with whom you are talking, etc.), and as a member of a specific category (e.g., grandmothers do not go to raves, priests wear clerical collars, etc.), so, too, are certain spirits expected to talk about certain things, perform certain functions, wear certain kinds of clothes, and exhibit certain preferences. Apart from the constraints ensuing from these and other general expectations, however, what the possessed hosts say and do is spontaneous. There is no specific, fixed sequence of actions to which the performer must adhere, and against which the observer can assess the author of the behavior. There is no reference against which the intentionality behind the words can be verified. It is impossible, therefore, for the observer to confirm that the behaviors and statements are attributable to an originating mind that is external to the host. As such, behaviors are potentially attributable to the possessing spirit, but they are also potentially attributable to the host. Hence, it may be clear that the "Great-grandmother is the spirit" (Bloch 2004: 73), but it may not always be clear that the actions of the host are attributable to the great-grandmother and not to the medium. The source of the utterances remains ambiguous.

A poignant example of this kind of ambiguity is given in an account by Wafer, in which he relates some of the behaviors of two Candomblé *exua* spirits, Corquisa and Sete Saia, and their host, Taís.

> Taís once said that Corquisa and Sete Saia are really the same *exua*, with different names. In fact, I found Taís, Sete Saia, and Corquisa adopting each other's characteristics so frequently that it became difficult for me to separate them completely. Corquisa would some-times use Sete Saia's coarse mannerisms, just as Sete Saia would lapse into refinement. On one occasion, as Corquisa was drinking a glass of spirits, she said that when she drinks *cachaça*, it is not herself but Sete Saia who drinks, since her own preferred drink is champagne.
>
> I also recall a couple of times when the *exuas* acted as though they were Taís. Once Corquisa was telling me about herself, and said *"eu sou muito educado"* ("I am very refined"). But she used the masculine instead of the feminine form of the adjective. . . . I did not regard it necessary to consider the lapses in the performances of Tais's *exuas* as evidence of *equê* [false trance]—although it may have been. I simply took it for granted that, since the three of them used the same body, they would find it hard not to get in each other's way. (1991: 34)

In this example, Wafer recounts explicit thoughts and reflections gener-ated by specific possession behaviors, focusing on aspects of the performance that triggered doubts about false trance. I, too, can recall having similar doubts. One such occasion was during a visit to a medium's house. On arrival, the medium, who was possessed with his chief spirit, greeted me in the usual Belenense fashion with a kiss on both cheeks and some casual chitchat. He returned to his work with clients, and I continued chatting with various other visitors arriving at the house. Some time later, he emerged from his consul-tation room, now "pure" (*puro*), that is, no longer possessed, and greeted those visitors who had arrived in the meantime. I, however, was not greeted by the medium. I was quite confident that I was not an unwelcome guest, nor was there any possibility of being inadvertently overlooked as he went around the circle of people gathered. I could think of no other explanation than that the medium was aware of having greeted me. This immediately raised doubts about the possession I had witnessed. Although false trance was not consid-ered commonplace among *terreiro* participants, there is no doubt that regular observers were much more attune to the subtleties of a compelling possession performance than I was.

But there is much more to perceiving agency than the kind of explicit reflection illustrated in these vignettes. Based on ethnographic data and evidence from the field of social psychology, I claim that attribution of intentionality is not only reflectively considered in terms of genuine and false trance assessments. It is not solely influenced by the success, or otherwise, of the performance (e.g., by "lapses"). The attribution of intentionality to either the possessing agent or the host-agent is informed by factors pertaining to the inherent social character of possession. Implicit psychological mechanisms and social perception biases inform both reflective and nonreflective thoughts and behavior toward the possessed person. As we shall observe, it is because of these tacit mental processes that it is unlikely that the "consciousness of deference" will ultimately disappear, as Bloch claims (2004: 72). In fact, these processes may be partly responsible for the *absence* of deference that is so often apparent in possession contexts in the *culto afro*. Although deference to supernatural entities (as, for example, semi-gods, healing masters, African ancestors, intrepid explorers, and skilled warriors and soldiers) certainly characterized people's explicit discourse, it was not always a feature of behavior and apparent attitudes toward the spirits when they came to possess their *filhos*. In this chapter, I present evidence from fieldwork and from social psychology that supports these claims. It is helpful to preface this with a brief consideration of some of the cognitive mechanisms and processes that are fundamental to the representation of intentionality and agency in general.

Representing Agency: Reading Behaviors, Mind Reading Intentional States

In the previous chapter, I argued that the way people think about spirits is fundamentally continuous with the way people think about agents in general. Spirits are represented the world over as animate, intentional beings who invariably possess human-like qualities, tastes, and tendencies, but who also possess a few nonhuman special qualities (e.g., the characteristic special quality of incorporeity that potentially allows spirits to invade the bodies of humans). That spirits are agents automatically invokes a fundamental capacity that all humans have for interpreting the behavior of other agents, namely "Theory of Mind" (ToM) (see Baron-Cohen 2001). ToM, also referred to as the ability to "mind read" (Baron-Cohen 1995), and "folk-psychology" (see Dennett 1987), is the set of mental mechanisms that enables us to make inferences about the desires, motives, intentions, and dispositions of others. Since we cannot directly observe people's thoughts and mental states, we infer them from behaviors. Speculating about the reasons for someone's behavior and predicting what he or she will do next is a basic, universal human capacity. Dennett writes, "We use folk psychology all the time, to explain and predict each other's behaviour; we attribute beliefs and desires to each other with confidence—and quite unselfconsciously—and spend a substantial portion of our lives formulating the world—not excluding ourselves—in these terms. Folk psychology is about as pervasive a part of our second nature as is our folk physics of middle-sized objects" (Dennett 1987: 47–48). ToM is so fundamental to successful communication and so effortlessly and universally used that Dennett has described it as our "intentional stance."

Furthermore, as Simon Baron-Cohen (1995) has pointed out, ToM is employed even in the absence of specific behavioral cues, such as when one is reasoning about the mental states of supernatural beings. The knowledge that an entity is agentive mobilizes a huge amount of nonreflective information and inferences about the psychological properties of that entity without recourse to explicit instruction, direct observation, or even conscious reflection (e.g., the entity has thoughts and acts on the basis of desires, motivations, etc.). In fact, this nonreflective knowledge is such a standard part of our cognitive apparatus that explicit instruction that contradicts these automatically generated inferences and expectations potentially presents problems for mental representation, comprehension, and memory. For example, on hearing for the first time, "God sent his son down to earth from heaven," I can easily theorize about the motives behind God's intentions until I arrive at a personally satisfying explanation. I may not come up with the "theologically correct" (Barrett 1999) answer, but it is accepted that my ability to reason about possible explanations surpasses the potential reliability of my conclusions. If someone then tells me that God and his Son are one in the same entity, certain implicit assumptions are violated regarding the indivisibility of agency, the unitary intentionality of the person, and so on. My default assumptions for the ontological category of agent, or person, are challenged, a lack of fit is detected, and a new set of ideas must be reflected upon. Actions that would normally be attributed to God are now attributable to both God and Son, not as a combination of two entities, but as a single whole.

Notions of spirits automatically trigger intuitive, nonreflective beliefs, expectations, and inferences for their ontological, stereotypical, and individual level properties. At the basic, ontological level, spirits are agents that are represented as possessing minds. Even without specific behavioral cues, people can employ ToM to attribute mental states to the invisible spirits. They are also represented as possessing certain traits. Some of these characterize their group category (whether as spirits in general or as a particular family of spirits). Some characterize their individual "personality."

We have seen that some concepts that violate ontological category expectations are easier to represent cognitively than others (e.g., minimally CI concepts are easier to grasp than maximally CI concepts). Possession is an example of an easily acquired concept. As stated above, the mind of the host is displaced by that of the spirit, and the bodiless spirit gains a body. A new "person" is formed who (setting aside considerations of special-agent qualities for the moment) squares with basic ontological expectations for the category of PERSON (i.e., body + agency). We have observed, however, that for the observer of actual possession episodes, the intentional agent responsible for the possessed hosts' actions is potentially ambiguous. Possession, therefore, gives rise to a situation that is atypical in social interaction.

To help us appreciate this complex situation more clearly and the role of personality and character trait expectations in social perception,[2] certain parallels can be drawn with the common experience of viewing actors' performances in films, theatre shows, and operas. Inverting the possession-theatre metaphor, Rouget has compared aspects of Renaissance opera and spirit-possession trance. He states, "From the spectator's viewpoint, the entire event happens in such a way that the opera singer is seen to be truly embodying his character, or is, in other words, totally possessed by that character. Indeed, if the spectators believe in this incarnation, the singer is a great actor" (1985: 244). For Rouget the successful opera *is* possession—"lyric possession"—and is appreciably equivalent to a possession ceremony. I take film not as an instance of possession, but as a situation that is analogous to possession. As with all analogies, there are limits to the similarities one can reasonably draw. At the very least, however, it enables us to consider some of the factors that influence observers' assessments of agency when there are potentially two candidate agencies.

The Name's Bond (Isn't It?)

In a film, an actor assumes a role that displays different qualities from his everyday personhood. For example, in the film *Fight Club*, Brad Pitt becomes Tylor Durden. When the performance is convincing, observers readily represent the person as Tylor, not as Brad. A convincing performance is one in which it is possible and natural for the observer automatically and without conscious effort to suspend existing impressions and beliefs about the person who is acting. Therefore, what makes a performance convincing—in that the observer perceives the person as Tylor and not Brad—may be contingent on existing constructs [or "person-files" (Boyer 2001: 219), i.e., impressions, memories, etc.] that the viewer has for the actor. Such constructs, based on the impressions generated through direct contact, media gossip, other films, and so on, are resistant (but not impervious) to change. It will therefore be more difficult for the actor's wife to perceive him as another character, no matter how good an actor he may be by objective standards, than for someone who is unfamiliar with his character offscreen. Likewise, those who are consciously reflecting on the fact that he is acting, such as aspiring young actors looking for helpful acting tips, are less likely to be captivated by the new person he has become. Whatever the case may be, at any moment, there is only one intentional agency represented—one mind and not two—as operating within the body, to which outward behaviors are attributable.

The notion that someone can become another person, in this sense, appears to be grasped intuitively—the mechanisms allowing us to represent a person as having sometimes several, discrete personas operate easily and automatically. We do not have to remind ourselves consciously that the character is no longer Brad but Tylor. However, some contextual factors can interfere with this cognitive capacity. Even when a performance is convincing (i.e., one in which the observer readily perceives the actor as being the person/role he is playing), certain cues may trigger spontaneous and conscious reflection on the situation, reminding observers of the fact that a role has been assumed, for example, when an actor's performance suddenly deteriorates and becomes poor, or when a particular gesture matches the actor's mannerisms in real life or in the scene of another film. Also, it is common for people to have strong feelings of attachment to an actor performing a particular role or kind of role (i.e., the actor becomes typecast). When the same actor appears in other shows, performing different roles, the new match seems bizarre or below par or "out of character." All these circumstances can impinge upon the degree to which the viewer accepts the verisimilitude and realness of the character being performed.

In the same way that there is potential for difficulty in representing the same actor performing many roles, the film world reality of substituting deceased or retired actors with new ones in order to keep characters "alive" may also confound the observer's conceptual schema for that character. The James Bond character provides a well-known example. The personality of Bond, as one has come to know it, is anchored to the body of a particular actor. When Bond ceases to be played by one actor and is assumed by another, the identity of the character as distinct from the body is brought to awareness. What is important in all these cases is that, on reflection, the observer is reminded that the role is pretence. The actor's behavior is pretence, mimicry, or impressionism and is not attributable to the actor's internal mental states. This may not diminish the lack of continuity one first perceives when the character discards the old body for a new one, or when the actor switches roles, but it certainly enhances the immediate credulity and coherence of the situation on the reflective level.

Juxtaposing possession performances and film performances provides many points of comparison for thinking about how observers represent the transference of personhood. As with the actor, the possessed person's agency is replaced by, or eclipsed by, an alternative agency. In both possession and film contexts, behaviors and statements are no longer attributable to the intentions of the actor. Possession, however, is not pretence. The possessed person is said actually to incorporate a new character or person, not simply to ape another person or an imaginary role. The spirit agent and the body of the host are combined. Nevertheless, as with the actor, the person in the possession context satisfies biological, physical, and psychological criteria for the ontological category of "person," having both body and mind.

When we deal with an agent in front of us, whatever that agent may be and whatever the body it inhabits, the interaction is governed by normal ontological assumptions we hold for agents. These are automatically delivered by our cognitive systems. The character of Bond as performed by two people simultaneously would be difficult to conceptualize consistently. We know that Smith in the Matrix trilogy is a computer program. But this does not eradicate the difficulties that we sense in conceiving it as infinitely replicable, caused by our intuitive representation of it as human (as it possesses unmistakably human characteristics and behaviors). Likewise, the twist at the end of *Fight Club,* in which we are forced not only to reflect on the dual personalities of a person suffering from Dissociative Identity Disorder, but also to accept that they coexisted simultaneously; yet autonomously both mentally and physically, is more than our mental tools can cope with. Workable concepts of people are constrained by implicit ontological assumptions that intuitively tell us that people are indivisible, individual, nonreplicable, and continuous.

Therefore, while the possessed person satisfies basic assumptions for the category of PERSON, the transformative act of possession entails the idea that minds are detachable from their bodies. The idea of migrating minds is catchy and memorable and is supported by a fundamental cognitive tendency to view ourselves and others as immaterial minds, or souls, occupying bodies. Recent research by developmental and cognitive psychologists suggests that we are "natural Cartesians—dualistic thinking comes naturally to us" (Bloom

2004: xii). Minimally counterintuitive notions about "migration" exploit in very salient and often humorous ways our early-emerging notions about the autonomy of minds, or "souls" (ibid.: xii), from the bodies they occupy. Unsurprisingly they are employed widely outside the context of possession. The notion that minds can swap and change between individuals has been capitalized on by the film industry (e.g., *Freaky Friday*). It is also commonly invoked to explain extreme irregularities in others' behaviors as illustrated by such familiar phrases as, "he was out of his mind" or "she was beside herself" or "his mind has gone" or "she's not her usual self today." Although such statements and films don't require much belief, possession provides a "real" example of migrating agencies.

There are, however, crucial inference systems in the mind of the observer that influence perception of the "real" migrant-mind situation. Although there is no significant cognitive impediment to notions about mind transfer,[3] further principles of social perception may be responsible for constraining the ways people represent the transference of personhood in practice. In the context of possession, established impressions of particular hosts, of spirits, and of particular spirits as possessing particular hosts mediate observers' perceptions of agency and behavior toward hosts. In the above analogy, we observed that constructs, or "person-files" (Boyer 2001: 219), which normally help us understand who we are dealing with in daily interaction, may create perceptual difficulties for viewers representing a novel character as played by the same person. Even though the viewer recognizes the transformation of character at an explicit level, it seems that implicit expectations delivered by the person constructs are difficult, perhaps impossible, to shut off. Similarly, once the possession is explicitly established as having occurred, the reflectively generated consequences (i.e., that the person is now hosting a different agent) may not necessarily or consistently govern intuitive representations of the properties of the particular agent present. If this is the case, then there should be some evidence from possession contexts that would appear to support this claim.

Observations from possession episodes in the *culto afro* do not provide sufficient evidence of what is going on at the implicit level, but they are at least suggestive of some incongruence between reflective and tacit perceptions of possession. The many inconsistencies that I observed between what people said about possession (i.e., in keeping with the "principle of displacement") and how they behaved toward possessed hosts initially raised doubts in my mind that observers actually believed that the hosts were really possessed. Closer observation, however, suggested that it was not the reflectively considered credibility of the host that was the issue. Even when people were apparently convinced that a host was genuinely possessed, they often behaved toward him and talked about him as though he was "his usual self." In the remainder of this chapter, I describe such situations more fully, presenting numerous examples from possession episodes in the *culto afro* in which the content of observers' implicit thought is apparently divergent from reflective, stated beliefs concerning the possessed person. I also suggest possible psychological and neurological factors that come into play, influencing people's behaviors and assessments of agency.

Observing Possession—What People Say

In Belém, I endeavored to pay attention to both verbal discourse and behaviors concerning spirits and possessed persons. The data suggest that what people observe in actual possession episodes frequently conflicts with the largely intuitively generated principles that people hold regarding agents in general, spirits in particular, and possession (e.g., the "displacement-of-control principle"). When two people are said to be possessed by the same spirit, differences in mannerisms and behaviors of the spirits are common. This generates a sense of incongruence because the personhood of the spirit, as the observer has come to know it, when possessing a certain individual, is anchored to the body of that individual and is perceived as relatively consistent. For example, when a spirit always behaves like a saint "in the head" (*na cabeça*) of one person, and consistently comes in another as a malevolent sorcerer, the observer may entertain doubts about the veracity of possession in one or both cases. The behaviors of the spirit in the new host do not fit with established impressions, or the "person-file" that the observer has for that spirit. Likewise, when two people are possessed by a spirit simultaneously, one is forced to think about the intuitive sense of incongruence that arises from violation of basic assumptions about the indivisibility of personhood.

Stark variations in the behavior and performance of one spirit as manifest in different individuals trigger reflection on possible explanations. That questions surrounding such matters arise frequently among the laity supports the claim that people intuitively represent spirits as indivisible agents, with fundamentally continuous character and behaviors. Some explanation must provide answers to the inconsistencies that arise for people to maintain a coherent understanding of the situation.[4]

Culto beliefs afforded a number of options. Participants might resolve such inconsistency, or dissonance, by showing that the perceived incongruence is illusory. Simple explanations may include judgments about the integrity of the person claiming to receive the spirit—maybe he is faking possession. Another possibility is that the spirit is deliberately disguising his identity. When two people are simultaneously possessed by the same *entidade*, one may be presumed to be the true entity and another to be the messenger of that entity. In the case of the *orixás*, both may be identified as "qualities" of that entity. In all these cases, *either* the spirit *or* the host is identified as the single, discrete agent behind all actions. The conceptual problems associated with the situation are therefore satisfactorily resolved—no ontological violations of intuitive expectations for the "person" category are invoked, and person constructs remain intact.

Subtle inconsistencies in the behavior of a particular *entidade* among various mediums may also be accounted for by appealing to what may be called "the principle of fusion." Receiving a spirit, especially for the first few occasions, is not as straightforward a procedure as the displacement notion would suggest. As a medium increasingly "gives passage" to his or her *entidades*, the spirit entity is said to become progressively more accustomed to the material it occupies.[5] This is not limited to a simple accommodation of a new skin, however. The "psychological material," or character, memories, knowledge, and personality, of the host is said to merge with that of the entity and vice versa. "When the spirit manifests itself," Pai says, "he changes, he performs alchemy, he mixes his structure with mine." (*Quando o espirito se manifesta ele muda, ele faz uma alquimia, ele mistura a estrutura dele com a minha.*) Gradually, the *entidade* is said to acquire qualities, mannerisms, and attitudes that characterize the medium, while the medium is believed to assume characteristics of the *entidade*. According to this rationale, behaviors of the possessed medium are not only reducible to the supernatural agent at any one time, but also are simultaneously attributable to the medium. This principle is presented as the "theologically correct" version of what happens when someone is possessed. On the basis of this principle, one can therefore explain why, when spirit X possesses person A, the performance will vary somewhat from when the same spirit, X, possesses person B. It is this principle that may also be invoked to explain features of mediumistic development (e.g., the need for training in mediumistic abilities).

Nevertheless, the notion of fusion does not accord with widespread claims outside of these specific analytical situations that in possession, the host is entirely controlled by the supernatural entity (see chapter 6). Furthermore, in practice, when a medium's behavior does not conform to the expectations that the observer holds for a particular spirit, the intentional agent is construed as either another spirit or the mistaken or deceiving medium, never as a fusion of two agents. It would seem, therefore, that the principle of fusion, or mutual influence of spirit and medium, is invoked as a (post hoc) reflective justification for certain events that contradict or violate participants' intuitive assumptions about how people think and act. When reflective recourse to these theories is not necessitated by the circumstances, automatic folk-psychological processes guide perceptions of agency—people operate with intuitive assumptions that govern normal human interaction: there is one agent, in one body, and not a merging of two agents. As we have seen, spirits are essentially represented as disembodied persons. Possession provides them with the missing physical property, whereby they become completed as persons. As a senior member of the *terreiro* community once told me, "It is the conjunction of the two parts that becomes, temporarily, a person." The body now accommodates a novel agent.

The notion that agencies can migrate between bodies and that the mind or spirit of the host is replaced by the spirit (i.e., "the principle of displacement") has become particularly widespread throughout possession cults around the world. The principle of fusion and other such ideas based on the combination of amorphous energies or on hybrid intentionalities are not intuitive and are less inferentially fertile in the real-time observation and interpretation of behaviors. Reasoning about the potential effects of dual agency within a single person is only possible at the level of conscious reflection. Even then, representing such a concept is complicated in practice. The notion of two intentional beings simultaneously sharing one body, to whose mental states all behavioral and verbal statements are simultaneously attributable, is not amenable to our cognitive capacities and intuitions in real-time situations.

The fusion concept, on this view, accounts for certain situations at the level of conscious reflection but contravenes a number of underlying assumptions and expectations that our mental tools effortlessly generate and that allow us to make sense of people's behaviors. Were the situations that violate these assumptions not to arise (e.g., were one never to be confronted with divergent performances that are said to be attributable to the same spirit) there would be no need for recourse to the theologically correct fusion principle. Its transmissive success is therefore determined by the demand for post hoc explaining and reasoning that such situations give rise to, but any other competing hypothesis that potentially satisfies intellectual logic could equally be devised. In contrast, ideas that square with the intuitions about the nature and limitations of minds and bodies fit with a broader range of mental tools, are always active in the observation and comprehension of possession, are invoked effortlessly and often largely unconsciously, and are therefore more likely to enjoy transmissive success with only minimal instruction or none at all. They can generally be employed readily and satisfactorily in thinking about agents, intentions, and persons. The fusion concept is neither intuitive nor readily applicable to real-time situations. However, when the assumptions underpinning the more intuitive ideas are violated and they no longer help one to make sense of a situation, the principle of fusion becomes relevant.[6]

Assuming then that the observer of the possession episode intuitively attributes any behavior to the intentions of *either* the host *or* the spirit, can we identify generalizable factors that influence which agency the observer selects? Are all judgments entirely reflectively generated? Do nonreflective thought processes also play a part? If so, do these influence explicit reflection? Is the observer always aware of his or her assessment?

Observing Possession: What People Do

Observer assessment of the intentional agent responsible for the actions of a host said to be in a state of possession is a potentially complex matter for examination. On the basis of widely accepted evidence from the field of social psychology, one can safely assume that the way agency is construed in the context of possession is not a simple question of the observer reflecting on all evidence to hand, on which basis he or she makes an informed judgment about whether or not the host is faking possession. The behavioral cues that cause the observer to behave in certain ways toward the possessed host may or may not be explicitly registered and reflected upon. Largely implicit intuitions and attribution biases concerning the host's character and personality may come into play.

Since the 1950s, social psychologists have been documenting the ways in which the processes of intuitive judgment are informed by simplifying heuristics that provide "quick and dirty" solutions to uncertainties in everyday situations (see Gilovich, Griffin, and Kahneman 2002). It is in this sense that humans have been labeled "cognitive misers" (Fiske 1995). These short-cut routes lead to real-world judgments that are often biased; the conclusion often departs from the objective value that careful and costly (in terms of mental processing) calculation of the facts would determine. The heuristics that are activated within social interaction are fundamental to social perception. Therefore the ways in which we interpret information about others, form impressions about them, and explain their behavior are often distorted by biases of which we are unaware.

Although I am not aware of any work directly relating to the issue of perceptions of alter agencies or dual personhoods, specifically in the context of spirit possession, it seems plausible that the biases that influence everyday interactions with other human agents are also operating in observer-actor relations in possession contexts. There are no special "supernatural social perception" procedures or mechanisms in our mental toolbox for interaction with spirit beings. Our intuitive notions of agency in general inform, constrain, and permit meaningful interaction with supernatural beings and their hosts. Many of these intuitions may not always (or *ever*) be entertained consciously. Nor can they be ascertained by the observer or by the anthropologist using standard methods of ethnographic investigation. Nevertheless, close and continuous participation in the daily possession episodes of the *culto afro* pointed to the presence of perception biases. These biases influenced people's attributions about the actions of possessed hosts, and, consequentially, their behavior and statements were often observably inconsistent with their explicit beliefs about possession.

The following are some observations from the field that typify the kinds of ambiguities and contradictions spoken of by some scholars of spirit-possession phenomena. Scholars emphasise the futility of searching for order amidst such ambiguities. Besnier, for example, writes, "Spirits and their world cannot be understood through a search for a *resolution* of such ambiguities and contradictions; rather, these qualities must be perceived as constitutive of the very nature of spirits" (1996: 76). I argue, however, that under the confusion we observe on the surface, the procedural operations of the mind that allow one to perceive spirit-possessed hosts are not qualitatively different from those that allow normal interpersonal interaction. Everyday judgments are also fraught with erroneous, biased, and inconsistent evaluations of ourselves and others. Findings from the field of social cognition may help us predict where, how, and why the ambiguities and contradictions are likely to arise in the possession context.

Observations from the Belém *culto* attest to the importance of morality and personality factors in observer representations of agency, both implicitly and explicitly, when dealing with a possessed host. As noted above, apparent inconsistencies in possession that occur regularly but are considered inoffensive (i.e., that are not perceived as crossing, or violating, accepted, moral boundaries) appeal at an explicit, reflective level, to the principle of fusion. The fact that Zé Pelintra is a nonsmoker in the head of one medium and smokes cigars by the score in the head of another may be reflected upon and explained by the notion that mutual influences are transferred between the spirit, Zé Pelintra, and the medium. Whether or not people actually consider one "manifestation" (*manifestação*)[7] to be the "true" one, and the other an imitation/false trance/pretender spirit, is difficult to determine through observation and direct-question interview techniques. Inconsistencies that transgress boundaries of orthodox possession behavior, however, are invariably accounted for by appealing to the misguided, scandalous, and disrespectful character of the medium even when the medium is considered to be possessed. Such accusations are often direct but may also be implied by absolving the spirit entity of blame as is illustrated by the following extract from a conversation with a *terreiro* member. Zé Pelintra, in the head of any other person that you see is totally different from when he is in the head of Pai. . . . It's totally different—he comes in the form of a vagabond [*malandro*], he is foul-mouthed, he comes smoking, drinking—this isn't Seu Zé. . . . He may have been a doctor once, but because they've used him so much for wicked deeds . . . he acquired an aspect of the sorcerer, an aspect of the crook. *Zé Pelintra, na cabeça de qualquer pessoa que você vê, não tem nada a ver na cabeça do Pai. . . . É totalmente diferente. Ele vem na forma de malandro, vem desbocado, vem fumando, vem bebendo, isso não é seu Zé. . . . Ele pode ter sido um doutor, entendeu, mas devido usarem muito ele pra fazer maldade . . . ele adquiriu o lado de feiticeiro, o lado de bandoleiro."*

In legitimate possession contexts, such as possession ceremonies of the *terreiro*, the spirits are the agents—said to "come into the heads" of their *filhos*. In an unorthodox setting, such as a drunken street party, a pay-hourly motel, or even at a crime scene, it is always the medium who is accused of "catching" or using his or her *caboclo*. The behavior of the guilty party is gossiped about and may be sanctioned accordingly. On such occasions, I observed that people were quick to show contempt toward the hosts. For example, on one occasion during fieldwork, Pai took me to visit a medium acquaintance, who, on this occasion, spoke with me in a less-than-refined manner. The possessed medium became increasingly amused by the audience's embarrassment of his uncouth language and conversation. "What's the best position to take a dump?" he/she asked me (the possessing spirit was female). Hoping it was a rhetorical question, from which the medium would elaborate upon some higher truth, I smirked, but kept my mouth shut. A second and a third time he asked until, without warning, he shifted his efforts to teaching me a string of Portuguese words that one is unlikely to find in any serious dictionary. Some time later, Pai recounted the incident to a group of people assembled in the *terreiro*. After some discussion about his personal objections to the practice and behavior of this medium in general, and of his fast-decreasing respect for his person, he exclaimed, "When [*spirit's name*] is in *my* head she is completely different! What sort of a thing is this? You [*referring to me*] are here to study religion and you are confronted with that. She should be saying, 'May you be blessed, may your path be opened to you, may you have success in your research.' " Although Pai was careful to refer to the spirit here, the full context of his statements left no doubt that it was the medium who was ultimately responsible for his own behavior, with a little help from the alcohol he had consumed. On such occasions, when I asked why the host should bear the blame for misdemeanors committed when possessed, people would often simply shake their heads and shrug their shoulders, reiterating the fact that such behavior is just wrong. Accusations of simulation are rarely made, nor did this appear to be considered as a likely explanation, unless corroborated by other kinds of evidence (e.g., if the person is known to have faked possession on other occasions).[8]

On one occasion, I asked Pai if he had any reflections on the unusual behavior of a person who was possessed with an *orixá* at a Candomblé ceremony. The person had failed to dance her turn and had remained seated, crying about an unwanted change to her ceremonial costume. Although she had clearly become possessed, Pai immediately blamed the behavior on the host's opinionated and stubborn character. When I quizzed who, then, had been crying in the ceremony, Pai responded that he didn't know, nor had he gone to any trouble to find out. After some thought, he went on to suggest that such behaviors may be the result of the errors inherent in the initiation procedure she had performed under an incompetent *mãe-de-santo* from another house. These errors exercise what he called a "social control," or restriction, on the authority and control of the possessing entity. Such a justification fits with the principle of fusion in which manifestation of an *entidade* is represented not as a clean substitution of agency, but as a fusion of two agents. It appears, however, that in this case and others alluded to above, observers tend promptly to attribute inappropriate behavior to the mental states and traits of the hosts.

Inadequate behavior elicits similar reactions. Observers' interactions with and statements about hosts' intentional states often seem inconsistent with their explicit statements and beliefs that the host is indeed possessed. Statements containing direct references to hosts' culpability when possessed were frequent; for example, "Flávia can't dance when she's possessed," "Márlia caused a scandal in the last *festa*," and "Paulo doesn't even know his own *doutrina*." Pai often teased and rebuked spirits for singing or dancing poorly or for singing a song that had not been "seated," or established, as an authentic number in the *terreiro* repertoire. He would also tell the spirits when it was time for them to leave, often lectured them on the failures of their *filhos*, and instructed them on the procedural details of ritual performances. This behavior does not appear consistent with widely held ideas within the *culto* that the *entidades* are superior to humans, possess more knowledge, and are the spiritual custodians of their own cult and distinctive practices.[9]

Furthermore, the degree to which Pai overtly demonstrated respect for the person when possessed correlated directly with the regard in which he held the person when not possessed, suggesting that interpersonal relational factors come into play in possession interaction. Two members of the *terreiro*, for whom Pai often openly acknowledged his dislike, were subject to his contempt even when they may have been possessed. One was suspected by the whole community of regularly simulating possession. The other was considered to be "crazy" and was often accused of behaving disrespectfully both within the *terreiro* and around the neighborhood. Nevertheless, when there were no doubts about the credibility of a person's possession state, there was a perceptible correlation between the questionability of that person's character in general, and the respect they were shown when possessed. This suggests that people's intuitive social judgments concerning the negative traits of particular hosts of the *culto* biased their implicit perceptions of hosts' personality and interpretations of their behavior when possessed.[10]

A simple questionnaire designed to access observers' and *filhos'* representations of the special qualities of possessed persons, particularly in regard to special access to certain kinds of knowledge, also suggests that the way people reason about the supernatural agency in possession is constrained by their character assessment of the individual undergoing possession. Participants were given a false belief task, in which the contents of a washing powder carton were removed and replaced with a t-shirt. They were then asked whether, on seeing the sealed box, (1) an *orixá*, (2) a *caboclo*, (3) an *orixá* possessing a medium, and (4) a *caboclo* possessing a medium, would know what the actual, current contents of the carton were. The purpose of the study was to access and compare participants' notions regarding supernatural agents' special access to hidden knowledge when *puro* (lit. "pure," or not possessing an individual) and when *"incorporado"* (possessing a host). Participants, however, had difficulty construing the situation for questions 3 and 4 without reference to a known medium. The most interesting discovery, perhaps, is that notions about the actual superhuman capabilities of spirits in specific possession contexts are often influenced by people's assessments of specific mediums. Variations in mediumistic capabilities are potentially rationalized by the theory that mediumistic ability develops over time. Yet people's answers were not guided by considerations of mediumistic experience and ability in a general sense. A number of participants spontaneously suggested names of specific, known mediums, and, on the basis of their knowledge and experience of these individuals, they made their assessment. This suggests that the criteria according to which people make such judgments are not entirely explicitly motivated but are generated by deep-seated, moral intuitions, motivational factors, and implicit representations and expectations that the observer holds for a particular host normally.

Wafer records instances of performance "lapses" that triggered deliberate reflection on the possibility of simulation (see above). Despite the nonparsimonious conclusion Wafer claims to have arrived at regarding false trance, perceptions of agency in possession—whether these are explicitly reflected upon or only implicitly registered—are not formed by distant observers making detached, calculated judgments. Deep-seated moral intuitions and attribution biases concerning character and personality drive and inform implicit representations, which in turn potentially inform explicit interpretations of behavior.

Evidence from Social Psychology

Research by social psychologists has shown that the meanings we attach to novel information about people are informed by our preexisting beliefs and knowledge of them (Fiske 1998; Gilbert 1998). People tend to form and hold implicit theories about other people and to perceive their behavior according to these theories. The established expectations and impressions, or schemas, we hold for individuals help us predict, interpret, and explain their behavior. These schemas have been shown to be particularly resistant to change, even in the face of novel information that violates expectations generated by the schema. Hence, impressions are slow to change and may lead to biases in social perception. The degree to which the person-schema is anchored to the memory of the physical appearance of the person has still to be addressed as an explicit focus of psychological investigation.

A potentially relevant series of studies by Susan M. Andersen et al. (1990; 1995) investigated the mechanisms underlying the everyday transference of mental representations of significant others[11] to new people. Recognizing the scholarly attention that has been given to the tendency for people to classify others according to social categories, such as stereotypes or traits, they point to the absence of any investigation into the potential for representations of known individuals, particularly significant others, to guide social perception of new persons. Their findings indicate that individual person-constructs for significant others are a powerful source of inferences in social perception (i.e., the interpretation and explanation of others' behaviors), even more powerful than other social categories, such as stereotypes and traits. Wegner and Bargh summarize the specific findings: "When we encounter people whose features resemble significant others in some important way, the representation of that significant other becomes activated without the perceiver's awareness by the presence of those features, and that activated representation becomes used to anticipate and interpret the behavior of the new acquaintance" (1998: 471). Although Andersen's research focused on the transference processes specific to significant others, there is evidence to suggest that familiar other constructs are also readily accessible within memory for the potential transference of representations to novel others who possess similar traits.

These findings are potentially relevant to our understanding of the mechanisms employed in people's perceptions of hosts said to be possessed. The possessing entity is expressly stated to take control of the host's intentional center of command, or agency; yet people regularly appear to represent the host as the agent responsible for actions and behaviors. As stated above, this is most obvious in the case of inappropriate or inadequate actions. Nevertheless, given the robustness of the impressions we have for others, it is, arguably, the default representation for all behaviors that are consistent with those impressions, or schemas. When schemas are violated, (e.g., when a person's behavior is dramatically out of character, or when the person performs some apparently superhuman feat, such as demonstrating awareness of some carefully guarded secret, or passing a naked flame across the body without appearing to cause any pain or injury), the observer may reflect on the possible explanations for such actions and swiftly reach the conclusion, or consciously remind himself, that the friend in front of him is "not here," but that the spirit entity has replaced him. Otherwise, given that the possessed host's physical and behavioral cues potentially activate information about the appearance and behavior of the host (as significant or familiar other) outside of the possession context, I predict, in the light of Andersen, et al.'s findings, that this information, stored in memory, readily and automatically informs observers' implicit interpretations of the host's behavior when possessed. A potentially analogous context might be the impressions one forms when one meets the identical twin of a close friend for the first time. Physical and other cues so strongly resemble those that one associates with one's friend that the mental schema one has for the friend is automatically invoked to understand the twin's behavior.[12] This may be ongoing despite conscious awareness that the twins are distinct persons and may lead to biased interpretations of behavior.

Evidence from Neuroscience

The ethnographic methods and observations that triggered this discussion limited investigation to observable behaviors and statements in natural settings. Inconsistencies were particularly evident when observers gossiped about the inadequate or inappropriate behavior of possessed hosts. It was also apparent that negative attitudes toward the host generally (e.g., personal dislike) "carried into" interactions between the observer and the host when possessed.

I have suggested certain social perception factors that may be responsible for these observable behavioral patterns. Nevertheless, these only help us explain the behavior patterns that the ethnographic methods permitted me to identify. Ethnographic methods cannot contribute to the investigation of the hypothesis that, even when the possessed host is behaving appropriately and adequately and is a good friend of the observer, the observer is indeed implicitly representing the host as absent and the embodied spirit as present. Clearly the *absence* of gossip about a developed, respectable medium, for example, does not constitute evidence that the observer implicitly comprehends that the medium is possessed by a new agency and is now a new person.

Some questions therefore remained: do implicit theories about the agency responsible for the possessed person's behaviors alternate between that of the host and that of the spirit in response to particular kinds of behavioral cues? When the possessed host's behaviors are appropriate, is the observer implicitly perceiving the host as the spirit, as a new person? When behaviors are inappropriate, does this act as a trigger that causes the observer implicitly to perceive the host as responsible? Or, is there a "default position," such that all behaviors are implicitly interpreted as being attributable to the host? Does the host really "fade into the background"? Neuroscientific investigation into the neural correlates of person identification powerfully support the hypothesis that there is an implicit "default position" in the perception of intentional agency present in the context of possession.

Briefly, we have seen that the observer may be consciously aware that the host is possessed but sometimes appears to perceive and interpret behaviors as though she is not. This, I suggest, is partly because there is a flow of information from specific modules in the brain that handle face perception, face recognition, and person identification that is rapid and automatic (Bruce and Young 1986; Burton et al. 1990; Leveroni et al. 2000; Shah et al. 2001). This means that on seeing a familiar face, one will generally retrieve person-identity information (e.g., long-term memories containing semantic and biographical information, emotions; the "person-file") without thinking about it. It is possible to have familiarity without identification. This happens when we get the frustrating feeling that we recognize a face but cannot remember from where. This is unlikely to occur, however, without pathology, for people we meet regularly. Indeed, even if one tried through conscious effort to block this neural pathway, it would be impossible. Recent fMRI[13] data provide evidence that recognizing a person involves automatic information flow from neuroanatomical areas of the brain that deal with face perception to familiarity checking to associated areas implicated in memory and emotion.

Consider the role of emotions (one of the components in our person-identity system) in person perception. The automaticity of the perception-identification process explains why someone with a deep-seated aversion to a particular individual is unable to shut off such feelings at will, even when the reflective belief that the person is possessed tells him or her that such attitudes and feelings are not appropriate. The collaborative operations of the various systems in our brain—our face-recognition systems, our person-file systems, and so on—which are working beyond the reach of conscious inspection, readily and automatically generate intuitive responses according to the coherent information gathered and delivered by these systems. Of course, the use of masks and costume—a practice common across possession contexts—may be an effective method of preventing the automatic retrieval of person specific memories and expectancies and of facilitating the implicit representation of the host as no longer present.

Conclusion

This necessarily brief and limited discussion shows that the factors that come into play in the perception of any possession episode are numerous and contextually variable. Neurological, cognitive, emotional, moral, and personality factors as well as others not explicitly considered here, such as motivational and social category (based on features such as authority, gender, expertise, etc.) factors, scarcely exhaust the list of possible influences on possession perception. The outputs of these factors produce seeming inconsistencies between the way people explicitly reflect on what is occurring when a person becomes possessed and the ways they behave toward *particular* individuals in actual possession episodes. Among *culto* participants, possession is said to refer to the governing influence of a spirit, specifically the spirit's agency, or mind, on the mind and body of a human being. Although this concept of possession is explicitly reported across all participants in the *culto* (and extensively across cultures), it seems that attitudes toward possessed people often appear to be inconsistent with this definition. This suggests that intuitive assessments of the agency responsible for the possessed person's behavior are informed by nonreflective thoughts generated by tacit mental biases and processes.

However people resolve these inconsistencies (e.g., by appealing to the principle of fusion), I suggest that we need to consider a number of underlying, fundamental psychological constraints, attributional biases, and relational and contextual factors for a more complete analysis of the kinds of concepts and representations that are workable in practice. These automatically generate inferences, predictions, and explanations in the actual observation of any possession episode. They underlie people's real-time conceptualizations of what is occurring, and more specifically, who is the responsible agent, when a person is possessed. The significant factors and their various outputs are potentially chartable by means of systematic testing in the natural setting.

Ultimately, why bother to probe deeply people's tacit mental representations of possessed people? Why not just listen to what they say and accept it? The aim of this research is to contribute to our understanding of cultural transmission, specifically the transmission of spirit-possession ideas and beliefs. Causes for the transmission of cultural concepts are not only—some would argue, not ever—located in their meanings, as these are explicitly and reflectively reported by people who hold those concepts. A growing body of evidence from the cognitive science of culture shows that people's implicit assumptions about how the world around them works inform and constrain the content, representation, and spread of ideas. Implicit assumptions, predictions, and intuitive expectations are generated by the cross-cultural regularities of the human mind-brain. Herein lies the key to explaining part of the complex phenomenon of spirit possession—that is, its widespread incidence across cultures, as well as at least some of its widely recurrent features. The area is ripe for further investigation of the specific contexts in which the underlying cognitive tendencies and social perception biases suggested here are activated. This chapter takes some tentative steps toward identifying patterns in—not "imposing order" on—the ambiguities and inconsistencies so apparent in the worlds of spirits and their hosts that we observe.

8

The Social Relevance of Spirits

Hoje em dia eu fico pensando, "Será que se eu não tivesse escolhido essa religião pra cultuar eu estaria bem agora, como eu estou? Será que eu não estaria com vários tipos de problemas? Doente? Será que isso tava no meu destino? Ser filho-de-santo?"

Nowadays I wonder, "If I hadn't chosen this religion would I be ok now, like I am? Would I have various kinds of problems? Would I be sick? Was this my destiny, I wonder? To be a *filho-de-santo?*"

—A filho

Counseling, orientation, guidance, clairvoyance, and curing are services frequently sought after in mediumistic traditions around the world. Even a cursory glance at the anthropological and statistical records of spirit possession and other trance phenomena worldwide reveals the high degree to which these phenomena occur in conjunction with practices involving such healing, therapy, and emotional support. Lesley Sharp, for example, describes two principal mediumistic forms among the Salakava of Madagascar. In the first, mediums are chosen by the royal ancestors to live as advisors to the living royalty. The second, which is far more widespread and popular, "involves a multitude of spirits who appear primarily in women living in town. Mediums for these spirits generally work as healers, serving the needs of local commoners" (Sharp 1999: 6). Taghi Modarressi describes the Zar of South Iran as a "possession cult devoted to healing" (1968: 149). Alan Howard relates how, following mis-sionization, the Rotumans "continued to perform rituals, such as kava cere-monies, pig sacrifices, and healing routines that presupposed the potency of spirits, in some instances invoking them directly through chants and prayers" (1996: 130). In Brazil, where some Pentecostal churches are designed to look more like hospitals, and the clergy and other personnel are dressed in medical garb, Andrew Chesnut records that, "prior to being possessed by the Holy Spirit, the majority of *crentes* [believers] adhered to the faith through the su-preme gift of faith healing" (1997: 97). Indeed, Winkelman's cross-cultural studies found that all societies sampled had altered states of consciousness associated with healing.

For Winkelman, "the universal presence of ASC associated with magico-religious healing practices, coupled with the functional relationships of ASC with the abilities of healing and divination, suggests that this is psychobiolog-ically based, derived from the characteristics of ASC" (1997: 405). He points to relevant research that indicates that a number of characteristics associated with the physiological changes of ASC have inherent therapeutic effects. Such states, for example, induce relaxation and reduce anxiety, tension, and phobic reactions (Lehrer, Woolfolk, and Goldman 1984); lower blood pressure (Ben-son, et al. 1974; Benson et al. 1981); and may increase placebo and other psy-chosomatic effects (Winkelman 1997; see also Sargant 1974). Winkelman characterizes the association between healing and trance as a functional corre-lation accounted for by the inherent therapeutic effects of the trance state. His explanation focuses exclusively on trance participants and on the neuropsy-chological mechanisms underlying the temporary dissociational states that often accompany possession.

In this chapter, I suggest that we turn our attention to particular cognitive mechanisms and psychological tendencies to explain cross-cultural features of the widespread association among spirits, possession, and "making better," that is, physical healing, financial assistance, and the improvement of life cir-cumstances generally (and by extension, the association among spirit beliefs, possession, sorcery, and coping with misfortune). Having looked at *how* people represent spirits, we now consider the causal processes underpinning some of the principal contexts in which they become relevant and valuable to both hosts and clients. This discussion focuses not on the experience of trance and on its therapeutic effects, but on specific, generic factors that account for the *appeal* of healing services provided by "magico-religious healers," to use Winkelman's term (1990). Why do shamanistic and mediumistic healing practices widely appeal to people across cultures and time? Why are these healers often sought out for counsel and guidance? More fundamentally, why do people attribute "religious" interpretations to everyday happenings? What are the mechanisms by which sorcery and divine providence and punishment are so readily accorded explanatory significance in daily affairs? The answers to these questions are partly located in the mechanisms and processes of everyday cognition. These underpin "theories of wondering why" for particular kinds of events (Malle and Knobe 1997) and the tendency for such theories to turn on notions of social causation (in general) and of supernatural agent causation (in particular). The mental steps taken—from subjective states of puzzlement for events, to agentive explanations in general, through to supernatural agent causation in particular, and factors in play, are outlined below.

- Reflecting upon puzzling events
  Attribution theorists have suggested that when a person is puzzled by an event, he or she is most likely to reflect upon possible explanations for the event if it is personally relevant, negative or surprising (see Malle and Knobe 1997). This is a culture-general response— surprising events anywhere, for example, are likely to trigger reflection because, by definition, they contradict prior knowledge or assumptions. Malle and Knobe state that nonunderstanding for negative or surprising events can lead to mild curiosity in some situations, but it can also be stressful and traumatic. They write, "people . . . are likely to wonder why the challenging event occurred. By implication, reaching an understanding of an event (i.e., finding an explanation) would, to some extent, reinstate control, predictability, self-integrity, and conceptual coherence" (ibid.: 289).
- Social-causal explanations
  Because we share our environment with other humans, actions they or we perform will often have social effects, that is, they will affect others. Because agents can make things happen, they are the highly probable targets of our causal attributions for disruption to an accepted state. Agent causation is intuitive and readily activated and may have some evolutionary basis. Alertness to the movements and actions of other agents (either as potential cooperators or threats) was vital to our ancestors' survival, both in evading predators and tracking prey (Atran 2002; Barrett 2004; Mithen 1996; Parker and McKinney 1999).
       Perceptions of agent causation are readily paired with assessments of intentionality. The tacit laws of exchange and fairness that govern human social interaction guide the ways people reason about the intentions behind other people's actions. On the basis of these principles,

people readily identify what is fair and what is not, what is cooperation and what is cheating, and so on. Psychological studies also suggest
that people also believe that the world in general *should* be—and
ultimately *is*—fair. According to this intuitive "just world belief"
(Lerner 1980), it is tacitly assumed that people get what they deserve.
Hence, if one suffers a grave accident, even though the immediate
cause may be known (e.g., one's own carelessness), an intuitive response is to consider the significance of the event in terms of fairness and retribution. When something is construed as "deserved" or
"unfair," it is being assessed according to the principles of social
exchange (e.g., if someone lost, then another person gained).

• Supernatural agent causation
Although much of the modern world may be largely skeptical of shamanistic and mediumistic healing techniques and appears to shun
explanations for misfortune in terms of supernatural design, it appears
that principles of exchange account for broad similarities across cultures in people's reasoning processes for personally significant,
salient events. "Why me?" is a common question often directed to
nobody in particular in Western societies (but notably often with eyes
raised toward the sky). Following theoretical claims advanced in the
cognitive science of religion, I argue that supernatural agent causation
for salient events is parasitical on our tendency to explain events in
terms of the actions and intentions of other humans (e.g., Barrett 2004;
Bering and Johnson, 2005; Boyer 2001; Slone 2004b). Where agents
are believed to exist who (1) are fundamentally similar to humans but
(2) have access to strategic knowledge about the lives and affairs of
people and (3) are conceived of as moral arbitrators of human affairs
and (4) possess the power to influence and act in those affairs, these
agents become particularly relevant to explanations of salient (e.g.,
negative, surprising, etc.) events. I further argue that the relevance of
spirits who possess (to explanations for salient events) is potentially
enhanced by their presumed close physical proximity to—and
involvement in—daily human affairs.
Understanding the ways in which people tend to interpret misfortune, that is, as an effect of the violation of tacit social exchange
principles (Boyer 2001: 201), is fundamental to understanding the
relevance of spirits. Whether an event is attributed to the intentions of
God, the spirits, or sorcerers, such explanations are intuitively satisfying. In the following sections, I show how these processes are relevant to activities in Pai's *terreiro*, and to the association between

possession and healing, and to the improvement of life circumstances more broadly. The cognitive account outlined above is discussed
more fully following a brief description of the daily work (*trabalho*)
in the *terreiro*, of clients' and *filhos*' explicit motivations for attending,
and of the social relationships that develop. Identification of the
mechanisms whereby spirits become relevant to people's everyday lives
is fundamental to explaining the widespread transmission of spirit-
possession concepts and phenomena described in the previous
chapters.

The *Terreiro* and Its Clients

The *terreiro* of Pai serves several functions. For many it is simultaneously a
house of worship, workplace, social club, hospital, sanctuary, spiritual retreat,
and home. All those who regularly use the limited *terreiro* space are expected
to earn their keep—whether that is defined as a place to lie one's head or by
the numerous *cafezinhos* consumed in the course of a visit—by attending to
the menial but essential tasks that allow the *terreiro* to fulfill all of the above
functions. This allows Pai to dedicate a great deal of his time to *filhos* and
paying members of the public who require consultation with him and frequently with the spirit entities who come to possess him.

Pai's hours of work and tariffs were posted just inside the front door of
the house. In practice, appointments and prices were flexible—it was not
unknown for Pai to assist people without anticipation of remuneration and,
despite the fact that official work hours stipulated an 8:00 PM finish, callers
were often received well into the early hours of the morning. Throughout the
muggy afternoons and evenings, lines of clients waited patiently to be called
into Pai's private, air-conditioned consultation room. Pai often complained
about the time consumed by this aspect of *terreiro* activity, as well as the com-
motion generated by the continuous stream of people entering and leaving
and calling by telephone. However, his renowned popularity was often proudly
invoked as an indication of his success and distinction as a competent *pai-de-
santo* and of his favor among the *orixás* and other spirit entities.

Access to these sessions for the purposes of research was understandably
restricted. Nevertheless, Pai agreed to complete a survey form for all meetings
with clients over a twenty-five-day period in September 2003.[1] During this
period, a total of seventy-three sessions with clients were recorded, with fourteen being the most in a single day. Given that some individuals' motives for
requesting counsel at any one session numbered more than one, a total of

seventy-eight complaints and problems were addressed. Issues to do with marriage, love, and family affairs had the highest representation, totaling 32 percent of all concerns. People expressed concerns relating to harassment from ex-partners and suspected sorcery by ex-spouses' new partners, problematic teenagers, and other marriage and family-related issues. Financial and health issues each occupied 24 percent of consultation time. One person reported difficulties with clients, another with workmates, another with the search for employment, and so on. There were eight meetings that addressed "spiritual" concerns, generally to do with the clients' questions about mediumistic development. In a number of cases, mediumship, or *mediunidade*, was declared to be *mal trabalhada*, or undeveloped. This, I was informed, occurs when a person is aware that he or she is a medium but is inexperienced and does not develop this mediumship, for example, in possession ceremonies or through ritual obligations to the spirits (*obrigações*). Alleged symptoms such as visions, confusion and dizziness, and unexpected and chaotic trance states are often reported. A small number of people enquired after the health and well being of a family member. Finally, a couple of clients desired to know about events in the immediate future (e.g., whether a planned trip was favorable). (See table 8.1 for summary.)

In all cases, advice was given and a remedy prescribed. All remedies amounted to ritualistic acts that appealed to the supernatural powers of the *entidades*. Clients were instructed to take baths with ritually prepared herbal infusions (*banhos*), to light candles wrapped in paper onto which their requests had been inscribed, to talk more with the *entidades*, to participate in the weekly propitiatory ritual to Exu (the *orixá* who "opens up the wa,y" *abre o caminho*), and so on. Some treatments (*tratamento*) were simple one-off acts. Others required repeat and follow-up sessions. More cumbersome, or "heavy" (*pesado*),

TABLE 8.1. Frequency with Which Issues (Grouped into Themes) Were Addressed in Consultation Sessions over a Twenty-Five-Day Period

Categories of Issues Attended To	Frequency and Percentage of Total	
	Number	Percent
Marriage, Love, and Family	25	32.05
Financial	19	24.36
Health	19	24.36
Spiritual	8	10.26
Family Member Enquiry	5	6.41
Future	2	2.56
Total	78	100

work such as undoing the effects of sorcery (as described in chapter 1) was an important part of Pai's service.

Toward the end of my period of fieldwork, I asked Pai for his view on what it is that brings people to religious experts like him in search of remedies to their problems. He responded:

In my opinion, there are many problems that we prefer to attribute to spirituality than to our own powerlessness. We prefer to say that we aren't rich because someone cursed us than to admit that we are doing things wrongly. People want to get rich quick, but there's no such thing as this. Now, all these cases, even the cases in which I want to get rich whatever the cost, but I prefer to think that someone is doing something against me, the *culto afro* works with this. I mean in order to free people of these thoughts there are aromatic baths, etc., so that the person can become aware that *he/she* is doing things wrongly and is on the wrong path. So, for us, there's always going to be a spiritual side to everything. Even the illnesses referred to the doctor have a spiritual side because we believe that people first become sick in their spirit and then physically [lit. *in the material*]. . . . Therefore, there are treatments that combine spirituality and medicine.

Na minha opinião, existe muitos problemas que é preferível a gente atribuir à espiritualidade do que à nossa impotência. Prefiro dizer que a gente não é rico porque fulano faz feitiço pra gente do que a gente querer admitir que a gente tá procedendo errado—que a gente quer ficar rico só numa hora e que não existe isso, né. Agora, todos esses casos, mesmo nesses casos em que eu quero ficar rico a todo custo e prefiro admitir que alguém esteja fazendo alguma coisa pra mim, o culto afro, ele trabalha em cima disso, quer dizer, pra desobstruir a mente da pessoa, né, banhos aromáticos, tudinho, pra que a pessoa se conscientize de que ela está procedendo errado, de que ela está no caminho errado. Então, pra nós, sempre vai ter o lado espiritual em todas as coisas. Mesmo as doenças que são encaminhadas a médicos têm o lado espiritual porque nós acreditamos que primeiro a gente adoece no espírito pra depois na matéria. . . . Então, há tratamentos que você combina a espiritualidade com a medicina.

The content of this message contributed to a great deal of confusion and misunderstanding for both *filhos* and clients. On the one hand, Pai clearly believed that the *orixás* govern one's steps and that everything has a spiritual side. Yet, he frequently instructed them not to become fanatical about explaining everything in spiritual terms. "Whatever happened to free-will?" he would question. "We get so . . . whatever . . . that everything that happens to me, I address it as mystical. So, let's say, I've got a pain here in the corner of my eye: 'Ah, you know what this is? It's a negative energy that I picked up!'" Kitchen discussions, such as this one, demonstrated that a number of people had trouble distinguishing between the problems of everyday life that could be presumed to be naturally occurring and which should try to resolve by their own effort and those caused by sorcery and supernatural intervention. It was also clear that, as Pai stated, people were reluctant to find fault in their own actions and were not satisfied with natural causes when explaining the misfortune that had befallen them. According to Pai, a frequent claim among clients with health complaints was, "The doctor has done *all* the tests and every single one has come up negative." When Pai asks such clients to bring the results of the tests, they rarely return.

Not all cult specialists were as conscientious in their diagnostic and treatment procedures. The clients' ignorance and suggestibility about the particular causes underlying their misfortune afforded a degree of latitude to the cult experts that potentially led to unethical and ill-fated consequences. One of the many stories to circulate the regulars assembled in the kitchen each evening told of a *mãe-de-santo* who was approached by a client who had been diagnosed as HIV positive. He was instructed that his condition was the direct effect of a demand of the *orixás*, that he should pay a series of *obrigações* to the *orixás* and terminate his medical treatment. He did, and he died. While the *mãe-de-santo* was widely accused of grossly unethical behavior, Pai often drew out an additional moral from this kind of event which he directed to clients:

> When you make requests, they must be within reason. If I want this
> lamp here, I can pray for a year for this lamp to levitate into my
> hand or I can take steps toward it myself. The *culto* is about creating
> a better place for you here. If I earn 240 reais and a *mãe-de-santo*
> charges me 240 for a bath, it would be ludicrous to pay it and then
> end up in an even worse situation without even the means to pay
> my monthly bills. Now, if I've worked all day with clients and I ask
> the *orixás* for a few beans, that's a just cause.

Pai's privileged access to the knowledge and intentions of the *orixás* through divination and what could be called "spiritual inspiration" or "mystical intuition," afforded him the peace of mind of knowing which situations should be interpreted as coincidental and which were spiritual. It was perhaps difficult for him to appreciate the position of those who relied on his expertise for the diagnosis and potential resolution of existential concerns. Telling other people that "fanatical superstition" was undesirable had limited effect. Immediately following the very lesson quoted from above, one *filha* described to me the financial and health problems she had been experiencing. Nothing seemed to be going right for her. Wondering if it might be connected to demands the *orixás* were making, she had phoned Pai, only to be told to stop making such a fuss. She told me that she had been coughing up blood all week, but, hurt and offended, she did not get in touch with him again. She was now considering paying for Pai to throw the *búzios* (divining cowry shells) to question the *orixás* directly. Because of their insider status as members of the religious community, and their contribution to the daily running of the *terreiro*, *filhos* generally did not wait their turn for consultation along with other clients. Appointments and informal meetings were generally set up outside of the consultation hours, in which Pai would teach and advise *filhos* collectively and individually without price. This *filha* was now thinking about paying the full price for a divination appointment.

Nevertheless, despite his often abrasive manner, Pai often boasted that he had always had the blessing of a steady clientele without investing any resources in publicity. The clients advertised the success of his treatments, telling of how employment opportunities had opened up, how their health had improved, how they were happy in love, and so on. Pai read the tarot cards, threw the cowry shells, effectively channeled the messages from the spirit entities, and provided the counsel and ritual expertise by which clients could correctly follow the entities' orders. Many clients informed me that they were attracted to Pai partly because his *entidades* had the *força*, or power, required for effective healing evidenced by the spectacle and success of the curing ceremonies. The decision regarding which spirit would attend a particular concern did not generally lie with the client. What was significant was that it was Pai who was channeling the advice and the assistance of the spirit.

Filhos and clients enter a three-way exchange relationship from the moment that they make a request and attribute the resolution of their problems to the *pai-de-santo*'s expertise and the powers of the *orixás*. The clients require more than just a listening ear. Pai advises them and guides them in soliciting the supernatural intervention of the *entidades*. He, in turn, depends upon the *entidades* to bring him clients. The income generated from this work keeps the *terreiro* doors open. Obedience to the wishes of the *entidades* is expected to win their cooperation and to bring rewards. For the client, rewards and resolutions confirm the competence of the *pai-de-santo* and the power, or *força*, of the *entidades*. For Pai, a problem solved is the confirmation of his calling and mission and the assurance of a return visit from the client. Given a high rate of success, the business of changing misfortune into fortune builds momentum. A circle is formed, of petitioning, surrendering, and expressing gratitude to the *entidades* and the *pai-de-santo*, followed by further petitioning. It increasingly encompasses the countless downs and ups of day-to-day life until, as some said of others, it becomes like an addiction.[2]

All *filhos-de-santo* in the *terreiro* were once clients. The resolution of their problems and difficulties would have required, or led onto, the establishment of a personal, intimate bond with their *orixás* and *guias* through initiation. Subsequent ritual obligations maintain this bond and the "balance," or equilibrium (*equilíbrio*), that characterizes a life that is governed and sustained by the *orixás*. In most cases, this direct relationship with one's *orixás* and other spirit beings does not diminish the need for guidance from Pai and the *entidades*. Pai commanded knowledge of divination methods and ritual procedures, traditionally transmitted between spiritual father (*pai-de-santo*) and initiated son (*filho-de-santo*). In all stages of his career, he could point to *filhos* who became greedy for the privileges that this knowledge would bring (e.g., paying clients) and who went their own way, later claiming that the spirit entities were their instructors in *culto* practice. This claim potentially authorized any innovation and divergence from the established practices of their initiating *terreiro*. Such assertions were rejected by those who recognized the tradition of incremental learning at the foot of their initiator (*boca à ouvido*) and the importance of maintaining the distinct *culto* traditions of the lineage and *egbe*, or community.

One of the more senior *filhos* described Pai's role in his personal relationship with the *orixás* as follows:

> In my point of view, before having contact with the *orixá*, we must first have contact with the *pai-de-santo*, with the "caretaker" (*zelador*, lit. the one who watches over) of the *orixás*. . . . In order for me to dedicate myself, give myself over to a ritual in his house, to an initiation, it is necessary to have some mutuality, that I respect his person. . . . The *pai-de-santo* is our intermediary. It is only through him that we have contact with the *orixá*. That's why I prioritize the *pai-de-santo*, respect and look out for (*zelar*) him, because he has the capacity to offer us the necessary knowledge regarding the *orixás*. We come here to pay our *obrigações* because it is with these *obrigacões* that we acquire the strength necessary for our security in the day-to-day things.

No meu ponto de vista, antes de nós termos contato com o orixá, nos temos contato primeiro com o pai-de-santo, com o zelador do santo.... Pra mim me dedicar, pra mim me entregar a um ritual na casa dele, a uma iniciação, é preciso que eu tenha afinidade, que eu respeite a pessoa dele.... O pai-de-santo é o nosso intermediário entre nós, só através dele é que nós temos o contato com o santo. Aí o porquê d'eu priorizar o pai-de-santo, respeitar e zelar para o pai-de-santo, pra que ele tenha, desde que ele tenha essa capacidade pra nos oferecer o conhecimento necessário sobre o santo. Aqui vem pagar obrigaçãoes porque é com essas obrigações que nós vamos adquirindo as forças necessárias à nossa segurança no dia-a-dia.

For all participants, finding a wise, personable, and honest *pai-de-santo* was a matter of great consequence and a blessing that was usually attributed to the care and protection of the *entidades*. Nevertheless, it is important to note that when relations between *filhos* and *pais-de-santo* turned sour, or when the inefficacy of the rituals raised the clients' and *filhos'* suspicions about the *pai-de-santo's* qualifications, filhos would tend to seek out the services of another ritual expert. One's *pai-de-santo* was far from dispensable, but it was between the *filho* and the supernatural agents that the enduring and fundamental flow of exchange existed.

This triangular relationship among *filho*, *pai-de-santo*, and spirit is often established at the first indications of possession and the onset of mediumship. Across the world, spirit-possession phenomena are often interpreted against a backdrop of belief that people's misfortune is a direct consequence of their possession by the spirits. These notions do not on the whole call into question the utility of the spirits as counselors, protectors, and judges. The anthropological literature shows with striking frequency that, where possession by spirits is believed to exist, it is frequently invoked as the explanation for certain physical and psychological maladies (e.g., Lambek 1981). Spirits are not only perceived as pulling the strings of one's fate according to moralistic, disciplinary motives. They may be perceived as causing trouble for rather more self-interested reasons.

Local accounts of spirits frequently describe them as beings that possess humans to satisfy a desire temporarily to return to earth. Reasons given may vary, from notions that they were once humans and now grieve or pine for earth, to accusations of malicious intent to cause havoc among the mortals. The spirit is not generally summoned initially but is believed to make his or her presence felt of his or her own accord and in his or her own time. Depending on the immediate circumstances of the host selected, and the local interpretations that accompany the event, the spirit may or may not be made welcome. Arrival of the spirit is frequently described in negative terms, as embarrassing, inconvenient, or incriminating. Spirits tend to make their presence felt by interfering with the host's quality of life, whether by causing ill health, trance or trance-like states, strange dreams, or irregular behaviors. Whatever the case, the spirit's arrival demands the attention of a qualified spirit expert or ritual specialist.

In the *culto*, *filhos* describe the first approximations of the spirits as erratic, untimely, and uncontrolled cases of trance, or as the onset of chills, headaches, or nausea when observing a possession ceremony, or as the message behind a series of ill-fated incidents. The person afflicted would inevitably be forced to seek out the guidance and instruction of a local *pai-de-santo* in order to confirm his or her doubts and to remedy the situation. On confirmation that a spirit had chosen the individual as a potential host, the individual would ideally begin to cultivate the requirements of the spirit and to develop his or her mediumistic competencies. In keeping with intuitive principles of exchange, cooperation would reap its own benefits. Failure to cooperate could exacerbate the difficulties one was presently experiencing. With obedience to the desires and demands of the spirits, and appropriate guidance, preparation, and schooling with the *pai-de-santo*, the host would eventually become a competent medium.

Social Exchange and Supernatural Agents

The foregoing account describes some basic properties of interaction between humans and gods that are repeated time and again across many of the world's religions. One encounters people in all societies who request counsel and guidance from supernatural beings. People all over the world also petition the gods for assistance, and the gods are expected to act in response to or in advance of some behavior or act that merits their kindness. Likewise, the gods are believed to punish those whose behavior falls short of their standards and expectations. The precise details of the causes, remedies, and the social ties that emerge may differ, but there are fundamental principles at the heart of these phenomena.

Crucial here are the tacit laws of exchange that govern everyday human social interaction. People socialize, communicate, form groups, and negotiate according to a set of principles by which they distinguish cooperation, reciprocation, commitment, opportunism, cheating, defection, and unequal exchange. These principles operate largely unconsciously, organizing the ways we behave toward others and readily enabling us to assess and explain the ways others behave toward us. For example, if I give something to someone but do not receive anything in return, I can readily and intuitively define this as unbalanced exchange. This may lead me to investigate my exchange partner's intentions in order to assess whether he or she intended that the situation should be so and to consider the implications for subsequent interaction. On confirming that negative reciprocity was fully intended, tacit principles of morality and inferences about the wrongness of the behavior are mobilized.

The defining principles of exchange are therefore closely connected to intuitive morality. When the give-and-take regularities that characterize fair exchange are distorted and the principles of social exchange are violated, something wrong is detected. The party from which more was taken than received often *feels* wronged (Barrett 2004: 53). A client, for instance, is aggrieved when it transpires that the *pai-de-santo* she has confided in, and paid good money to, is in fact a fraud and a charlatan. The specific cues that can be interpreted as cooperation and cheating may vary cross-culturally, but the connection between morality, emotional states and social interaction is universal (Boyer 2001:187).

These principles of social exchange may have bestowed adaptive advantages upon ancestral human beings. Other agents, both human and animal, were of crucial significance to our ancestors' survival. Agents' capacity to act and cause things to happen meant that they were potentially valuable (as friends) or hazardous (as enemies) in a competitive, social environment. Failure to detect the actions of these agents, and accurately to interpret them, brought grave risks. Detecting agency and then making sense of it are basic mental processes facilitated by the highly sophisticated tools of our evolved mental architecture. As Daniel Gilbert points out, "We care about what others do, but we care more about why they do it" (2002: 167). But the rapid and efficient, implicit processes by which we readily comprehend our social environment also potentially lead to biased reasoning for everyday occurrences. We detect agency even on the basis of minimal cues, and, at times, against the weight of evidence. The predisposition to over-employ the concept of agency and agent causality in everyday situations is widely documented in social psychology literature. E. Thomas Lawson writes,

> It seems to be the case that human beings have the propensity to
> overextend attributions of agency even when the situation does not
> require such attribution (Ross 1977). What is involved here is not
> so much the error of over attribution as it is the preoccupation that
> humans seem to have with agent causality. Conspiracy theories

abound. Blame is placed even when it is not required. Human beings' preoccupation with agent causality typically results in their un-
derestimation of the role of the environment and their overestimation
of human responsibility and the role of personality traits when assessing the causal dynamics of social events. (Lawson 2001: 164)

People all over the world are highly sensitive to the threat of shady deals,
breaches of contract, fraudulence, deceitfulness, and other forms of cheating,
particularly when they might be among the victims. This, of course, makes
good adaptive sense. Human agency is often sufficient in the search for a satisfactory and plausible cause for events. For example, when I get home from
work to find a mountain of dishes by the kitchen sink, I can assume that neither the cat nor the ghost is the cause (given that there are more relevant human
agents around). If a driver crashes into another car, I might assume that he is to
blame. We are constantly making judgments about everyday situations that
satisfactorily identify human agents as the perpetrators. As Barrett says, "When
appeals to human agency seem to do the job and are salient, then that is where
the credit lies" (2004: 52). In some cases, however, accident or chance, mechanical accounts, or even human causation do not satisfy as explanations. For
example, if the driver crashes into *me*, I may acknowledge immediate causation,
but even an explanation that gives an account of the mechanics of the crash,
and which confirms the driver's actions to be unintended, may not entirely allay
my state of nonunderstanding. Outstanding questions of personal significance
may remain; "Why me?" and "Why now?" for instance. From a young age,
children bemoan situations that "aren't fair." "What did I do to deserve this?"
is a common sentiment when things go wrong against all one's best efforts.

   Our bias toward agent causation is demonstrated in our tendency to represent salient and unfortunate events, even in which there is no immediate
social element, in terms of fairness and exchange, as though they were social
things (Boyer 2001). Once social causation is triggered, design is implied, and
intentions, or intentionality, are often inferred. Ideas about luck turn on similar reasoning processes. As Jason Slone writes, "The belief in luck is a by-
product of this cognitive capacity to identify events in the world and to infer,
often quickly and from incomplete data, their cause(s)" (2004a: 386). In all
such cases, people implicitly and readily attribute design (and, by inference, a
designer) to random events and may invoke exchange principles to assess the
reasonableness of the situation. Barrett points out that appeals to agency are
particularly satisfying because when events can be explained in terms of intentions, no further reasons are required (2004: 53). When misfortune is treated as

the effect of violations of fair exchange, explanations are informed by the guiding principles of social interaction and reciprocity. They are therefore closely linked with moral judgments. For example, the notion that someone else's fortune is gained at the expense of one's happiness, health, wealth, opportunities, and so on, not by chance but by design, is both intuitively plausible and emotionally upsetting.

But why do people ask why in the first place? The perceived lack of satisfactory explanation is individually subjective and may be contingent on several factors. Barrett has suggested that the level of personal significance attached to the event increases its salience and the tendency to reflect on possible explanations beyond "cold, statistical reasoning" (2004: 51). Numerous studies in psychology have shown that people are motivated to wonder why an event happened if having no explanation challenges their goals, particularly their need for control and prediction or for conceptual coherence (see Malle and Knobe 1997). Negative and improbable events are therefore most likely to elicit reflection on possible causes as such events challenge people's needs for control and prediction and for cognitive and affective balance (ibid.: 289). I further suggest below that the special context of superhuman involvement in the lives and affairs of *culto* participants increases the potential for agency to be detected in everyday happenings. But these explanations appeal to a special kind of agent.

Boyer (2001) claims that the centrality of agents with special qualities (such as gods and spirits) to the explanation of events is parasitical on the central preoccupation with agents in human judgment in general. Precisely because the gods are represented as engaging in social exchange with people, they are potential causes of misfortune, just as are all the other people with whom one interacts. What sets the supernatural agents apart as particularly suggestive is their knowledge of all the strategic information relevant to social interaction between humans (Boyer 2001: 201). For example, if I do something wrong, no other human may ever find out, but I can assume that the gods saw it. Furthermore, the gods have the power to punish misdemeanors. "In the case of misfortune," Boyer writes, "our propensity to think of salient events in terms of social interaction creates a context where supposedly powerful agents become more convincingly powerful" (ibid.: 202).

Tamar Gordon's (1996) ethnography on Tongan possession provides one of many examples found in the cross-cultural anthropological record of the readiness with which people explain salient events in terms of moral justice. Direct disciplinary intervention, including possession, by the spirits is prompted by the contravention of social taboos. According to Gordon,

> Tongans say that the dead are even more morally outraged than the
> living by social transgressions. The spirit's desire to exert moral re-
> straint over a person intensifies when specific *tapu* are violated.
> For example, one young woman I knew officially died of heart fail-
> ure; the explanation going around at her funeral was that the spirit of
> her recently deceased father had entered her body and had "*a vea'i
> ia,*" "taken her away." This girl had been extremely close to her
> father and had lovingly nursed him in the final months of his fatal
> illness. Her mother, aunts and sisters said that she died because
> she had broken the *tapu* on handling her father's bodily wastes.
> (Gordon 1996: 56)

Appeals to putative supernatural agent causation are particularly satisfying. As this ethnographic example illustrates, supernatural beings, such as
gods and spirits, not only have the power to act, but also are often thought to
be privy to all kinds of knowledge that enables them to adjudicate a particular situation fairly. Hence their frequent position as monitors, arbitrators, or
meddlers in the deeds of humans. When reasoning about their intentions for
sending misfortune, I can assume that the gods know my circumstances (e.g.,
what I have been getting up to) and have their reasons for sending affliction
my way.

The ways people reflect on the gods' reasons are continuous with the ways
people reflect on everyday social action. Principles of exchange that govern
ideas about fairness in daily life are equally relevant to how people think about
gods—as social beings—and about appropriate ways of interacting with them.
The anthropological record of religious practices worldwide repeatedly shows
how human exchange provides the template for exchange with the gods.
"When I ask for something," says Brazilian sociologist, Roberto da Matta, "and
sacrifice something precious to make an offering to the saint of my devotion,
social logic obliges the saint to resolve my problem" (1984: 111, my translation).
Da Matta describes the result as a pact between the two sides. Similarly, *culto*
participants often defined the exchange of prayers, candles, offerings, and
obrigações for the daily assistance, guidance, and friendship of the spirits as a
pacto, or pact. In the following passage, Lambek describes the negotiations that
result from confirmation of first possession of a Mayotte person:

> Once a spirit has made its presence felt, it is then up to the host to
> respond. . . . The spirit is asked to state its conditions for releasing the
> patient from her suffering. The spirit makes a list of excessive, if
> predictable, demands, and there ensues a process of bargaining and
> exchange, which stabilizes the relationship between spirit and host.

The intent is not to exorcise the spirit but to come to an understanding with it, to negotiate the removal of the unpleasant symptoms rather than the spirit itself. . . . There is an underlying tension
here between the best interests of the host and those of the spirit.
The reappearance of illness functions as a control mechanism,
turning the host back to a consideration of the spirit's demands.
(Lambek 1981: 46–47)

The notions that the dead become outraged at the transgressions and misdeeds of social actors, and that this results in some form of retribution, re-
cur again and again across cultures. For some evolutionary psychologists, this
widespread recurrence raises important questions as to the possible evolutionary role of such notions in enhancing genetic fitness. Jesse Bering and
Dominic Johnson (2005) have suggested that, in the ancestral past, perceiving
one's social behavior as being under the watchful and just eye of a powerful, moral adjudicator bestowed selective advantages on human beings living
within complex groups. Fear of supernatural punishment encouraged the inhibition of selfish actions. Such actions contravene social-exchange principles
of reciprocity and cooperation and tend to be deemed socially objectionable
and immoral. And "because human behaviors are unconsciously motivated
by genetic interests, individuals should have evolved to be motivated to refrain from any behaviors that are believed to threaten inclusive fitness (i.e., the
representativeness of one's genes in current and future generations)" (ibid.:
127–28).

Bering and Johnson describe some of the implicit expectations operative in
causal reasoning that may result from such tacitly held interests. For example,
extensive evidence has been found that people hold to beliefs that the world is a
"just place" (see Furnham 2003 for a review of recent research). People behave
and reason about events with the tacit assumption that they get what they deserve. What goes around comes around eventually, whether in this life or the
next. When a person breaks a moral rule or taboo, he or she often appears to
anticipate punishment. The waiting and expecting is often accompanied by
guilt, which, if not discovered, is often expunged only with the liberating self-
declaration of culpability.

The ethnographic record points not only to the widespread representation
of supernatural agents as a source of danger, but also to their role as protectors and guides and spiritual, emotional, physical, and financial benefactors.
Bering and Johnson observe that "prosocial actions, or actions that foster cooperation between in-group members and generally help grease the wheels
of social harmony, should lead actors to have expectations for positive life

events" (ibid.: 129). According to the principle of reciprocal altruism, people who consider themselves to have done no wrong (before men and gods), who perceive themselves as morally upright, and believe that they do more than their average altruistic bit for others, potentially assess personal unhappiness and ill-fate as being unprovoked and unwarranted. The gods are sure to be party to everything from the public display of the charitable philanthropist down to the humble offerings of the unprofessed almsgiver. And just as they have the power to return punishment for transgression, the gods also have the power to protect, heal, and mete out good fortune as rewards for righteousness. The old adage "cheaters never prosper" satisfies the intuitive, tacit principles that operate in any complex social situation. Furthermore, when a direct appeal to the gods is followed by success and fortune, the chain of causation is simple and clear. In such cases, belief in the power of the gods is confirmed and reinforced. Barrett describes the general mechanism implied earlier in this chapter by the term *momentum:*

> The properties gods typically have encourage us to incorporate gods into thinking about fortune and misfortune. They provide much-desired explanations for why peculiar and otherwise inexplicable things happen. But this tendency to incorporate gods into thinking about fortune and misfortune in turn reinforces belief in gods. Each time we satisfactorily understand an episode as being the work of a god, another memory is created affirming the existence of the god, and the mental tools responsible for such problem solving have more tightly woven the existence of the god into its operating assumptions. (Barrett 2004: 55)

The Relevance of Gods Who Possess

O contato direto com os deuses e a preparação do corpo para que esses deuses possam voltar a se manifestar pra dar conselhos é o ponto máximo do culto afro.
     Direct contact with the gods and the preparation of the body so that these gods can return and manifest themselves to give advice is the crucial point of the *culto afro* (Pai).

When the gods and spirits speak directly through divination methods and are believed to possess people and speak through them, the causes for misfortune and fortune become potentially knowable. For a reasonable fee, both believers and nonbelievers in the *culto* can directly ask the *entidades* what they know. One friend in the *culto* defined possession for me as "a means of communicating more quickly, of them [the spirit entities] coming and talking. Whether or not they talk, just by coming, they are there responding to something... through possession they are giving the fastest response." (*É um meio de comunicar mais rápido, deles virem e comunicar. Ou se comunicar ou não falar, eles já deram só de vir tá alí respondendo por alguma coisa... então eles já tão dando pela incorporação uma resposta mais rápida.*) The *entidades* are not expected to be aware of everything that may be relevant to one's problem, but there is always a chance that, with their bird's-eye view of the world and their elevated wisdom, discernment, and foresight, they will be able to contribute to the successful identification of causes and remedies for one's misfortunes. As one participant told me, "When the *entidade* is chatting to you, she perceives your life [lit., has clairvoyance]. She peels you like a banana; she sees what happened; she has a deep connection with what happened. It's as if everything were being shown on television." (*Na hora em que a entidade está conversando com você., ela tá tendo uma vidência na tua vida. Ela faz, ela te descasca como se você fosse uma banana, ela ta vendo o que aconteceu, ela tá numa ligação profunda do que aconteceu. É como se fosse uma televisão passando do lado—ela vê tudo aquilo.*) This alleged ability made them potentially excellent counselors. They were neither distant spectators nor disinterested judges of the affairs of humans, however. They were often tangibly in attendance as full-time partners in those affairs. I suggest that, when contemplating the potential causes of misfortune, this increased their relevance as potential perpetrators.

These spirits occupied a space that straddled both the human and supernatural exchange arenas. Monetary donations were placed directly into their hands. Requests were whispered into their ears at ceremonial possession parties. *Filhos* negotiated dispensations from attending the *terreiro* activities when it was unsuitable. Lodgers requested late curfews. Friends and *entidades* exchanged secrets, gossip, and jokes. The *entidades* were recognized as owners of the *terreiro*, having bought it with donations they had been offered. They dealt insults, and those on the receiving end took offense. Blessings, counsel, and comfort were exchanged also. In short, almost everything that the *terreiro* was, had, and did was owned and commanded by the *entidades*. This brought them into intimate, regular, and immediate contact with the human social circle of exchange. The supernatural agents were present, interested, watching, powerful, intentional, and often incarnate human beings. They would not only know about the difficulties one was enduring and have the power to cause them or to intervene; there was also great potential for them to be the party cheated, offended, and irritated by one's insensitive behavior, immoral deeds, disrespect, and failings.

Mediums in the *culto* often appeared to use the power of the spirits to their advantage, attempting, through possession, to add the authority of the spirits to their statements. When scolding, planning a ceremony, and garnering support for a particular project or task, a useful and effective strategy—frequently used by Pai—was to add the authority of the spirits to their statements by becoming, or appearing to become, possessed. The respect that apparently resulted from people's deference to the *entidades'* superior status was also a calculated attempt to curry *the entidades* favor. Saying no to the specific request of a spirit could run its own risks and limit one's chances of assistance in the future. Whether in casual conversation or in ritual acts, *filhos* were aware of the potential to displease the spirits. In such situations, the familiar saying, "What goes around, comes around," evokes a fundamental exchange principle for the justification and anticipation of retributive punishment.

It is important to note that the threat of punishment did not always *deter* people from misconduct. In the previous chapter, we observed that the deference and respect shown toward mediums when possessed by ancestral spirits and African semi-gods rarely matched the level of deference in discourse about the *entidades* outside the possession context. But when problems arose, the spirits were a regular target of causal attributions. In this context, simple occurrences are potentially quickly reflected upon as goal-directed events (rather than merely random occurrences) and easily explained in terms of basic like-for-like exchange principles. "Perhaps," one thinks, "it was that snide retort," or "perhaps it's because I didn't attend yesterday's ritual obligation (*obrigação*)." Otherwise insignificant and random occurrences and happenings are thus rapidly perceived as events that can be readily explained in terms of punishment, retribution, and revenge. In comparable human social situations, when the people with whom one interacts are offended or angered and desire to seek vengeance, they are restricted by physical and other normal, human limitations. Returning the harm done to us by others is often desirable but not always attainable. Cost-benefit considerations will also come into play. The victim weighs up the delayed costs of getting revenge against the immediate, certain rewards to be gained through correcting the situation (Baron and Richardson 1994; Baumeister 1998). For example, a potential cost of "sweet" revenge is that one becomes the target of countervengeance. In contrast, one can assume that with the lifting of human limitations, spirits will have little difficulty in retaliating, whatever the offense. And, as the feeble sight of man shaking his fist at the heavens aptly portrays, humans are no match to the superior might and wisdom of the supernatural "powers that be."

Sorcery—The Occam's Razor of Misfortune

In the context of the *culto*, a further option is available for the explanation of misfortune. People frequently reflect on whether or not spirits have been stimulated into action by the evil and selfish intentions of another human agent. Was one's misfortune a consequence of another person's envy? When sorcery is speculated, the gods are not the intentional source of the action. The gods are the medium of power by which the misfortune occurs, but human agency and intention lie behind it all. When it comes to seeking explanations for misfortune, both direct supernatural intervention and sorcery or witchcraft are often equally plausible options—both the gods as disciplinarians and humans that can exploit the powers of the supernatural beings are potentially salient, satisfying, and relevant causes. I argue, however, that even assuming the high potential for people to relate their misfortune to their direct dealings with the gods, particularly in the context of the possession cult, the latter scenario is particularly attractive.

This is because sorcery accusations do not only appeal to the biases that one's mental tools generate for interpreting and explaining misfortune (e.g., the tendency to look for causes for misfortune and an inclination toward social explanations). They also play to a further bias that has been widely documented by social psychologists. Attribution theorists have suggested that people attribute negative outcomes to external factors in an effort to maintain their self-esteem (e.g., Baumeister 1998). We have seen how supernatural punishment for one's misdeeds is a cognitively plausible, easily inferred explanation for misfortune. But the blame for the negative situation ultimately rests with the person punished (assuming that the gods are privy to all evidence and are justified in their actions). Sorcery accusations, in contrast, potentially diagnose the sum of one's difficulties as being wholly attributable to the intentions of other people and not to one's own shortcomings. Putting one's failures and misfortune down to someone else's evil intent absolves one of all blame for the supernatural intervention of the spirits. Consider the following interview extract in which Pai, possessed with Mariana, discusses the ritual aberrations of some *pais-de-santo* in the city:

> One doesn't cut [immolate] anything on Fridays. One doesn't spill blood on Fridays—the African Friday begins at sunrise and when the sun sets, after the sun sets, you can cut, but before this you can't cut anything. [This is] in homage to Oxalá because Oxalá doesn't accept the color red, also because you can't kill an animal on a day

that is devoted to the lord of life. It would be a contradiction, isn't that right? But there are *casas* that don't obey this. It doesn't matter if it's Friday—"Ah! C'mon, let's cut now today so that tomorrow we can eat"—and many times the *obrigações* become an excuse for a barbecue. So, I tell you that you need to give a pig at your *obrigação*, and I don't consult the *orixás* because I feel like eating roast pork—I cut the pig, all that, tomorrow we do a barbecue, tomorrow I eat the roast pork and oftentimes, my daughter, the person doesn't give even a piece of that animal to the *santo*. . . . They want to eat everything and don't give anything to the *santo*.

But they don't suffer at all?

They suffer, they definitely suffer.

Because, I know that the pai-de-santo often says that there is no right or wrong way [i.e., ritual orthodox for the whole *culto*] but it seems that it's wrong to eat all the food that should be given to the orixá, the santo?

They suffer, my daughter. They suffer terrible consequences, but when they are afflicted by these things, they attribute them to sorcery, magic. . . . They don't know how to throw [i.e., to divine using the cowry shells], they don't want to throw, and they would never see in the cast that the *orixá* is annoyed with them because they killed a ox and ate it all and didn't give a piece to the *santo*. The consequences are terrible—the *festa* finishes in fights, financial situations. . . .

Não se corta nada dia de sexta-feira. Não se derrama sangue dia de sexta-feira. A sexta-feira do africano começa no nascer do sol e quando o sol se põe, depois que o sol se põe, pode-se cortar, mas antes disso não se pode cortar nada, em homenagem a Oxalá, porque Oxalá não aceita a cor vermelha e até porque, porque não pode matar um animal num dia que é votivo ao senhor da vida. Seria uma contradição, não é isso? Mas tem casas que não obedece isso, não interessa que é sexta: "Ah vumbora cortar logo hoje pra amanhã a gente comer," e muitas vezes as obrigações se tornam motivo pra fazer churrasco. Então eu digo pra você, que você precisa dar um porco com a sua obrigação, e não consultei os orixás, porque eu tô com vontade de comer porco assado. Corta o porco tudinho, amanhã faz um churrasco, amanhã como do porco assado e muita das vezes minha filha, a pessoa não dá nenhuma parte daquele animal para o santo, . . . não, eles querem comer e não dão nada pro santo.

Mas eles não sofrem assim?

Sofrem, com certeza sofrem.

Porque, eu sei que muitas vezes o pai-de-santo fala que não tem um jeito certo e errado [ou seja, procedimento padronizado para o culto], mas parece que é errado comer toda a comida que deve ser dada para o orixá, o santo?

Sofre minha filha, eles sofrem consequências terríveis. Só que eles, quando são atingidos por essas coisas, eles atribuem ao feitiço, magia . . . não sabem jogar, não querem jogar e jamais vão olhar no jogo que o orixá tá chateado com ele porque ele matou um boi e comeu todo o boi e não deu um pedaço pro santo, as consequências são terríveis. Termina a festa em briga, situação financeira. . . .

If the self-serving bias described here is relevant as a predictive measure of the kinds of attributions of misfortune that appeal to supernatural agency, one should find that, all else being equal, sorcery practices are entertained more readily as potential explanations for misfortune than ideas about the punishment of the gods. Throughout my fieldwork, the perceived threat of *feitiço*, or sorcery, was fully evident in *filhos'* and clients' conversations and preventative practices. Garments, belongings, a lock of hair, or a photograph could potentially be used by the *feitiçeiro* to bring about misfortune and disadvantage. Other than carefully guarding such items, one could do little to stymie the effects of envy and vengefulness of someone somewhere. Work colleagues, ex-spouses, and unfaithful partners were particularly suspect candidates. Unknown competitors were also culpable in the grand system of one's exchange partners. Other human agents were a real danger and potentially injurious to one's fortunes and ambitions. The anthropologist, a relatively peripheral and temporary presence in the group, was a particular hazard, with her cameras clicking at every opportunity.[3] Overall, eighteen months of participation in *terreiro* life (and in Belenense society in general) confirmed the immense popularity of sorcery explanations for misfortune.[4]

Even if these observations are suggestive, the frequency with which practices of sorcery and human intention are actually invoked as causing one's misfortune remains an empirical question, answerable through systematic data gathering. For example, one could record all instances of client complaints over a specific time period, their suspected causes, and stated reasons for particular speculations made. Although participants are unlikely to be aware of their implicit motivations for suspecting sorcery or divine punishment, the reasons that they explicitly state may indicate whether other factors are in play that could potentially confound results. For example, if a person has failed to "pay" a ritual obligation (*pagar obrigação*) to the chief *entidade* and this is swiftly followed by a period of personal crisis, the apparent contingency of the two events may influence the person's reasoning toward divine-punishment explanations. Likewise, if someone has a history of sorcery attacks and counter-attacks with a particular person, but has no firm commitment to the religious and ritual life of the *terreiro*, it is likely that he or she will tend toward sorcery explanations when misfortune arises. Research that shows statistically significant evidence of a tendency toward sorcery explanations over supernatural punishment explanations, in which both are equally plausible, would lead on to precise and systematic testing of the hypothesis advanced above to account for this pattern. Since the theoretical rationale lies in biases of social cognition that are universal across all social interaction, it is potentially testable in any context in which sorcery beliefs and beliefs in supernatural punishment exist as equally plausible explanations for misfortune.

Conclusion

In a recent communication, a Brazilian friend of mine speculated on the factors that give rise to the widespread belief across Brazilian society in spirit causation for personally significant events. According to this friend, the principle protagonist is ignorance, or lack of education. Ignorance, according to this rationale, causes people to invoke superstitious lines of reasoning when attempting to explain what is really their own incompetence. In addition, he argued, "In Brazil most people don't assume their responsibilities. On committing an error, they blame others, or lie, or say that something or other invaded their body." These two factors, along with some consideration of specific features of Brazil's colonial history, were said to make spirit beliefs particularly plausible and attractive to sectors of Brazilian society.

Despite being a widely popular theory, it is clear that it is not for want of an educated, natural explanation that people invoke supernatural causation when making sense of their surroundings. I reminded my friend of an individual case close to home, in which accusations of sorcery were seriously considered during a particularly difficult spot in a relative's business career. Although everyone around perceived the situation as being the logical, natural outcome of a series of normal events, the relative was concerned with explaining the specific nature, timing, and recurrence of these negative circumstances in his life. Sorcery provided some fit with these more personally significant questions that the situation posed (Boyer 2001: 197; also see Evans-Pritchard

1937). My friend's explanation begs another important question that I have attempted to answer here: "Why spirits?"

As minimally counterintuitive agents, spirits are easily thought about, and are relevant to explaining ambiguous events, particularly those that are negative, surprising, and personally significant. Knowing the causes of such events can enable one to predict and control the kinds of circumstances that may lead to their future recurrence. As will be shown in the following chapter, there are numerous contextual factors that motivate people to think about gods and spirits and that lead to such concepts becoming widespread and even endemic across a population. I have specifically argued here that intuitive reasoning, by means of which misfortune is so readily attributed to the intentional agency of supernatural beings or to human adversaries who can manipulate supernatural powers, is continuous with generic, tacit beliefs and expectations that people everywhere hold for the social world that they are a part of.

The presence of supernatural agents extends the parameters and possibilities of that world to encompass a special kind of inferentially powerful social causation. Gods have special access to information about morally valenced social behaviors and are potential arbitrators of human affairs. They are commonly attributed the power to punish and reward where appropriate. Other humans are always potential threats to our chances of gaining positive opportunities, prospects, and return in life. Where they are able to manipulate the powers of the gods, they become equally, and probably more, suspect in one's search for causes. These factors become particularly relevant to situations in which people seek explanations for personally consequential events, especially those that threaten well-being and survival. Chapter 9 considers in more depth the cognitive mechanisms that underpin these processes and factors that act upon them, giving rise to clearly identifiable correlations between the incidence of spirit phenomena, including possession, and particular features of the ecological contexts in which such phenomena appear.

9

Explaining Distributions of Spirit Concepts and Spirit Possession

Emma could open up a *terreiro* over there in Ireland, be a *mãe-de-santo*! Do you have *terreiros* over there?

A Emma pode abrir uma casa lá na Irlanda, né—ser mãe-de-santo! Vocês têm pra lá?

—A filho, informal conversation

I have suggested that the spread of spirit phenomena is in part explained by universal micromechanisms of cognition that generate predispositions and tendencies toward certain patterns of thinking and behavior. Basic cognitive processes involved in perception, representation, interpretation, explanation, and prediction are fundamental to our comprehending the world around us. Generating inferences about the way things in the world work is a basic human capacity, enabled by highly sophisticated mental tools such as the "object detection device," "agency detection device," Theory of Mind, "social exchange regulator," "intuitive morality," and so on (Barrett 2004). Because of the pressures under which these tools process the play-by-play of everyday movement, action, and interaction, many inferences, or mini-theories, and immediate conclusions are generated only as fleeting or oversimplistic heuristics. For example, I can recall a number of occasions on which I have been momentarily and mildly startled even at my desk by what has turned out to be the shadow of my pen as the desk lamp has caught and reflected its movements. The agency detection device operates so rapidly and automatically that it often infers animacy where there is only movement. On reflection, one can take time to bring more evidence to bear on the false positives generated by one's implicit mental processing.

It is the universality of our mental tools and the automaticity with which they process information from the world around us that make them indispensable for the explanation of the form and spread of cross-culturally recurrent concepts and practices. The point of departure for the claims made in this book is that, all else being equal, concepts that diverge considerably from inferences generated by the tacit operations of the mind, that are conceptually "heavy," and that require effortful conscious reflection for mental representation, are less likely to be transmitted than concepts that fit with the inferences and intuitions generated nonreflectively and rapidly by regular mental mechanisms. Yet, if, as I have suggested, these universal mechanisms find such a natural output in the form of spirit phenomena, such as spirit sickness, possession, mediumship, sorcery, supernatural-agent causation for misfortune and fortune, and so on, why are these outputs more widespread in some societies than in others?

Why, for example, do we find that spirit phenomena are ubiquitous and everyday in certain sectors of some African societies (see Comaroff and Comaroff 1993), for example, in Southern Sudan ("Witchcraft is ubiquitous. It plays its part in every activity of Zande life"; Evans-Pritchard 1937: 63), while there is much less evidence that such phenomena are regarded seriously or become institutionalized in other parts of the world, for example, in North America and Northwestern Europe (Bourguignon 1968: 45, 160)? Why do women figure more prominently in spirit cult activities than men (Lewis 1971; Harris 1957; Messing 1958)? Why are superstitions, witchcraft beliefs, spirit possession, and mediumistic activity especially rife in conditions of political conflict and socioeconomic change (for South Africa, see Kohnert 2003; and for Kenya, see Dolan 2002)? If the mental mechanisms described here are constant across societies, then what other factors might account for the patterns of geographical and contextual variation in spirit possession, and spirit phenomena more broadly, that are so apparent in the anthropological literature? Bourguignon's (1968) survey identified 74 percent of 388 societies as having some form of institutionalized possession trance, but what of the other 26 percent?

Cognition has been described as "a nexus of relations between the mind at work and the world in which it works" (Lave 1988: 1). Cognitive capacities and predispositions must not, therefore, be mistaken for determining factors. Showing that all humans have the capacity to think readily about the

properties of spirits and the predisposition to invoke agentive-causal explanations for ambiguous events is not sufficient to explain the variable incidence of these notions across different societies. All people everywhere, for
instance, have the capacity to acquire the structures of language required for
verbal communication without explicit instruction, as well as the potential to
learn how to record language in writing. Yet the presence of writing systems, and even simple writing technologies, is not ubiquitous across cultures.
We must not confuse necessary with sufficient conditions in our predictions
and explanations of cultural phenomena. Even if one demonstrates that regular mental architecture is something one must have to conceptualize spirit
possession—a *necessary* condition—it does not follow that having this architecture is enough—a *sufficient* condition.

When generating hypotheses for cultural transmission from a cognitive
perspective, we can begin by making predictions about the relative chance that
an idea will have in cultural transmission, all else being equal. Consider the
two scenarios of spirit possession described in chapter 6. All else being equal,
the first scenario has a higher chance in cultural transmission than the second. It is unlikely that the more conceptually complex and inferentially impov-
erished spirit-possession scenario would enjoy success in cultural selection,
but it is certainly not impossible. It is conceivable that with deliberate instruction, or with sufficient mental rehearsal, or by some other mnemonic means,
such ideas could be remembered and subsequently transmitted intact across
and between generations. A cognitive explanation for the transmission of such
complex concepts would necessarily incorporate these contextual factors in
accounting for memorability (e.g., Whitehouse 2004). Similarly, features of a
particular situation could serve to enhance the relevance (and therefore the
transmission) of the easy-to-grasp concepts of the first scenario (e.g., a spirit
that can know people's secret thoughts and deeds). An appreciation of significant contextual factors that inhibit and encourage the spread of such concepts can only help to refine a theory's predictions, making clear what would
count as counterevidence for the claims proposed. Ideally then, further significant factors in cultural transmission (e.g., specific ecological conditions),
previously grouped under the "all else" heading, are distinguished from random, arbitrary features and incorporated into our increasingly precise and
detailed predictions.

In this chapter, I suggest that certain correlations between institutionalized and endemic spirit phenomena (e.g., possession, magico-religious healing, etc.) and particular contextual and demographic conditions (as identified
by extensive cross-cultural surveys) are causally significant. I focus on the correlation between spirit possession and suggested effects of social complexity,

such as political oppression, marginalization, and stress. I also propose a causal account for the unequal participation of men and women in certain forms of religious activity in general, and spirit-possession cults in particular. The claim that these well-attested correlations are causally significant is by no means novel. Explanations for the incidence of such phenomena have often taken for granted a chain of causation. Yet, we shall observe once again that few attempts to generate explanatory theories have succeeded in formulating hypotheses in such a way that the mechanisms that are suggested as accounting for pertinent patterns and correlations are specified precisely enough to allow for systematic testing and evaluation. I do not claim to describe all, or even the most significant, factors accounting for these cross-cultural patterns. I do, however, present a limited, but potentially testable, range of hypotheses that could contribute in some small way to more comprehensive and useful accounts of the spread of spirit possession and associated phenomena.

In their accounts of the incidence and prevalence of particular cultural phenomena, anthropologists, sociologists, social psychologists, historians, and other social scientists often exclusively select or prioritize features of local contexts (e.g., political, economic, etc.) that appear to encourage the public presence and standardization of ideas, attitudes, or practices within a group or society. These "population scale macro-phenomena" (Sperber 1996: 2) are often attributed some special power or "force" of their own which can bend and shape human culture into infinitely variable forms (see chapter 5). Of all the material constraints that are said to obtain in the selection and transmission of ideas, human cognition—in which ideas, or "culture," reside—has tended to be overlooked. We have seen, however, that some aspects of cognition are not as flexible as the standard social science model tends to assume. It, too, exerts its own "force," or, as Whitehouse more eloquently writes, "patterns of mental activity, rooted in the biology of brain functions and their developmental contexts, have direct effects on the elaboration of all domains of human culture" (2004: 16).

Taking as our point of departure the precisely described, regular machinery and capacities of the mind—specifically agency detection and Theory of Mind—I ask, what are the general factors that might further encourage or discourage the appearance and transmission of the kinds of concepts (e.g., supernatural agency, supernatural causation, etc.) generated by our mental tools? In posing the question this way, one finds that recent advances in the cognitive sciences may have significant relevance to long-running debates about the subtle variations in the transmission of spirit possession and spirit phenomena.

Ethnographic Survey Data: Where Do Spirit Beliefs Arise?

As a cognitively optimal—that is, largely intuitive, memorable, and easily transmittable—concept, spirit possession requires little by way of deliberate instruction or other special conditions for its transmission across cultures. It should transmit easily in the absence of any institutional framework, specialist expertise, authoritative instruction, elaborate technologies, and so on, all else being equal. Unsurprisingly, therefore, we find that spirit possession is widespread across the world. Indeed, it is likely that the concept of spirit possession is universal, but that specific environmental and historical factors further promote the generation, spread, institutionalization, and persistence of possession belief and practice within a society.

The extent of the incidence of possession belief and the identification of environmental factors contributing to its spread has been the focus of a number of cross-cultural surveys. Using a broad sample of societies[1] from all major regions of the world, Bourguignon reported that institutionalized possession could be found in 360 of the 488 societies surveyed. Figure 9.1 shows the distribution of possession belief[2] recorded by Bourguignon across the

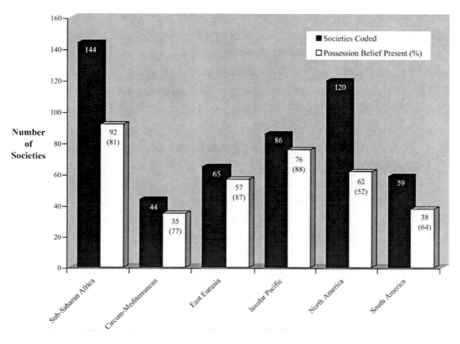

FIGURE 9.1. Distribution of Belief in Spirit Possession (Bouguignon, 1968)

sample of societies. A total of 74 percent of the societies were recorded as having possession belief (including both possession associated with trance and possession not associated with trance, in which trance is defined as involving "alterations or discontinuity in consciousness, awareness, personality, or other aspects of psychological functioning" [ibid.]), with the Insular Pacific region showing the highest incidence at 88 percent of societies sampled, closely followed by East Eurasia (87 percent) and sub-Saharan Africa (81 percent). One quarter (26 percent) of sample societies have no possession beliefs, an absence which is most marked in North America (48 percent).

Where the possession concept is invoked to account for the trance state, this is defined as possession trance (PT). 251 societies had some form of possession trance, making up 51% percent of the total sample. Again we find a large discrepancy in incidence between North America (25 percent) and sub-Saharan Africa (66 percent).[3] Bourguignon's survey registers coded measures of societal complexity in all societies sampled, and the final report includes discussion of correlations between these features and possession. Such features include indicators of socioeconomic inequality, such as class stratification, levels of jurisdictional hierarchy, and slavery.

Investigation of the possible factors contributing to the distributional pattern worldwide yielded significant correlations with a number of these societal complexity dimensions. The study reports significant positive relationships of possession trance to class stratification and jurisdictional hierarchy above the local level. Taking a sample of 114 societies from sub-Saharan Africa, Lenora Greenbaum (1973) also found that the presence of slavery (or recent slavery) and the presence of a system of stratification (more than one social class) were significantly related to the presence of possession trance. In a more recent survey of the incidence of possession in the training of shamanistic healers, Winkelman (1986) found a positive correlation between possession and all of the societal complexity variables from Murdock and Provost (1973). The strongest significant correlations were with political integration, population density, and social stratification.

Interpretations of the correlations between these societal variables and possession trance were framed largely within considerations of social change and cultural innovation. In a collection of papers bringing together qualitative and quantitative data on possession trance, Bourguignon writes, "What appears to emerge clearly from our discussions ... is that altered states in general and, perhaps, possession trance in particular represent potentially important and dramatic instruments of social power and, thus, of social change" (1973: 338). In the same volume, Greenbaum investigated the specific role of "societal rigidity" in an attempt to develop a more precise understanding of the specifically relevant correlates and features pertaining to the broad variable of complexity. Taking the degree of "role and structure differentiation" (Greenbaum 1973: 54) and "fixed internal social status distinctions" (ibid.: 50) as indications of societal rigidity, and arguing that such rigidity was more likely to be a characteristic of complex societies than of simpler, nonstratified ones, she predicted that, "where individuals have little opportunity for achievement and little control over their daily activities, possession trance is more likely to occur" (Bourguignon 1976: 31). The causal mechanism proposed was that possession trance represents a "safety valve," providing, as Bourguignon says, "some elbow room" (ibid.), and offers the medium some authority. This broad-spectrum hypothesis resonated with the findings of many anthropologists who subsequently employed and refined it, appropriating its generalizable claims to their explanatory and interpretive analyses of possession and race, class and gender inequality (see chapters 4 and 5).

As observed in chapter 5, however, Bourguignon's theory and accounts that were subsequently developed from its premises have not sufficiently described the mechanisms proposed to account for the correlations identified, much less suggested procedures for their systematic evaluation. How, for example, are "role and structure differentiation" and "fixed internal social status distinctions" to be defined? In what ways, if any, does the societal rigidity of complex societies share characteristics with the societal rigidity of simple societies? How can such rigidity be measured? How could one define and measure "opportunity for achievement" and "control over daily activities"? Could one definitively characterize the "degree of leeway" (Bourguignon 1976: 31) that possession trance is said to provide in order to confirm its significance? Scientific precision and rigor demands that such claims be unpacked, rendered testable, and ultimately put to the test before one may affirm their validity.

Psychologists, by adopting a more precise empirical approach, have made interesting discoveries and claims about the kinds of situations in which paranormal beliefs in general tend to be invoked. Drawing from studies ranging from Malinowski's (1954) description of Trobriand Islanders' fishing practices through to Padgett and Jorgenson's (1982) findings on superstition and economic threat in Germany from 1918 to 1940, psychologists have noted that superstitious and magical beliefs tend to increase during periods of ambiguity, uncertainty, or uncontrollability (see Dudley 1999: 1058). Eschewing imprecise predictions and unjustifiable assumptions that the domain of magical and paranormal activity is chiefly among primitive tribes (Frazer 1890, 1959; Malinowski 1954), young children (Freud 1919, 2003; Piaget 1929), or individuals suffering from mental health disorders (Klein 1946, 1987; Wilder

1975), these scholars have sought to identify the psychological factors that may be significant for the emergence and rise of religious, magical, and superstitious thinking (see Albas and Albas 1989; Dudley 1999; Gmelch and Felson 1980; Keinan 1994, 2002; Matute 1994, 1995; Rothbart and Snyder 1970; Vyse 1997).

Stress and Control

Psychologists have shown that the belief that one is in control of one's own fate is strongly associated with emotional well-being and mental health (James and Wells 2003; Thompson, et al. 1993; Thompson and Spacapan, 1991). Thompson, et al. discovered that in uncontrollable situations, for example, in the event of terminal illness, individuals use numerous strategies to maintain a sense of control, even if only over the consequences (e.g., emotional, relational) of the negative life stressor rather than over the stressor itself (Thompson, et al. 1993: 302). Indeed, control over one's environment may have had a functional evolutionary adaptive value for our ancestors. The pursuit of regularity and order through everything from agricultural tools, to hunting maps and weapons, to astronomy and science potentially, increases a sense of perceived control by rendering harsh, unstable, or unpredictable environments more hospitable and less uncertain (Denton 1999).

In some recent experimental studies, Giora Keinan (2002) found that exposure to stress correlated with an increase in the incidence of magical ritual behavior. In another study, Keinan showed that during the Gulf War, there were higher levels of superstitious and magical thinking among residents living in areas most likely to be hit by a missile than those living in low-stress areas (1994). Refining the mechanism suggested by Greenbaum concerning possession behavior in particular, and consistent with the findings of other experimental studies (e.g., Dudley 1999; Rothbart and Snyder 1970), the research also indicated a "tendency toward magical thinking and superstitious behavior in situations in which control is reduced or lacking" (Keinan 2002: 106). In these studies, variables such as stress and control were measured according to a Subjective Stress Scale and a Desirability of Control Scale (Burger and Cooper 1979). Keinan's results support an explanation in terms of desire for control that is commensurate with correlations and interpretations from Bourguignon and her successors. This explanation, he writes, "posits that stress undermines individuals' sense of control and that resorting to superstitious behavior may provide a means of regaining control" (2002: 106). This explanation is also consistent with the ethnographic data and predictions presented in chapter 8 of this book.

These studies suggest that lack of perceived control and the desire to regain control are precipitating factors in leading people to embrace religious and magical and superstitious ideas and practices (James and Wells 2003; Keinan 1994, 2002; Thompson, et al. 1993). Religious specialists the world over, such as healers, shamans, and mediums, offer techniques for restoring control to people whose lives are believed to be influenced by supernatural powers. The techniques range in levels of sophistication, from prayer and simple divination measures, through to elaborate rituals of fortification and protection.

In the *culto*, a large repertoire of ritual activities, including healing, bestowing of positive energies, and receiving the powerful, fortifying force of Axé, could restore equilibrium to imbalances (*desequilíbrio*) that affected people's (control over) marriages, financial situations, health, and so on. Likewise, baths of herbal infusions for protection (*banhos de proteção*), the wearing of bead necklaces representing one's guardian angel, and the "closing of the body" (*fechamento de corpo*) ritual were common means of protecting oneself against the evil intent of sorcerers and malevolent spirits that could inflict physical, emotional, and financial harm. "*Fechamento de corpo*," one informant explained, "is like a vaccine . . . so that when a negative energy comes her way, she is not fragile and weak. . . . She might feel something, but she's going to be stronger and better prepared." (*Fechamento de corpo . . . é como, por exemplo, você toma uma vacina . . . quando a carga negativa vem, ela pode até sentir alguma coisa, mas ela vai tá mais forte, vai tá mais preparado pra aquilo.*) Such rituals were provided on a supply-on-demand basis. As another member of the *terreiro* once said, "You don't get involved in a religion in order to learn. You do so out of necessity, in search of some help, some kind of help with a problem of illness, or health, or a problem with love, or whatever. You pay for a product . . . and that's it." (*Você não entra numa religião pra aprender. Você entra por uma necessidade, a procura de alguma ajuda, ajuda de alguma maneira—ou um problema de doença, de saúde, ou um problema amoroso, enfim. Foi algum problema, tá, você vai pra pagar um produto . . . e acabou.*) This statement may not reflect the variable motivational aspects of involvement among all *culto* frequenters throughout ongoing and long-term participation in *culto* activities. It does, however, resonate with the experience of most, if not all, adult participants when they first enter the *terreiro* doors.

Practices such as prayer, sacrifice, and vaccination against sorcery develop from concepts that capitalize on ordinary cognitive processes and inferences.

The idea that powerful, knowing agencies exist, and that they can be petitioned for rewards in return for appeasing and pleasing actions is largely intuitive; it fits with a vast number of assumptions that our mental tools generate. As such, these ideas are easily remembered. Furthermore, it is the agents' minimal counterintuitiveness that makes them particularly attention grabbing. Just as important is their significant ability to generate explanations and predictions for events that have triggered a sense of nonunderstanding and uncertainty for the perceiver. But there are certain contexts in which these ideas, once present in an individual's mind, become even more compelling.[4] In the following section, I provide a more comprehensive description of our "agency detection device" (Barrett 2004) introduced in previous chapters. This tool is fundamental to the attribution of agent causality and intention to ambiguous events. Insofar as its sensitivity is encouraged by factors such as urgency and stress, I suggest that this device may be instrumental in explaining apparent variations among people and across populations in attributions of supernatural agency to events and happenings in their lives.

The Hypersensitive Agency Detection Device

Barrett coined the term "Hypersensitive Agency Detection Device" (HADD) to refer to the mental mechanism responsible for a tendency to (over)attribute agency to events in our environment. Developmental psychologists have shown that young infants can distinguish between agents and nonagents (Gopnik, Meltzoff, and Kuhl 1999; Premack 1990; Leslie 1996 [1995]; see Lawson 2001), indicating that this is an early-emerging, basic cognitive capacity. In studies of adults' perceptions of moving shapes on a screen, observers are reported to have described the objects' movements in terms of mental states and personalities (Heider and Simmel, 1944; Michotte 1963, in Barrett 2004: 32, 44f).

Once HADD is activated, it searches for a likely candidate agency. Unless an external agency can be detected and identified as acting upon the object, the apparently goal-directed movements are attributed to the object itself as agent (Barrett 2004: 32–33). Furthermore, as Barrett points out, there need not be an object present for HADD to detect agency. When HADD fails readily to identify human or animal agency responsible for an event, other kinds of known agents may make intuitive sense. This is where supernatural agents may become relevant. Agents with superpowers are particularly salient when explaining events that appear to be intentionally and purposefully caused, but for which no visible or human agent fits well. Indeed, rather than their counterintuitiveness promote disbelief, it is this property that enables their perfect fit with the evidence to hand.

Consider the following portion of a *terreiro* member's life story. As a child, Fátima enjoyed hearing the stories from her friends about the *orixá* deities. The "enchanting" events of the legends kindled a desire to know more about the *orixás* and about their continued spiritual existence, if indeed it was real. She recalls, however, that at seven years of age, she first began to have particularly disturbing experiences. She recounts,

> I felt, I felt—I told my mother and she told me to close my mouth... "Mummy, this man is...". It was a footstep like that of a man, a really tired man, who used to hang around me. But I never saw him, I only listened—just a child. If, as an adult, you don't see the thing, just imagine what would go through your mind, because you can hear it. But you can't see it—the thing you will see is that which you imagine.
>
> *Eu sentia—eu sentia— eu dizia pra minha mãe, ela mandava eu calar a boca... "Mamãe, esse homem tá," era um passo como se fosse de um homem, um homem muito cansado que vivia ao meu redor, só que eu não via, só escutava—uma criança. Se você, adulto, não vê uma coisa, você imagina, imagina o quê que não passa pela tua cabeça, né, porque você não escuta mas você não vê—você vai, o que você vai ver é aquilo que você imagina.*

Fátima's mother refused to accept her stories and fears about the footsteps. Fátima could hear and feel them right beside her but never saw the person responsible for making them.

Some time later, she became ill to the point of losing the power in her legs. At the hospital, no conclusive diagnosis was reached. Finally, a domestic maid in the neighbor's house took her to a *terreiro*. The *pai-de-santo* called her mother for the diagnosis:

> Look, what she has is not for the attention of the doctor. You aren't going to cure this at the clinic. She has got *encosto*... someone is doing work [*fazendo um serviço*, i.e., doing sorcery, the consequences of which are generically referred to as "encosto"]. It was done for you [Fátima's mother], but she is the person who is receiving it. Everything they send to you, she gets it. She is the one who hears—she doesn't see, but she feels and hears.

Olhe, o que ela tem não é pra medico, que a senhora não vai curar no
médico. Ela está com encosto, ta . . . Estão fazendo um serviço, foi feito
um determinado serviço para a senhora e só quem está recebendo é ela.
Tudo o que mandam para a senhora é ela que recebe e ela que escuta. Ela
não vê mas é ela que sente e escuta.

In order to get Fátima back on her feet again, a "remedy," or potion, was massaged into her legs, prayers were said, and by the next day, the feeling had returned to her legs and she was walking again.

The next tragedy—a near-fatal swimming accident in the river—was readily accredited to evil intent. Fátima developed a simple theory for what was occurring: if someone sends something bad to another person, and yet another person "has a weaker and lesser spirit, without security"—a child, for example—the latter will be vulnerable to attack. As Fátima matured, she began to frequent *terreiros*, meet mediums, and converse with the *entidades* about her problems. One *entidade* in particular, Mariana, was instrumental in bringing her closer into the *terreiro* community: "Everything that she did for me at that time was a success, and I saw that things were really turning out right." (*Todo que ela fazia na época dava certo. Aí eu fui, realmente vi tá dando certo, né.*) Fátima is now one of the most loyal *filhas-de-santo* at Pai's *terreiro*.

This particular life path started with a startling and frightening event caused by the failure to match HADD to a candidate human agent. To Fátima's young mind, all evidence pointed toward there being a person with no body responsible for the noises that she readily identified as footsteps. The fact that, until then, her entire experience of persons indicated that the property of physicality was normal did not stop her from thinking that this person was factual. Indeed, since person-agency was so undeniable, only such a being *could* be responsible.

What doubtless caused most perturbation was the failure to discern the purpose of the person's actions. Being able to infer something about the intentions of others is an indispensable capacity because it helps one predict and explain their behavior. Much as in the case of diagnosis for a physical complaint, these underlying causes could highlight a legitimate cause for concern. They may guide subsequent action for the restoration of a sense of control over the situation. Reasoning about superhuman agents' ability to make things happen, and to do so for a reason, naturally leads to the *kinds* of responses described in chapter 8 and life stories like that of Fátima. The nuanced differences between specific responses may vary widely, but they naturally spring from a common source.

So, how do the commonalities in human mental architecture help one explain the variability, if not of the specific and nuanced forms that such responses take, then of their *incidence* cross-culturally? I predict that the HADD mechanism described above, with its sensitivity to particular features of the environment, is a relevant (but not the only) causal factor in these patterns of distribution. HADD, by definition as "hypersensitive" or "hyperactive," is always on the lookout for agency. But certain situations put it onto "high alert." Much as the anticipation of a visitor increases the likelihood for us to (mistakenly) think we hear a knock on the door, and as the information that a room is haunted heightens our attentiveness to every creak of the floorboards, so, too, agency detection for events can be particularly sensitive under situations of high stress. Stress is a psychological and physical response to a situation of pressure, known as the stressor. As such, it pertains to the individual and is measurable at the level of the individual. Yet, in that a stressor may be population wide (e.g., a natural disaster) and long-standing (e.g., a harsh political regime), its effects may be experienced at a collective level (i.e., by multiple individuals). One of these effects, I suggest, in high-stress situations, is the increased invocation of supernatural-agent causation and remedy for high-stress, low-control events. HADD for events is the mechanism that may potentially explain, in part, the correlation between stress/oppression/uncontrollability, on the one hand, and the high incidence of spirit phenomena and superstitious and paranormal beliefs, on the other hand.

HADD and Urgency

As yet little is known about the precise processes involved in agency detection, and much less about the contextual factors that might increase its sensitivity. Nevertheless, extant predictions are currently being considered for experimental evaluation. Barrett identifies individual background and dispositions as important variables acting on HADD's sensitivity: "People who believe in ghosts are more likely to see ghosts than non-believers. Being a believer—or merely open to believing—in a god makes one more sensitive to detecting the god's action or presence" (2004: 39). Another significant variable, he suggests, is the immediate context. To put it simply, situations in which one is particularly aware of the potential to become prey (e.g., walking in a dark alleyway), or in which one is deliberately tracking down potential prey (e.g., seeking an intruder), affect HADD so that it detects agency with minimal or even zero environmental cues. Its frequent coupling with situations of urgency is natural and develops very early in infancy.

Barrett thus associates contexts and situations of urgency and uncertainty with increased tendency to detect agents easily and rapidly. When agent causation fails to deliver a satisfactory explanation, then superhuman agency may be a salient and intuitive explanation, particularly where the perceiver is already a believer. This leads Barrett to conclude that, "in more traditional societies, such as those tied to subsistence hunting or farming, where life is filled with nonhuman dangers, life is also filled with forest spirits, ghosts, witches, and ancestor spirits constantly and obviously at work" (ibid.: 40).

Nevertheless, the literature reviewed above suggests that the degree to which one is surrounded by other humans is less relevant to the rate at which one may perceive nonhuman dangers than the degree of perceived danger and uncontrollability in general. We have noted that, even where people find plausible explanations for events in terms of human agency, a subjective state of nonunderstanding will often persist under certain circumstances. Nonunderstanding potentially threatens basic needs to predict, explain, and control critical situations (Malle and Knobe 1997). A further condition that needs to be satisfied for people to reason about the explanation for an event is its personal relevance, or its potential to threaten the positive outcome of a personal goal. When that goal is as crucial as survival, by means of a fertile crop or the avoidance of illness, for example, threats to the situation are likely to trigger agentive-causal thinking, with high frequency on only very modest information, and therefore further to support existing beliefs in spirits and gods. This prediction is consistent with findings from experimental psychology and anthropology (e.g., see Keinan 1994, 2002; Malinowski 1954; Padgett and Jorgenson 1982). Whether it is the effects of pestilence, flood, and drought, or of economic decline, gang warfare, and government corruption that one is trying to make sense of, all such situations potentially appeal to supernatural agency as the ultimate cause and cure, even if humans are known to be immediately involved and at least partly responsible.

Thus, on the assumption that HADD and environmental contextual conditions, such as survival and urgency concerns, are causally associated, I predict that, all else being equal, the incidence of phenomena that invoke the special powers of supernatural agents for explaining and predicting events increases under environmental pressures that threaten immediate survival and control. This prediction holds, first, that HADD is a panhuman tendency to invoke intentional agency for events for which the actor is in a perceived state of nonunderstanding, and that magical, superstitious, and much religious thinking capitalizes on this tendency. In that stress (whether caused by crop failure, ill health, unemployment anxiety, etc.) and uncontrollability may contribute to the emergence of such beliefs, one should expect to find higher levels of institutionalized forms among individuals and populations in situations that contribute to such stress (e.g., lower-class/marginalized/unemployable/oppressed sectors of society). Second, one should detect in particular the rate of occurrence increasing at points of transition that threaten previously taken-for-granted survival and welfare. Third, practices that restore control or perceived control over these environmental "stressors" would tend to accompany these causal beliefs.

The possession concept is by no means representative of all kinds of spirit-related phenomena that a truly comprehensive survey would encompass for the naturalistic evaluation of the HADD prediction. However, it is hugely widespread across the world, probably universal. A range of environmental and historical factors are clearly correlated with the successful spread and institutionalization of possession beliefs and practices within a society. One of those factors, according to the HADD prediction, is environmental pressure on survival, whether man-made or otherwise. The evaluation of the above claims could be initiated in highly controlled studies, testing the predicted correlation between HADD and urgency in a laboratory setting or in a controlled study.[5]

However possession specifically is interpreted (e.g., as a safety valve, a means to claim power and authority, a form of resistance to man-made pressures outside one's control, etc.), its presence is potentially explainable, in part, by generalizable psychological factors. Stress related to survival at the level of populations, for example, through war, famine, socioeconomic inequality, and exploitation, may promote (in tandem with other factors) the emergence, increase and institutionalization of beliefs and practices associated with spirits and supernatural agents that are normally already present in the wider society. What the new cognitive science of religion contributes to this discussion is a description of the possible fundamental mechanisms of cognition that explain why, in particular, supernatural and magical agency become so germane in such contexts. These mechanisms evolved in our ancestral past, developing a survival system by which people automatically and intuitively arrive at certain conclusions about the world that surrounds them; even—or perhaps especially—when that world is uncertain, their place in it is vulnerable, and the threat of their own mortality is particularly vivid.

Women in Spirit-Possession Activity

Our description of the propensity of the mind to attribute events to the actions of agents would be unduly truncated if concluded at this point. Once agency is detected, reasoning about the intentional states of the agent is automatic. We are more concerned about the reasons for people's actions than the actions per se (Gilbert 2002: 167). Description of the mechanisms that enable us to make inferences about what is going on in the minds of other people is the domain of increasingly sophisticated Theory of Mind (ToM) scholarship (see chapter 7). It is important to note that agency detection and ToM are mutually supporting, regardless of how distinct the mechanisms seem in the descriptions of their respective functions. Barrett explains it thus: "[I]f ToM can suggest the agent's desires and aims relevant to the event, it affirms to HADD that the event was goal directed, increasing HADD's confidence that agency has been discovered. Thus, HADD's work is not in isolation, and ToM's flexibility and readiness to explain subtle signs of agency encourage HADD's touchiness" (2004: 42). Following Barrett, I suggested in chapter 8 that, just as the ToM mechanism is employed in reasoning about the dispositions, motivations, and intentions of other people, it is also fundamental to reasoning about the intentional states of supernatural beings. I conclude this chapter with some tentative suggestions and considerations regarding the possible role of ToM in contributing to a further well-established demographic trend in the incidence of spirit possession.

The preponderance of women in possession cults is a widely acknowledged fact among anthropologists (Boddy 1989, 1994; Kapferer 1991; Lambek 1981, 1993; Landes 1947; Lerch 1980; Lewis et al. 1991; Ong 1987; Pressel 1980; Raybeck et al. 1989; Spring 1978; Wilson 1967). Undoubtedly, as with any complex and differentiated cultural phenomenon, there are many significant factors that come into play, giving rise to this demographic pattern. Different questions have been explored at different levels of analysis, generating various claims. Interpretivist accounts, for example, have looked to the local discursive processes and to common themes, idioms, and meanings, concerned, as Boddy says, "to trace the informal logic of everyday life ... to find both the coherence and the indeterminacy in what villagers see as commonsensical, to uncover the intrinsic and the natural in quotidian interactions" (Boddy 1989: 7). This has been the endeavor and hallmark of modern ethnographic fieldwork for several decades. Ruth Landes was one of the first American students to gather data on the women-centered cult houses of Brazilian Candomblé through fieldwork methods that prioritized participant observation and involvement in the day-to-day lives of her research participants. In the now-celebrated ethnographic classic, *The City of Women*, (1947, reprinted in 1994), Landes describes how "the ritual life of the candomblés mirrored the economic and social autonomy of the women and the female-centeredness of Afro-Brazilian households in Bahia. Removed from political and economic representation in Bahian society, Afro-Brazilian women endowed their domestic lives with meaning through creative elaborations and modifications of the possession religion" (Cole 1994: xii).

Landes's unconventional approach to fieldwork and her apparent failure to frame the analysis within a broader historical context came in for heavy criticism from a seasoned Africanist, who argued, "The basic thesis is wrong . . . because of the misreading of an economic cause—that is, few men are initiates, in Bahia no less than in Africa, because they cannot afford the time it takes, because in Africa it is easier to support a woman in the cult-house than to withdraw a man from productive labor for months on end" (Herskovits 1948: 124). That such demands impinged on freedom to participate in cult activities was corroborated by Eduardo da Costa's contemporaneous descriptions of the demanding initiation rites in his classic *The Negro in Northern Brazil* (1948). He writes, "The West African period of complete seclusion for several months which is also found in the Bahian cult houses is here limited to eight days, and formal instruction is limited to a minimum. . . . [M]any of the women must make their own livings and fear to lose their jobs if they absent themselves during the period of seclusion" (1948: 75–76). Landes, however, operated within an alternative framework that characterized the Candomblé as a cultural expression that was vitally Brazilian and, more particularly, that appealed specifically to the women of the Bahian urban poor. Landes's perspective afforded an alternative to the focus on African survivals and integration into the New World society that predominated in studies of African-derived traditions in Brazil at the time.

Psychological explanations, meanwhile, that were proposed within anthropological scholarship on possession more widely, tended not to take women's widespread prominence in possession activities to be derivative of social differences and divisions. Rather, these explanations often leaned toward, or explicitly articulated, essentialist arguments premised on a "weaker sex" assumption. For Oesterreich, women (along with the lower classes, "primitives," and the uneducated) were more susceptible to "autosuggestion" (1930: 28) and therefore were more likely to believe in spirit entities that could possess people. In his functionalist interpretation of "demonic" or "unsolicited" forms of possession, even Lewis describes the healing cult as a "feminist sub-culture," which the "weaker sex enjoys as a religious drama" (1989: 80). In this "cult of feminine frailty," "women are, in effect, making a special virtue of adversity and affliction, and, quite often literally, capitalizing on their distress" (ibid.: 79). It was not long, however, until the unfounded "hysterical propensity of women, the mysterious powers of their yin-dark nature, and other magico-scientific explanations" (Kendall 1987: 24) were rejected as implausible and unpromising causal accounts. Continuing scholarship attempted to provide answers to the question of elevated female participation by looking to the social domains, divisions, and differences of women's worlds.

Almost half a century after Landes's unconventional, fine-grained descriptions of women's everyday lives had scarcely found a publisher, meaning-centered approaches were now dominant in anthropological descriptions and analyses. Scholars returned their focus to the appeal and relevance that spirit-possession cult activities had for women, through fine-grained, local, and individual-level analyses. "An obvious approach," Boddy claimed, in her discussion of female participation in the *zar* cult in Northern Sudan, "is to ask whether the range of experience that possession constructs is more common to Hofriyati women than to men" (1989: 138). Boddy suggests that this indeed is the case because "possession is closely linked to fertility with which women are identified and for which they bear responsibility" (ibid.). Many anthropological studies showed how possession addresses and meets the needs pertinent to the social domains and activities for which women were traditionally and typically (though not exclusively) responsible, such as family health, "domestic religion" (Sered 1999), the reproduction of social communities, and the contestation of social injustices (Boddy 1994: 416; e.g., Alpers 1984; Brown 1987; Constantinides 1982; Lambek 1980; Lerch 1982).

There has also been continuing discussion within modern psychological scholarship on the possible causes of gender differences in religious involvement and commitment more generally. Indeed, the conclusion that women are more religious than men has been described as one of the best-attested findings in the psychology of religion (Francis and Wilcox 1996). Here we find two main groups of theories, approaching the problem in a similar vein to anthropologists over the years. In her review of empirical research on the issue of gender and religion, Leslie Francis categorizes them as follows: "The first group of theories concentrates on social or contextual influences which shape different responses to religion.... The second group of theories concentrates on personal or individual psychological characteristics which differentiate between men and women" (1997: 81–82).

In the first, gender differences in religiosity are predicted to have a sociological basis. It has been claimed, for example, that girls are socialized into religiousness more than boys (Mol 1985; Nelson and Potvin 1981). Factors that overlap significantly with those suggested in the discussions above have been predicted also; the family-centered position of women (Moberg 1962), the nature of the domestic division of labor (Azzi and Ehrenberg 1975), men's and women's unequal participation in the secularized world (Lenski 1953; Luckmann 1967; Martin 1967), and the social support offered by participation in religion (Moberg 1962) have all been suggested as relevant factors to women's greater involvement in religious activities (see Francis 1997 for a comprehensive review).

Of the second group of theories, Francis shows that there has been mounting support for "gender orientation theories" in particular. These theories predict a positive relationship between psychological femininity (measurable by sex-role inventories, such as Bem [1981] or Antill, et al. [1981]) and religiosity. This is an emerging field of enquiry, for which little cross-cultural investigation has been carried out, and for which as yet no data are available on nonwestern societies. Findings from the United States and the United Kingdom, however, strongly suggest that the association between women and religiousness is a function of gender (i.e., femininity) rather than being female (Thompson 1991; Francis and Wilcox 1996). Yet, as Rodney Stark (2002) has pointed out, the fundamental source of these gender differences has been left unexamined. Considering highly significant results from a cross-cultural survey that compares religiousness in men and women in forty-nine nations, Stark claims that there "is only one other gender difference similar to the one involving religion" (2002: 501). He draws from evidence in the field of gender and criminality that point to fundamental physiological sources for men's heightened risk-taking behavior and proneness to violence and impulsive behaviors. He links this to Miller and Hoffman's (1995) findings that intragender measures of risk aversion correlate significantly with religiosity—those who score highly on risk aversion are more religious. Stark concludes his analysis, "If we assume with Miller and Hoffman that irreligiousness is simply another form of risky behavior to which certain kinds of men are given, then there seem to be grounds for proposing a link between physiology and faith" (ibid.: 504).

Stark claims that he looked to insights from physiology with a great deal of reluctance, and only after he found "every cultural and social alternative to be inadequate" (ibid.: 496). It is, however, somewhat premature to write off the predictions from these fields. The fluidity of the social contexts in which women's roles are played out complicates the application of generalizable models within populations, not to mention across time and across populations. Notwithstanding, these approaches have made interesting advances and are not bereft of serious predictions that, once substantiated, may provide a more economical answer to the question of gender differences and religiosity than Stark's proposed physiologically based association between risk-taking and irreligiosity. Furthermore, contrary to Stark's claim, there *is* at least one other significant psychological difference that is predicted as a causally significant dimension in differential behaviors of men and women.

A recent model advanced by Simon Baron-Cohen (Baron-Cohen, et al. 2003; Baron-Cohen 2004) proposes an alternative, though perhaps complementary, source for gender differences; namely, men's and women's variable performance in empathic and Theory of Mind skills. The importance of ToM for the generation and acquisition of religious concepts, particularly agent-concepts, has already been discussed. Recent research suggests that strongly attested sex differences in ToM are relevant to respective differences in behavioral tendencies and cognitive skills (ibid.). I suggest that this may be a fruitful place to further our inquiry into the differential ratio of men's and women's involvement in religious activities in general, and spirit possession in particular. Sociological, psychological, and anthropological approaches have contributed much to the discussion concerning women's religious involvement but have failed to elucidate the mechanisms whereby this cross-culturally recurrent pattern comes about. We need a generalizable, testable hypothesis—or set of hypotheses—that fits with the evidence on the ground, whether in urban New York or among the emancipated slave populations of northeastern Brazil. As with any widespread phenomenon, universal patterns are strongly suggestive of the presence of panhuman causal factors. Given the crucial importance of the ability to infer the intentional states of other agents to spirit and other (supernatural agent) phenomena worldwide, I suggest that we consider the explanatory potential of well-attested gender differences in cognitive abilities.

The Empathizing-Systemizing Theory

Baron-Cohen's central claim is that there are essential sex differences in the mind, for which systemizing and empathizing are the two major dimensions of relevance. It is by systemizing, on the one hand, that we most successfully understand and predict the behavior of a law-governed system, such as the relatively stable, inanimate world that surrounds us, including technical (e.g., a sundial), motoric (e.g., a tennis stroke), and abstract systems (e.g., mathematical), among others (Baron-Cohen 2003: 361–62). Empathizing, on the other hand, is our most powerful tool for analyzing and predicting the social world, that is, for making sense of other people's behavior. It is composed of both a cognitive and an affective component. The cognitive component is the ability, or drive, to infer other people's mental states from their behaviors (i.e., Theory of Mind). The affective component is the drive to respond to these inferred states with an appropriate emotion (Baron-Cohen 2004: 28). Through a series of studies, Baron-Cohen and others (Baron-Cohen, et al. 1997, 1999,

2001, 2003) found that females tend to score higher on empathy measures than males (measured by the Empathy Quotient [EQ] questionnaire).
Males, however, tend to score more highly on systemizing measures than
females (measurable by the Systemizing Quotient [SQ] questionnaire). These
results do not, however, indicate an absolute, essentialized difference between
males and females. Rather, the poles are divided according to the "brain type"
an individual has, whether male or female. Individuals who are average to
high systemizers are defined as having a brain of Type S. Individuals who are
average to high empathizers are referred to as Type E. These two dimensions
are not mutually implicated (i.e., low EQ does not necessarily follow from
high SQ), but the higher score will predict the brain type classification. Individuals who score equally on both quotients are referred to as Type B. As
stated, there is evidence to support the claim that *more* males than females are
Type S, and *more* females than males have a brain of Type E (Baron-Cohen
2004).

One important finding that has emerged from this application of cognitive
and affective mechanisms to sex differences is the strongly significant correlation between individuals with a high-systemizing quotient/low-empathizing
quotient—mainly males—and autism. This has led to an associated theory
called the extreme male brain theory (EMB) of autism (see Baron-Cohen 1995,
2004; Baron-Cohen, et al. 1999, 2002, 2003). There has been somewhat less
consideration of the potential applications of high-scoring EQ, low-scoring
SQ individuals, a possible effect is that these individuals (mostly women)
would have difficulty analyzing variables in a system and deriving underlying
rules (see Baron-Cohen 2004, chapter 12). Their hyperempathetic tendencies
could also drive them constantly to speculate about the mental states of others,
but with a high degree of accuracy, perhaps resulting in seemingly uncannily
precise insights into others' minds.

With regard to empathizing and systemizing differences between Type S
and Type E individuals at the less extreme ranges of the scales, the crucial question is: are there any broader applications for the Empathizing-Systemizing
theory to well-established, widespread, and generalizable gender differences in
patterns of religious behavior (as well as perhaps criminal tendencies and other
differential behavioral patterns)? I suggest that these findings are significant
for explaining, in part, the demographic patterns found in religious involvement cross-culturally, with specific relevance to spirit-possession activity and
the particular demands it places on empathizing abilities (as defined by Baron-
Cohen). My argument is premised on two main claims.

First, as we have noted, HADD and ToM are fundamental mechanisms
for the generation, acquisition, and spread of supernatural agent concepts that

populate our religious traditions and everyday worlds. Although I am not aware of evidence to suggest that there are any essential male-female differences in the operations of the HADD mechanism and its activation, Baron-Cohen's work suggests that ToM, with which HADD mutually interacts in affirming the goal-directedness of perceived agents, displays gendered (or male/female brain) differences in both the readiness with which it is activated and in the sophistication of interpretations and predictions it generates. Hence, as Barrett has suggested, since females more readily reason about the beliefs, desires, motivations, dispositions, and intentions of others, and use these ToM inferences to respond appropriately, negotiate social exchanges, and easily strike up social alliances, we would expect women more readily to explain and react to HADD's detections of agency, including supernatural agency (Barrett 2004: 43).

Indeed, this prediction is consistent with structural role predictions that correlate the female parent role with increased participation in religious activities. The source of both causal models may be found in the possible adaptive advantage that mothers had to "read the minds" of their infant children, establish social networks beyond the genetic group, and benefit from reciprocal relationships within stable communities. Baron-Cohen writes, "Anything that contributes to community stability can only increase the survival chances for both children and women. Since women are the sex that invests far more time and resources in parenting, one can argue that such benefits of reciprocal relationships will be more relevant to them" (2004: 127). From this perspective, socialization hypotheses, predicted social-role causes, and women's sociability factors may have identified important patterns, for which the adaptive advantages of empathizing tendencies and sophisticated ToM in females is a possible causal source. While parenting practices have changed dramatically in many societies in modern times, the mechanisms selected for survival in our evolutionary past persist as basic components of our mental architecture.

Thus, the general claim here is that differential levels of empathizing between males and females contribute to their differential levels of involvement in religious groups (and by extension, other social groups that contribute to community—and therefore—family stability). The prediction that has particular relevance to our understanding of the cognition of supernatural agent concepts, however, is that the ToM differences between males and females in their ability to understand and predict the behaviors of others is a causal factor in the high incidence of female sensitivity to the actions and intentions of supernatural agents. We should therefore find that, all else being equal, Type E individuals, of whom the majority are female, predominate in religious activities in which spirits, gods, and other supernatural agents also participate, and with whom intimate relations are developed through prayer and devotion. The ethnographic data on women's participation in spirit-possession activity appears to attest to this claim. In order empirically to test the causal mechanism predicted, however, one would need to control for social effects predicted by the more general claim above (e.g., that women are more likely to participate in social group activities more generally). This would necessarily require experimental methods of investigation that can control for potential confounds that naturalistic environments would inevitably yield.

Second, a further suggestion for high rates of female participation in spirit-possession, particularly mediumistic, cults specifically draws again on the sex differences in the mind proposed by the E-S (Empathizing-Systemizing) theory. The evidence for the claim that more males than females have a brain of type E includes the finding that "women are better at decoding non-verbal communication, picking up subtle nuances from tone of voice or facial expression, or judging a person's character" (Baron-Cohen 2003: 362), suggesting that women are not only more accurate in their "mind-reading" capabilities, but also more likely to detect and decode social information, where men would fail to notice it. As described in chapter 7, perception and interpretation of a possessed host's behaviors are potentially complicated by numerous factors. One of the most significant factors is that the physical (and often the behavioral, e.g., voice, mannerisms, etc.) characteristics of the host continue into the possession episode. In this sense, the host both is and is not the actor in any possession episode. The ability to maintain a coherent perception of the agency present requires heightened sensitivity to the often subtle cues that confirm the presence of that agency, despite competing cues from physical appearance and other continuities with the host's normal behavior. More fundamentally, the ability to infer the intentional states of the spirit agency from behaviors that can only be expressed through the body of the host when in possession requires a highly sophisticated theory of mind. Undoubtedly, the majority of individuals, including males, would score sufficiently well on the EQ to be able to reason at some basic level about the intentional states, emotions, and motivations of a person while possessed. However, since women tend to score more highly on the EQ, they should more readily be able to infer the mental states of the possessing entities and to respond appropriately. Although neither accurate nor sophisticated inferences are a necessary condition for communication between possessed hosts and observers, it is more likely that Type E individuals will be more sensitive than Type S individuals to the perspectives, motivations, beliefs, and desires of the spirits that possess others as well as of the spirits that they themselves are host to, and will therefore enjoy more understanding and satisfying relationships with these entities. The causal mechanism proposed here is potentially partly responsible, therefore, for women's participation in possession-cult activities, both as clients, or devotees, and as hosts to possessing spirits. For the purposes of evaluation, this two-pronged claim would need to be uncoupled and each prediction refined for independent testing.

Conclusion

We have now considered a range of factors that might explain some of the variation in the incidence of spirit phenomena cross-culturally. Could the sensitivity of our agency detection device in high-stress/low-control situations account for population-wide incidence of paranormal and religious beliefs? Could gendered differences in mind-reading abilities explain women's prominence in the kinds of spirit-cult practices described in this book and across the world? Are these real possibilities, or are they just fanciful speculations?

There are limitations on what we can say with confidence and on the claims that we make on these topics. First, our predictions must be consistent with the observable facts. Second, they must be commensurate with the hypotheses of neighboring disciplines that have been substantiated through scientific methods. And third, their predictive value must be ascertainable and ultimately put to the test. "The rate of the development of science," Feynman writes, "is not the rate at which you make observations alone but, much more important, the rate at which you create new things to test" (1998: 27). When things do not turn out as we predicted, then we are free to look in new directions for more powerful explanations.

The claims that I have tentatively advanced in this book are of little scientific interest if not appreciably uncertain and potentially testable. Testability demands precision and measurability. Surveys, statistical analyses, controlled laboratory experiments, naturalistic studies, and ethnographic data gathering are all indispensable to this potentially arduous and prolonged investigation. Rigorous, precise, scientific investigation, interdisciplinary collaboration, and varied methodologies are needed to assess the factors proposed for the variable incidence of spirit possession cross-culturally. Yet, how much more fulfilling it would be to say something about the transmission of spirit phenomena (and cultural transmission in general) with even a tiny measure of certainty than with none at all; to be able to hold to some provisional knowledge that something is the case (or that something isn't the case) than to seek refuge in some cherished hunch, fashionable vogue, or imaginative—but untestable—construct.

Appendix

Prioritizing exercise: *terreiro* activities.

PROCEDURE

Nineteen participants (twelve males, seven females) performed the exercise. Each participant was given ten strips of card on which the following statements were printed:

Prioritizing Exercise: *Terreiro* Activities

	Statements Given in Portuguese	Translation into English	Mean Ranking
A	Pagar obrigações aos orixás e entidades	Pay ritual obligations to the orixás and entidades	4
B	Cumprir responsabilidades ao egbe/familia	Fulfill responsibilities to the community	5
C	Ler e aprender as lendas	Read and learn the stories (of the orixás)	8
D	Aprender a prática ritualistica—procedimento correto	Learn the rituals—correct procedures	3
E	Aprender os fundamentos dos orixás	Learn the fundamentos of the orixás	2
F	Lutar contra preconceito	Fight against prejudice	9
G	Respeitar e zelar para o pai-de-santo	Respect and attend to the pai-de-santo	1

(continued)

Prioritizing Exercise: *Terreiro* Activities (*continued*)

	Statements Given in Portuguese	Translation into English	Mean Ranking
H	Aprender a história da religião—entidades, personalidades, etc.	Learn the history of the religion—entidades, personalities, etc.	6
I	Aprender os cântigos, danças e lingua dos orixás	Learn the songs, dances, and language of the orixás	7
J	Transmitir a religião para outros ainda de fora	Transmit the religion to others	10

Participants were asked to place the cards one above the other, according to their subjective evaluation of the order of importance of the activity or behaviour inscribed. No time constraints were imposed, and participants performed the exercise in private. The chart below demonstrates the mean ranking for each of the activities.

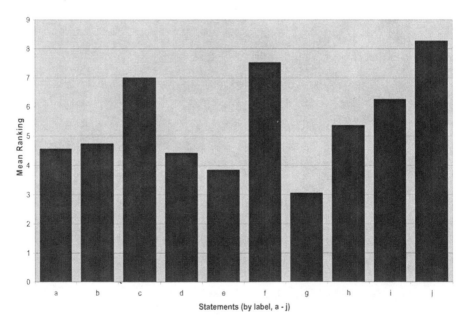

FIGURE A.I. Chart Showing the Mean Ranking of Each of Ten Statements Ordered according to Degree of Priority

Glossary

This glossary contains terms that may be used more than once in the text and that are not accompanied by a translation in each instance.

Babalorixá: The Yoruba term that translates literally to *pai-de-santo*, or father-of-saint. An initiated male is called Pai, or Babá, from the point at which he receives the right to initiate his own sons- and daughters-of-saint. (Female counterparts are known as *Iyalorixás*, or *mães-de-santo*.) Although the precise time at which an initiated member of the community should receive this right is widely disputed, it is generally considered to be at the seventh anniversary of initiation and is marked by a ceremony. In Pai's *terreiro*, no one had yet received this right despite there being initiated members of ten years and more. One of the reasons, according to Pai, was that they did not have the financial resources required to set up their own *terreiros;* and until such time, there was little point in performing the ceremony that would give them the right to do so. Nevertheless, they were still called "Pai" by the more junior members.

Banho: Literally translates as "bath" (or "shower" as in the phrase "to take a shower"). In the *culto*, it also refers to herbal infusions (of variable concentrations and ingredients) that are ritualistically prepared for the purposes of spiritual cleansing, strengthening, protection, attracting money and love, and so on. Baths for cleansing, for instance, are taken with these infusions in the *terreiro* before participation in

religious activities in order to eliminate any negative energies picked up outside the *terreiro*, or "on the street" (*na rua*). Baths for attraction (*banhos atra-
tivos, banhos cheirosos*) may be taken at home and are sold in the *terreiro*.
Mediums may take certain *banhos* to attract the spirits that possess them.

Boca à ouvido: "Mouth to ear" learning was said to be the means by which
foundational knowledge (*fundamento*) of the *culto* is transmitted from spiritual
father to son. The phrase connotes individual dedication to seek that knowledge from one's initiating *pai-de-santo*, secrecy in the method by which it is
revealed, and the exclusivity or peculiarity of the knowledge to each individual
and his or her needs.

Búzios: The *búzios* are cowry shells, or conches, used as an instrument of
divination. The concave part of the shell is cut off, leaving a two-sided object
that when cast may fall either "open" or "closed." The simple method by
which four shells are thrown, for example, may yield the combination 1:3
(open: closed), in which the response is interpreted as negative. A more complicated method, using sixteen shells is also used to converse with the *orixás*
and to determine to which *orixá* one belongs. Pai called the *jogo de búzios*
(throw of the cowries) his "internet to the *orixás*."

Caboclo: *Caboclo* may be translated as "indigenous backwoodsman." As such,
this term refers to native dwellers of the interior, for example, the Amazon
region. Within the *culto*, the term is often used more broadly to refer not only to
spirits of indigenous origin, but also to the collective of spirits that may have
lived on earth once and who now come to possess mediums within the *culto*.
People often refer to spirits of European origin as *caboclos*. The term is not
interchangeable with *orixá*, however. The female form of the term is *cabocla*.

Cargo: Within the *culto*, positions of responsibility and hierarchical titles are
referred to as *cargos*. Most of these are only open to initiated members and are
allocated following consultation with the *orixás*. In Pai's *terreiro*, some people
were appointed to their cargos by the *orixá* of the house (*orixá da casa*), Oxalá,
while possessing Pai.

Casa: A general term for house, often used interchangeably with *terreiro*, or
Afro-Brazilian religious center.

Culto Afro: This was the shorthand term for the *culto afro-brasileiro*. *Culto* may be
translated into "cult," but I have chosen to leave it in the original Portuguese,

as it has a less pejorative significance in Brazilian usage. Most members are content to describe their religious expression using this term, although some have recently campaigned for the *culto* to be regarded by outsiders as an acceptable religion like any other (e.g., Roman Catholicism, Assembly of God, etc.), thereby encouraging members and others to call their practices and faith a "religion."

Culto indígena: The strand of religious practice in the *terreiro* specifically dedicated to indigenous spirits, for example, spirits of the forest (*da floresta*).

Doutrina: A generic term for songs and verses sung during possession ceremonies, for example, to announce the arrival of a spirit, or family of spirits, and during ritual activities, for example, when the *pai-de-santo* applies a herbal infusion (*banho*) to a medium's head in order to facilitate his or her mediumistic development. The term *canticô* is more commonly used to refer to verses and song in the context of ceremonies and rites concerning the *orixás* and *voduns*.

Encantado: These are spirits that are said to have lived as human beings but who have passed through "the portal" into the dwelling place of the spirits, the *encantaria*, without undergoing physical death.

Entidade: A generic term for all spirit beings. Some people distinguished between *entidades* and *orixás* (and *voduns*), however. They would, for example, discuss their faith in the "*entidades* and *orixás*," apparently differentiating between the African spirit beings of Candomblé and all the other members of the spiritual pantheon.

Feitiço (feitiçeiro): In *culto* use, *feitiço* most commonly refers to an act of sorcery, in which a prescribed series of steps are followed—a ritual recipe—to cause misfortune in the life of another person. It also refers to the physical form that the sorcery takes in the body of the victim, which could be removed by a curer (*feitiçeiro*; *tirar feitico*, "to take out," *feitiço*).

Filho-de-santo (feminine form: filha-de-santo): Literally means "son-of-saint," or son of *orixá*. One becomes a *filho-de-santo* following initiation, in which a bond is established between the initiate and the *orixá* and the initiator. The term is often abbreviated to *filho* and as such may be used to refer to "sons of the house/*terreiro*" (*filhos da casa*) or sons of Pai X (*filhos do Pai X*, thereby identifying the *filhos* with a particular community). As such, it is often used more unrestrictedly to refer to those people who frequent a house and who may also participate in the ritual activities of the house, but who have not yet been initiated.

Fundamento: *Fundamentos* are said to be deep truths about the *culto afro*, specifically about the *orixás* or *voduns* to whom one belongs, that are transmitted privately and incrementally from the *pai-de-santo* to the initiated cult members.

Incorporação: Literally meaning "incorporation," this is the term that corresponds with "possession." *Possessão* is not normally used other than to refer to possession by evil spirits (said to be an extremely rare phenomenon).

Linha: The different strands of religious practice in the *terreiro*, with their variable histories, origins, and theologies, are referred to as "lines." The same term is sometimes used similarly to "family" to refer to a group of spirits who are associated by origin, familiar relationships, or function within the cult.

Nação: The word *nation* is used to refer to different Candomblés, claimed to be traceable to various African origins (cities and regions). Candomblé Nagô, for example, is said to originate in Yoruba, now Nigeria, and Candomblé Angola in Angola, etc.

Obrigação: This refers to rites of many different kinds, ranging from simple cleansing and purification baths to the demanding series of rituals performed at initiation. Participants were keen to point out that although the term connotes obligation, they fulfilled their ritual responsibilities willingly.

Pai-de-santo (see also *babalorixá* above): Lit. "father of saint," or "father of orixá." The *pai-de-santo* is typically the leader of a *terreiro* community. He officiates at initiation ceremonies and determines the day-to-day activities and ritual calendar and practice of the *terreiro*. He liaises with the *orixás* to solicit their advice and will concerning these activities. He offers consultations and advice to *filhos* and clients and should be knowledgeable in *culto* history, ritual, and mythological traditions. He should also possess the *fundamentos* (see above) that enable *filhos* to develop in their faith and relationships with their *orixás* and other possessing spirit entities. The term *pai-de-santo* is often employed more broadly to signify anyone who receives clients for consultation (but who does not necessarily initiate) or to members who have received the right to initiate their own *filhos* (normally seven years after initiation).

Pajelança: This is an indigenous form of shamanistic healing that is frequently part of *terreiro* activities in the northern regions of Brazil. Curing spirits are often called *mestres* and are typically animals (e.g., river dolphins) although they generally appear to act as persons when possessing their hosts. In many *terreiros*, the methods and instruments of *pajelança* are used in healing rituals (e.g., the cigar and maraca), but *encantados* and *caboclo* spirits may perform the cure (*cura*).

Povo de santo: This term, meaning "people of the saint," is most frequently heard within the context of public rallies and campaigns tackling religious intolerance toward the *culto*. It refers to members, clients, and often supporters of the *culto afro* as a united collective.

Terreiro: The *terreiro* is the physical nucleus of a particular community of *culto afro* members (i.e., *filhos* and *pai/mãe*) and clients. The term is used interchangeably with *casa*, or house.

Notes

CHAPTER I

1. Pronounced as "pie" in English, meaning "father." The full title is *pai-de-santo* (lit. "father-of-saint") for cult house leaders if often so abbreviated.

2. Adjectival form of Belém.

3. Brazilian white rum.

4. The ill effects of sorcery (*feitiço*) often take a physical form in the body of the victim. Common items removed by the healer from the victim include fish bones, dress pins, and small insects.

5. An *obrigação* signifies any ritual action, or "obligation," that is "paid" to the spirit entities, for example, offerings, propitiatory rites.

6. This practice reflected the normal customs that regulated the inter-*casa* comings and goings of the majority of participants who were settled in any one *terreiro*. Although relations between *terreiros* and their leaders were often friendly, defection to another community would invariably generate negative feelings of betrayal and suspicion.

7. Lit. "sons/daughters-of-saint." Like the term "Pai," this is also abbreviated to *filhos* (meaning "sons" or "sons plus daughters") and *filhas* (meaning "daughters"). These terms are used to refer to the broad category of participants in *terreiro* activities and religious rituals. Strictly speaking, however, a *filho* is a member of the Afro-Brazilian religious community who has been formally initiated into one of the "nations" through a series of ritual acts.

8. Many of the claims put forward in this book, especially in chapter 6, are currently being experimentally investigated by the author in collaboration with Justin Barrett.

9. A generic term commonly used by research participants to refer to Afro-Brazilian religious practice.

CHAPTER 2

1. Pronounced "o-ree-SHA."

2. "Whitening" (*embranqueamento*) of blacks through intermarriage and miscegenation was central to the ruling classes' theories of social and racial evolution. As Johnson writes, "Progress and modernization were tied to 'whiteness'; backwardness and indolence to 'blackness' and the significant African presence in Brazil" (2002: 84).

3. Person of mixed race.

4. But see Darcy Ribeiro; "We are a mixed-blood people in flesh and spirit, for miscegenation here was never a crime or a sin. We were made through it and are still being made that way. The mass of natives originating in miscegenation lived for centuries with no awareness of themselves, sunk in nobodyness. That was how it was until they were defined as a new ethno-national identity, that of Brazilians, a people in the making, in search of its destiny even today" (2000: 321; original Portuguese version, 1995).

5. *Race* here, of course, is not taken to signify natural biological-categorical variability, but is a social designation.

CHAPTER 3

1. A widespread term throughout Brazil that is synonymous with "white person" (*gringo* being the male form of the adjective) or "American," "westerner," and so on.

2. *Pai-de-santo* is the most frequently used term among both members and the wider population for the owner/head/leader of the cult house. The term is equivalent to Yoruban *babalorixá*. A literal translation renders "father-of-saint." *Sacerdote*, meaning "priest," is also used frequently. Initiates and frequent participants in terreiro activities are known as *filhos-de-santo*, or "sons/daughters of saints."

3. "*Aquilo me apanhou sem eu precisar de cantar, algo terrível dentro de mim, algo que me jogava pro lado, me batia, eu sentia que aquilo ali me sacolejava por dentro.*"

4. Afro-Brazilian priestess, or "mother-of-saint."

5. Umbanda, considered the most Brazilian and most widespread on the spectrum of Afro to Brazilian traditions, originated in the Niteroi area of Rio in the 1920s. Possessing spirits comprise four groups: old blacks (spirits of former slaves), *caboclos, ere* child spirits, and *exus* (mischievous and malevolent spirits, of which the female *pomba giras* are perhaps most famous). African *orixás* are also honored as leaders, or chiefs, of families of spirits.

CHAPTER 4

1. See Gilbert Lewis's *A Failure of Treatment* (2000) for a worthy attempt at transparency of authorly choices.

2. This was noted in Boddy's 1994 review. Since that date, however, there has been a resurgence of studies that take spirit beliefs and spirit possession as their principal focus; for example, Stoller (1995), Mageo and Howard (1996), and Behrend and Luig (1999).

3. These are discussed further in chapter 5.

4. "It is also sometimes disturbing to insist on honesty when honest representations would detract from the romantic depictions we might be tempted to provide" (Rosenthal 1998: 9).

5. "The way we picture and talk is bound to a dense set of representational gimmicks which, to coin a phrase, have but an arbitrary relation to the slippery referent easing its way out of graspable sight" (Taussig 1993: xvii).

CHAPTER 5

1. See Grace Harris, "Possession 'Hysteria' in a Kenya Tribe," *American Anthropologist* 59 (1957): 1046–66.

2. Temporal lobe structures in the brain include the amygdala and hippocampus, connected with such functions as face recognition, emotional reaction, and hearing and understanding human speech (see Livingston 2004 for a summary of neurological research on temporal lobes and its relevance to religious experience, for example, meditative states, mystical experiences such as visions, and so on).

3. Ohayon, et al. etymologises the terms: "The term 'hypnagogic' from *hypno* (sleep) and *agogos* (induced), was introduced by Maury in 1848, to designate the illusions heralding from sleep. The term 'hypnopompic.' From *pompe* (act of sending), was first used in 1918 by Myer to describe these phenomena during the transition between sleep and awakening" (1996: 459).

4. "Along the perception-hallucination continuum of increasing arousal of the sympathetic nervous system (ergotropic arousal), man—the self-referential system— perceptually-behaviourally (cortically) interprets the change (drug-induced or 'natural') in his subcortical activity as creative, psychotic, and ecstatic experiences" (Fischer 1971: 897)

5. See Firth, whose account describes various cases of locally defined mental illness, strange behaviors, and mediumistic abilities as being attributable to possession. For the Tikopia, "the line between madness and spirit mediumship was by no means a rigid one" (1967: 298). Any case of possession could rarely be wholly attributed to mental illness or to the sociocultural context. For Firth, participation in spirit mediumship may include a number of factors that are of differential influence according to each individual, for example, history of mental disturbances, personality characteristics such as "suggestibility," family, and wider social dictates and pressures, and so on.

6. Shamans, shaman healers, mediums, and healers, according to this model, are distinguished from one another by variations in their *selection and training, magico-religious activities, power*, and *trance states and characteristics*. For a tabulated description of these distinctions, see Winkelman 1990: 316–17.

7. The mutual exclusion of the incidence of different magico-religious practitioner types evidenced by the data surveyed raises doubts concerning the diffusion hypothesis.

8. Lambek contends, "It is time students of spirit possession stopped apologizing for not doing EEG's in the field and accepted the social reality of what they observe" (1989: 46).

9. See Raybeck et al. (1989) for a reexamination of the calcium-deficiency hypothesis and an alternative account that considers the significance of psychological stress as a factor contributing to women's participation in spirit-possession cults.

10. A similar, not unrelated, situation is described by Edward Norbeck (1963) in his examination of Max Gluckman's (1954, 1959) descriptions of rites that he interpreted as expressing social conflict. Using the same ethnographic data that Gluckman had used to substantiate his hypotheses concerning ritual and rebellion, Norbeck suggests possible interpretations that diverge from those of Gluckman.

11. Lindsay L. Hale, for example, rejects the reification of Umbanda as a religious system, describing it as a means by which individuals variously engage with self, situation, feelings, and being in the world. According to this view, Umbanda is "not so much . . . an object or system of beliefs, but rather . . . idioms, and poetic ones at that, used by people to mediate life and make it meaningful" (2000: 111).

12. For example, the cognitive approach to certain aspects of possession-cult activity proposed here is commensurate with Burdick's proposals for the study of social movements, an area that is clearly relevant to possession analyses. Generalizing the sociological perspective from which he conducted his study of women, race, and popular Christianity in Brazil, he writes, "Although a particular group activity may be understood from an academic perspective as a social movement, it is, more often than not, perceived by local people as but one of a number of concurrent, and . . . more or less coequal activities occurring in the neighborhood. Grasping this phenomenological reality has positive consequences for the analysis of social movements. One of the chief aims of such analyses has been to trace the processes through which *ways of thinking* and living that contest socially dominant ones *come into being, evolve, become influential,* and move people to various kinds of social action" (1998: 199, emphasis added).

CHAPTER 6

1. This story is taken from Pierre Fatumbi Verger's *Lendas Africanas dos Orixás* (1997) and translated here from the Portuguese. Verger's are perhaps the most widespread and widely available written versions of *orixá* stories. They were collected during extensive data collection in Africa and Brazil over more than two decades.

2. Candomblé participants.

3. In Portuguese, the verb may be used unaccompanied by the pronoun. The inflection (in this case, third-person singular) of the verb does not specify gender.

4. This anthropomorphic tendency is evident in representations of animal spirits also. The everyday tendency to interpret the behavior of animals in terms of human social interaction is often enhanced in the case of MCI animals (see Guthrie 1993,

1997; Winkelman 2002). In the *culto*, animal spirits were distinguishable from nonanimal categories of spirits by their title, for example, dolphin (*boto encantado*). In all other respects, they were represented similarly to other nonanimal spirits, even when possessing mediums. They were often called *mestres*, or masters, and were generally associated with *pajelança*-derived curing practices.

5. MCI concepts here abbreviated to MCIs.

6. Our intuitive mental tools automatically and rapidly process information and generate inferences about things we experience (e.g., sights, sounds, feelings, etc.). The nonreflective assessments that result from these rapid mental processes enable us to make implicit sense of things around us. Reflectively available information, such as learned theological or scientific principles, sometimes diverges from our implicit assumptions, however. When our minds are "under pressure" to generate inferences and conclusions about a situation, they will automatically access default intuitive assumptions (e.g., if it moves, it's alive), rapidly reaching conclusions about a situation before reflective knowledge is brought to bear. Hence, conclusions reached may be intuitively satisfying but may contravene reflective knowledge. A well-known example of this is the way we tend to process the earth's movements in relation to the sun. Despite (reflectively) knowing that the earth rotates around the sun, our experience of (apparently) following the sun's movements across the sky tells us otherwise. Reflective knowledge must be invoked to correct the assumptions generated in real-time observation. Thus, accuracy (according to explicitly acquired knowledge) often requires time for conscious reflection.

7. See Lambek's account of Mayotte representations of possession: "spirits enter the bodies of human beings and rise to their heads, taking temporary control of all bodily and mental functions" (1981: 40).

CHAPTER 7

1. I use the terms *actors, observers,* and *acts* to describe fundamental elements of the possession context. *Act* is employed here as a term of broad definition that potentially includes all behavioral events, that is, statements and actions. This makes no argument regarding possession as *fact* or as *act,* i.e., simulation or mimesis of possession trance.

I also use psychological definitions of the terms *actors* and *observers* in a general sense when referring to possession. In this case, the *actor* is the person performing the behavioral event, and the *observer* is the person perceiving the behavioral event. Note that all possession actors are also observers of their own and others' performances; they also perceive and represent the act, whether during it (in the case of partially conscious trance) or after it, or in generic representations of possession-trance behavior.

2. This is the term employed in social psychology to signify any perception that has a social element. According to the *Penguin Dictionary of Psychology,* it is used "with respect to an individual's awareness of the behaviors of others which are revealing of their motives or attitudes" (2001: 690). This leads to the forming of impressions about individuals, person-specific interpretations of behavior, and iden tification of reasons for behaviors.

3. See Johnson's (1990) developmental studies investigating children's understandings of hypothetical brain transfer scenarios.

4. Leon Festinger's cognitive dissonance theory holds that people want their
beliefs and attitudes to be consistent with one another and their behavior (1957).
Awareness of inconsistency, or dissonance, among these elements motivates people to
reduce the discrepancies and to make them more consistent. Because people often
find it difficult to change their behavior, dissonance is generally reduced by changing
the established beliefs and attitudes. Dissonance reduction is a strategic process
that requires conscious effort (Gilbert 1993). Reflectively generated beliefs may therefore satisfy motivations to resolve inconsistencies. These explicit beliefs may often
diverge from nonreflective, implicit intuitions, however. Therefore, dissonance reduction, motivated by factors such as self-esteem enhancement and mood regulation (see Smith 1998), may result in beliefs that do not fit with tacitly held
assumptions produced rapidly and automatically by our mental tools.

5. This is reflected in the increasing control with which people appear to enter
possession and the overall competence and performance as a host when possessed
(according to how this is assessed for each category of spirits).

6. These claims are currently being systematically investigated through a British
Academy-funded program of experimental research conducted by the author and
Justin Barrett.

7. Physical manifestation of the spirit through possession.

8. Talking about excessive drinking during possession ceremonies in other *terreiros*, however, one recent initiate stated that "this ends up harming the *filho* because
he is with the spirit but when he starts to drink, and becomes drunk, then the *guia*
goes away, the *guia* backs off and he [*the medium*] gets drunk. It actually isn't the
spirit anymore, it's the drink" (*isso acaba prejudicando o filho porque ele tá com o espírito
mas, de repente, ele começa a beber, a ficar bêbado, aí o guia vai embora, o guia se
afasta e ele fica bêbado. Na verdade já não é mais nem espírito, já é bebida*). The con-
sumption of alcohol was forbidden in *festas* at Pai's *terreiro*.

9. On one occasion, a *filho* publicly addressed Pai, possessed with Zé Pelintra, as
follows: "I hope that you continue to be this *caboclo* of great patience within our
house and, principally, to be a great friend, often making us think that we're dealing
with a human being" (*Espero que o senhor continue sendo este caboclo de grande
paciência dentro da nossa casa e principalmente sendo um grande amigo muita das vezes
fazendo nós pensarmos que nós estamos lidando com um ser humano*).

10. It is possible that by the same token, when Pai has no reason to dislike the
person, these positive attitudes may also carry over into possession episodes, in
which case Pai shows the host respect. Respect, in this case, is to acknowledge that
the person is possessed and to behave accordingly, showing deference to the supernatural agent and superior being believed to be possessing the host. Therefore,
this behavior cannot automatically be taken as evidence to support the assumption
that observer perceives the spirit as the agent.

11. "Significant others" here refers to important others in one's life, such as a
sibling, uncle, best friend, teacher, lover, or spouse (Anderson et al. 1995:42).

12. This remains an empirical question. As yet there has been no research focusing on the activation of SO representations specifically via physical/appearance cues.

13. Functional Magnetic Resonance Imaging is a form of brain imaging that registers blood flow to functioning areas of the brain.

CHAPTER 8

1. Pai attends clients throughout the year. Some periods are typically marked by reduced client *trabalho* due to the pressing responsibilities of preparing and participating in annual ceremonial activities and *obrigações*. These can involve up to two weeks of activities, such as *festas*, offerings, seminars, and other rituals, directed toward ("in honour of," *em honra de*) particular families or *linhas*, as described in the chapter 1. The largest of these are held in January (*Povo da Mata*), June (*Família de Legua*), and November (*Familia Nobre da Bandeira*). The twenty-five-day period in September, for which I record information above, commenced on the first of the month. The Day of Saints Cosme and Damião, on which the *terreiro* throws a large party for local children, is celebrated on September 27. Preparing for this day ends the month's activities with clients.

2. Although such claims may have been made tongue-in-cheek, or to excuse oneself for failing to attend the *terreiro* more regularly (in other words, what people are really saying is, "*she* only comes so much because she's addicted to the place"), it may be that the (perceived) control afforded by participation in magico-religious rituals, divination, and advice from gods and spirits, and knowledge of the unseen forces affecting one's life, is increasingly desired for random events as positive results are yielded. The robust predicative association between sense of control and physical and mental well-being has been demonstrated by decades of psychological and sociological research (see Skinner 1996). It is conceivable that the natural desire to avoid potential sources of misfortune and loss, and increasingly to gain knowledge and therefore predictability and control of factors influencing success and gain, could acquire aspects of compulsion, similar to other addictions and compulsions, such as pathological gambling (see Blanco et al. 2001; Toneatto 1999).

3. Permission to take photographs was invariably requested. Newcomers often refused, and I was frequently asked, even by good friends among the participants, about the storage, security, and end-purpose of the photographs taken.

4. According to Susan Reynolds-White's observation among the Nyole that "was the most dangerous cause of misfortune, and it was the cause to which death was most commonly attributed" (1991: 155).

CHAPTER 9

1. The sample of societies was drawn from the Ethnographic Atlas (Murdock 1962–67; 1968).

2. Possession here is defined as a belief that "a person is changed in some way through the presence in him or on him of a spirit entity of power, other than his own personality, soul, self, or the like" (Bourguignon 1976: 8).

3. It is important to note that this survey material identifies the presence of institutionalized forms of possession only. It does not register isolated cases or associated phenomena, for example, sorcery and witchcraft accusations. Furthermore, there is no indication as to which sectors of society the figures concern. Therefore, it is useful to juxtapose ethnographic data with statistical surveys and analyses in mapping out the intrasocietal contexts in which possession is most germane.

4. Certain contexts may encourage the inhibition of such cognitively intuitive concepts also. In an elaborate theory of religious transmission, Whitehouse (1995, 2000, 2004) identifies potentially generalizable cognitive and sociopolitical dynamics that he claims characterise and account for the successful transmission of cultural—specifically religious—knowledge cross-culturally. One prediction states that the kinds of cognitively optimal concepts that are easily generated and are globally widespread, such as those that often surround spirits, witchcraft, sorcery, and so on, are less likely to become established where the authoritative presence of a standardized set of doctrines and rituals excludes and forbids them. In traditions that require special learning conditions for the transmission of conceptually heavy, orthodox doctrines and standardized bodies of ritual exegesis, those whose responsibility it is to teach and uphold such complex bodies of knowledge often differentiate them from easily acquired, cognitively optimal concepts, such as superstitions. "Policing" of the orthodoxy is a frequent characteristic of such doctrinal systems, with sanctions on unauthorized innovation. This is a potentially testable hypothesis that may serve to illuminate significant and widespread features of the contexts that affect cultural transmission on the ground.

5. Consider, for example, Derren Brown's documentary production, *The Séance*, for Channel 4 Television, in which a group of participants believed that the spirit of an allegedly deceased woman was responsible for ambiguous events (e.g., noises) in the environment. The spirit was also believed to come and speak through one of the participants, named the "medium."

References

Albas, Daniel, and Cheryl Albas. 1989. Modern magic: The case of examinations. *Sociological Quarterly* 30 (4): 603–13.

Alpers, Edward A. 1984. "Ordinary household chores": Ritual and power in a 19th-century Swahili women's spirit possession cult. *International Journal of African Historical Studies* 17 (4): 677–702.

Andersen, Susan M., and Steve W. Cole. 1990. "Do I know you?": The role of significant others in general social perception. *Journal of Personality and Social Psychology* 59 (3): 384–99.

Andersen, Susan M., Noah S. Glassman, and Serena Chen. 1995. Transference in social perception: The role of chronic accessibility in significant-other representations. *Journal of Personality and Social Psychology* 69 (1): 41–57.

Antill, John K., John D. Cunningham, Graeme Russell, and Norman L. Thompson. 1981. An Australian sex-role scale. *Australian Journal of Psychology* 33:169–83.

Atran, Scott. 2002. *In gods we trust: The evolutionary landscape of religion.* Evolution and cognition. New York; Oxford: Oxford University Press.

Azzi, Corry, and Ronald Ehrenberg. 1975. Household allocation of time and church attendance. *Journal of Political Economy* 83 (1): 27–56.

Baran, Michael, and Paulo Sousa. 2001. On the possibility of different sorts of racial categories. *Journal of Cognition and Culture* 1 (3): 271–81.

Barkow, Jerome H., Leda Cosmides, and John Tooby. 1992. *The adapted mind: Evolutionary psychology and the generation of culture.* New York; Oxford: Oxford University Press.

Baron, Robert A., and Deborah S. Richardson. 1994. *Human aggression.* Perspectives in Social Psychology. 2nd ed. New York: Plenum Press.

Baron-Cohen, Simon. 1995. *Mindblindness: An essay on autism and theory of mind. Learning, development, and conceptual change.* Cambridge, Mass.: MIT Press.

———. 2004. *The essential difference.* London; New York: Penguin Books.

Baron-Cohen, Simon, Therese Jolliffe, C. Mortimore, and M. Robertson. 1997. Another advanced test of theory of mind: Evidence from very high functioning adults with autism or Asperger syndrome. *Journal of Child Psychology and Psychiatry* 38 (7): 813–23.

Baron-Cohen, Simon, Michelle O'Riordan, Rosie Jones, Valerie Stone, and Kate Plaisted. 1999. A new test of social sensitivity: Detection of faux pas in normal children and children with Asperger syndrome. *Journal of Autism and Developmental Disorders* 29:407–18.

Baron-Cohen, Simon, Jennifer Richler, Deraj Bisarya, Nhishanth Guunathan, and Sally Wheelwright. 2003. The systemizing quotient: An investigation of adults with Asperger syndrome or high-functioning autism, and normal sex differences. *Philosophical Transcripts of the Royal Society of London* 358:361–74.

Baron-Cohen, Simon, Sally Wheelright, Richard Skinner, Joanne Martin, and Emma Clubley. 2001. The autism-spectrum quotient: Evidence from Asperger syndrome or high-functioning autism, males, females, scientists and mathematicians'. *Journal of Autism and Developmental Disorders* 31:5–17.

Baron-Cohen, Simon, Sally Wheelwright, Rick Griffin, John Lawson, and Jaqueline Hill. 2002. The exact mind: Empathising and systemising in autism spectrum conditions. In *Handbook of cognitive development,* ed. Usha Goswami, 491–508. Oxford: Blackwell.

Barrett, Justin. 1998. Cognitive constraints on Hindu concepts of the divine. *Journal for the Scientific Study of Religion* 37:608–19.

———. 1999. Theological correctness: Cognitive constraint and the study of religion. *Method and Theory in the Study of Religion* 11:325–39.

———. 2000. Exploring the natural foundations of religion. *Trends in Cognitive Sciences* 4:29–34.

———. 2004. *Why would anyone believe in God?* Cognitive Science of Religion Series. Walnut Creek, Calif.: AltaMira Press.

Barrett, Justin, and Melanie A. Nyhof. 2001. Spreading non-natural concepts: The role of intuitive conceptual structures in memory and transmission of cultural materials. *Journal of Cognition and Culture* 1:69–100.

Bastide, Roger. 1971. *African civilizations in the new world.* New York: Harper & Row.

———. 1978. *The African religions of Brazil: Toward a sociology of the interpenetration of civilizations.* Johns Hopkins Studies in Atlantic History and Culture. Baltimore: Johns Hopkins University Press.

Baumeister, Roy F. 1998. The self. In *Handbook of social psychology.* Vol.1, ed. Daniel Gilbert, Susan T. Fiske, and Gardner Lindsey. 4th ed., 680–740. Boston: McGraw–Hill.

Bem, Sandra L. 1981. *Bem sex-role inventory: Professional manual.* Palo Alto, Calif.: Consulting Psychologists Press.

Benson, Herbert, and M. Carol. 1974. The relaxation response. *Psychiatry* 37:37–46.

Benson, Herbert, and Irene L. Goodale. 1981 The relaxation response: Your inborn capacity to counteract the harmful effects of stress. J. Fla. Assoc. 68(4): 265–67.

Bering, Jesse M., and Dominic P. Johnson. 2005. "O Lord . . . you perceive my thoughts from afar": Recursiveness and the evolution of supernatural agency. *Journal of Cognition and Culture* 5 (1–2): 118–42.

Besnier, Niko. 1996. Heteroglossic discourses on Nukulaelae spirits. In *Spirits in culture, history and mind*, ed. Jeannette M. Mageo, Alan Howard, 75–97. New York and London: Routledge.

Blanco, Carlos, Paulo Moreyra, E. V. Nunes, Jeronimo Saiz-Ruiz, and Angela Ibanez. 2001. Pathological gambling: Addiction or compulsion? *Seminars in Clinical Neuropsychiatry* 6:167–76.

Bloch, Maurice. 1974. Symbols, song, dance and features of articulation or is religion an extreme form of traditional authority? *Archives Europeenes De Sociologie* 15:55–81.

———. 1986. *From blessing to violence: History and ideology in the circumcision ritual of the Merina of Madagascar.* Cambridge Studies in Social Anthropology. Vol. 61. Cambridge; New York: Cambridge University Press.

———. 2004. Ritual and deference. In *Ritual and memory: Toward a comparative anthropology of religion*, ed. Harvey Whitehouse and James Laidlaw, 65–78. Walnut Creek, Calif.: AltaMira Press.

Bloom, P. 2004. *Descarte's baby.* London: Arrow Books.

Boddy, Janice P. 1989. *Wombs and alien spirits: Women, men, and the Zar cult in northern Sudan.* New Directions in Anthropological Writing, 407–34. Madison: University of Wisconsin Press.

———. 1994. Spirit possession revisited: Beyond instrumentality. *Annual Review of Anthropology* 23:407.

Bourguignon, Erika. 1968. *A cross-cultural study of dissociational states.* Columbus: Research Foundation, Ohio State University.

———. 1973. *Religion, altered states of consciousness, and social change.* Columbus: Ohio State University Press.

———. 1976. *Possession.* Chandler & Sharp Series in Cross-cultural Themes. San Francisco: Chandler & Sharp Publishers.

———. 1979. *Psychological anthropology: An introduction to human nature and cultural differences.* New York: Holt, Rinehart, and Winston.

Boyer, Pascal. 1994. *The naturalness of religious ideas: A cognitive theory of religion.* Berkeley: University of California Press.

———. 2001. *Religion explained: The evolutionary origins of religious thought.* New York: Basic Books.

Boyer, Pascal, and Charles Ramble. 2001. Cognitive templates for religious concepts: Cross-cultural evidence for recall of counter-intuitive representations. *Cognitive Science* 25:535–64.

Brown, Diana. 1979. Umbanda and class relations in Brazil. In *Brazil: Anthropological perspectives*, ed. Maxine L. Margolis and William E. Carter. Ann Arbor: University of Michigan Press.

————. 1986. *Umbanda: Religion and politics in urban Brazil*. Studies in Cultural Anthropology. Vol. 7. Ann Arbor: University of Michigan Research Press.

Brown, Diana, and Mario Bick. 1987. Religion, class, and context: Continuities and discontinuities in Brazilian Umbanda. *American Ethnologist* 14 (1): 73–93.

Bruce, Vicki, and Andrew Young. 1986. Understanding face recognition. *British Journal of Psychology* 77:305–27.

Brumana, Fernando Giobellina, and Elda Evangelina González Martínez. 1989. *Spirits from the margin: Umbanda in São Paulo: A study in popular religion and social experience*. Acta Universitatis Upsaliensis. Vol. 12. Uppsala; Stockholm: Uppsala University; Distributed by Almquist & Wiksell International.

Burdick, John. 1998. *Blessed Anastácia: Women, race, and popular Christianity in Brazil*. New York: Routledge.

Burger, Jerry M., and Harris M. Cooper. 1979. The desirability of control. *Motivation and Emotion* 3:31–393.

Burton, A. Mike, Vicki Bruce, and R. A. Johnston. 1990. Understanding face recognition with an interactive activation model. *British Journal of Psychology* 81:361–80.

Campelo, Marilú. 2001. *Candomblés de Belém. O povo-de-santo reconta sua história*. In X Encontro de Ciências Sociais do Norte e Nordeste, 2001, Salvador: UFBA.

————. 2003. *Tradição e inovação: Um estudo sobre a Mina e Candomblé na Amazônia*. Belém: Departamento de Antropologia/UFPA.

Campelo, Marilú M., and Luca, Taissa Tavernard de. 1999. Os espaços da memória: O povo de santo constrói sua cidade. In *VI reunião regional de antropologos do norte e nordeste (programa e cadernos de resumo)*. Belém: UFPA/Museu Paraense Emilio Goeldi.

Cardoso, João Simões. 1999. Uma Rosa à Iemanjá: Uma análise antropológica da Associação dos Amigos de Iemanjá. Belém: Departamento de Antropologia/UFPA.

Carneiro, Edison. 2002 [1948]. *Candomblés da Bahia*. 8th ed. Rio de Janeiro: Civilização Brasileira.

Chesnut, R. Andrew. 1997. *Born again in Brazil: The Pentecostal boom and the pathogens of poverty*. New Brunswick, N.J.: Rutgers University Press.

Cole, Sally. 1994. Ruth Landes in Brazil: Writing, race, and gender in 1930s American anthropology (Introduction). In *The city of women*, ed., Ruth Landes, vii–xxxiv. Albuquerque: University of New Mexico Press.

Colson, Anthony C. 1971. Perceptions of abnormality in a Malay village. In *Psychological problems and treatment in Malaysia*, ed. Nathanial N. Wagner and Eng-Seong Tan, 88–101. Kuala Lumpur: University of Malaya Press.

Comaroff, Jean. 1985. *Body of power, spirit of resistance: The culture and history of a South African people*. Chicago: University of Chicago Press.

Comaroff, Jean, and John L. Comaroff. 1993. *Modernity and its malcontents: Ritual and power in postcolonial Africa*. Chicago: University of Chicago Press.

Constantinides, Pamela. 1982. Women's spirit possession and urban adaptation in the Muslim northern Sudan. In *Women united, women divided*, ed. Patricia Caplan and Janet D. Bujra, 185–205. Bloomington: University of Indiana Press.

Csordas, Thomas J. 1987. Health and the holy in African and Afro-American spirit possession. 24 (1): 1–11.

Dennett, Daniel C. 1987. *The intentional stance.* Cambridge, Mass.: MIT Press.

Denton, Keith. 1999. Magical oracles and hand axes: Lessons for building self-confidence and employee ownership. *Leadership and Organization Development Journal* 20 (3): 147–53.

Dewhurst, Kenneth, and A. W. Beard. Sudden religious conversions in temporal lobe epilepsy. *British Journal of Psychiatry* 117:497–507.

Dolan, Catherine, S. 2002. Gender and witchcraft in agrarian transition: The case of Kenyan witchcraft. *Development and Change* 33 (4): 659–81.

Dudley, R. Thomas. 1999. The effect of superstitious belief on performance following an unsolvable problem. *Personality and Individual Differences* 26:1057–1064.

Dumont, Louis. 1975. Preface to the French edition of E. E. Evans-Pritchard's *The Nuer.* In *Studies in social anthropology,* ed. John H. M. Beattie and R. Godfrey Lienhardt. Oxford: Clarendon Press.

Edgerton, Robert B. 1966. Conceptions of psychosis in four east African societies. *American Anthropologist* 68 (2, Part 1): 408–25.

Evans-Pritchard, Edward E. 1937. *Witchcraft, oracles, and magic among the Azande.* Oxford: Clarendon Press.

Favret-Saada, Jeanne. 1980. *Deadly words: Witchcraft in the bocage* [Mots, la mort, les sorts.]. Cambridge; New York: Cambridge University Press.

Festinger, Leon. 1957. *A theory of cognitive dissonance.* Evanston, Ill.: Row, Peterson.

Feynman, Richard Phillips. 1998. *The meaning of it all: Thoughts of a citizen scientist.* Reading, Mass.: Perseus Books.

Figueiredo, Napoleão, and Anaiza Vergolino e Silva. 1967. Alguns elementos novos para o estudo dos Batuques de Belém. *Atas do Simpósio Sôbre a Biota Amazônica* 2: Antropologia: 101–22.

———. 1972. *Festas de santo e encantados.* Belém: Academia Paraense de Letras.

Firth, Raymond William. 1967. *Tikopia ritual and belief.* Boston: Beacon Press.

Fischer, Roland. 1971. A cartography of the ecstatic and meditative states. *Science* 174:897–904.

Fiske, Alan 1995. Social cognition. In *Advanced social psychology,* ed. A. Tesser, 149–94. New York: McGraw-Hill.

Fiske, Susan T. 1998. Stereotyping, prejudice, and discrimination. In *Handbook of social psychology,* ed. Daniel Gilbert, Susan T. Fiske, and Gardner Lindsey. 4th ed., 357–414. Boston: McGraw-Hill.

Francis, Leslie J., and Carolyn Wilcox. 1996. Religion and gender orientation. *Personality and Individual Differences* 20 (1): 119–21.

Frazer, James George. 1959. *The new golden bough: A new abridgement of the classic work.* New York: S. G. Phillips.

Freud, Sigmund, David McLintock, and Hugh Haughton. 2003. *The uncanny.* Penguin Classics. [Essays]. New York: Penguin Books.

Freyre, Gilberto. 1986. *The masters and the slaves—casa-grande and senzala: A study in the development of Brazilian civilization.* 2nd English-language, rev. ed. Berkeley: University of California Press.

Furnham, Adrian. 2003. Belief in a just world: Research progress over the past decade. *Personality and Individual Differences* 34:795–817.

Geertz, Clifford. 1983. *Local knowledge: Further essays in interpretive anthropology.* New York: Basic Books.

———. 1988. *Works and lives: The anthropologist as author.* Stanford, Calif.: Stanford University Press.

Gilbert, Daniel. 1998. Ordinary personology. In *Handbook of social psychology,* ed. Daniel Gilbert, Susan T. Fiske, and Gardner Lindsey, 89–150. Boston: McGraw-Hill.

———. 2002. Inferential correction. In *Heuristics and biases: The psychology of intuitive judgment,* ed. Thomas Gilovich, Dale Griffin, and Daniel Kahneman, 167–84. Cambridge: Cambridge University Press.

Gilbert, Daniel, and Patrick S. Malone. 1995. The correspondence bias. *Psychological Bulletin* 117:21–38.

Gilovich, Thomas, Dale Griffin, and Daniel Kahneman. 2002. *Heuristics and biases: The psychology of intuitive judgment.* Cambridge, U.K.; New York: Cambridge University Press.

Gil-White, Francisco. 2001. Sorting is not categorization: A critique of the claim that Brazilians have fuzzy racial categories. *Journal of Cognition and Culture* 1 (2): 221–49.

Gluckman, Max. 1954. *Rituals of rebellion in south-east Africa.* Manchester: Manchester University Press.

———. 1959. *Custom and conflict in Africa.* Glencoe, Ill.: The Free Press.

Gmelch, George, and Richard Felson. 1980. Can a lucky charm get you through organic chemistry? *Psychology Today:* 75–78.

Goodman, Felicitas D. 1988. *Ecstasy, ritual and alternate reality: Religion in a pluralistic world.* Bloomington: Indiana University Press.

Gopnik, Alison, Andrew N. Meltzoff, and Patricia K. Kuhl. 2001. *How babies think: The science of childhood.* London: Phoenix.

Gordon, Tamar. 1996. They loved her too much: Interpreting spirit possession in Tonga. In *Spirits in culture, history, and mind,* ed. Jeannette Marie Mageo and Alan Howard, 55–74. New York and London: Routledge.

Greenbaum, Lenora. 1973. Societal correlates of possession trance in Sub-Saharan Africa. In *Religion, altered states of consciousness and social change,* ed. Erika Bourguignon, 39–57. Columbus: Ohio State University Press.

Guthrie, Stewart. 1993. *Faces in the clouds: A new theory of religion.* New York: Oxford University Press.

———. 1997. The origin of an illusion. In *Anthropology of religion,* ed. Stephen D. Glazier, 489–504. Westport, Conn.: Greenwood Press.

Hacking, Ian. 1995. *Rewriting the soul: Multiple personality and the sciences of memory.* Princeton, N.J.: Princeton University Press.

Hale, Lindsay Lauren. 1997. Preto velho: Resistance, redemption, and engendered representations of slavery in a Brazilian possession-trance religion. *American Ethnologist* 24 (2): 392–414.

Harris, Grace. 1957. Possession "hysteria" in a Kenya tribe. *American Anthropologist* 59 (6): 1046–66.

Heider, Fritz, and Marianne Simmel. 1944. An experimental study of apparent behavior. *American Journal of Psychology* 57:243–49.

Herskovits, Melville J. 1948. Review of *the city of women*. *American Anthropologist* 50 (1, Part 1): 123–25.

Howard, Alan. 1996. Speak of the devils: Discourse and belief on spirits on Rotuma. In *Spirits in culture, history and mind*, ed. Jeanette Marie Mageo and Alan Howard, 121–45. New York and London: Routledge.

Jacob, Cesar Romero, Dora Rodrigues Hees, Philippe Waniez, and Violette Brustlein. 2003. *Atlas da filiação religiosa e indicadores sociais no Brasil*. Coleção Ciências Sociais. Vol. 7. Rio de Janeiro: Editora PUC–Rio; São Paulo, SP; Brasília, DF: Edições Loyola; CNBB.

James, Abigail, and Adrian Wells. 2003. Religion and mental health: Towards a cognitive-behavioural framework. *British Journal of Health Psychology* 8:359–76.

Johnson, Paul C. 2002. *Secrets, gossip, and gods: The transformation of Brazilian Candomblé*. Oxford; New York: Oxford University Press.

Kapferer, Bruce. 1991. *A celebration of demons: Exorcism and the aesthetics of healing in Sri Lanka*. Explorations in Anthropology Series. 2nd ed. Providence, R.I.; Washington, D.C.: Berg; Smithsonian Institution Press.

Kehoe, Alice B. 1983. Reply to Lewis and to Bourguignon, Bellisari and McCabe. *American Anthropologist* 85 (2): 416–17.

Kehoe, Alice B., and Dody H. Giletti. 1981. Women's preponderance in possession cults: The calcium-deficiency hypothesis extended. *American Anthropologist* 83 (3): 549–61.

Keinan, Giora. 1994. Effects of stress and tolerance of ambiguity on magical thinking. *Journal of Personality and Social Psychology* 67:48–55.

———. 2002. The effects of stress and desire for control on superstitious behavior. *Personality and Social Psychology Bulletin* 28 (1): 102–8.

Keller, Mary. 2002. *The hammer and the flute: Women, power, and spirit possession*. Baltimore: Johns Hopkins University Press.

Kendall, Laurel. 1987. *Shamans, housewives, and other restless spirits: Women in Korean ritual life*. Studies of the East Asian Institute. Honolulu: University of Hawaii Press.

Kiev, Ari. 1968. The psychotherapeutic value of spirit-possession in Haiti. In *Trance and possession states*, ed. Raymond Prince, 143–48. Montreal: R. M. Bucke Memorial Society.

Klass, Morton. 2003. *Mind over mind: The anthropology and psychology of spirit possession*. Lanham, Md.: Rowman & Littlefield.

Klein, M. 1987 [1946]. Notes on some schizoid mechanisms. In *The selected Melanie Klein*, ed. J. Mitchell, 176–200. New York: Free Press.

Kohnert, Dick. 2003. Witchcraft and transnational social spaces: Witchcraft violence, reconciliation and development in South Africa's transition process. *Journal of Modern African Studies* 41 (2): 217–45.

Lambek, Michael. 1981. *Human spirits: A cultural account of trance in Mayotte.* Cambridge Studies in Cultural Systems. Vol. 6. Cambridge; New York: Cambridge University Press.

———. 1989. From disease to discourse: Remarks on the conceptualization of trance and spirit possession. In *Altered states of consciousness and mental health*, ed. Colleen A. Ward, 36–61. Newbury Park: Sage Publications.

———. 1993. *Knowledge and practice in Mayotte: Local discourses of Islam, sorcery and spirit possession.* Anthropological Horizons. Toronto: University of Toronto Press.

———. 1996. Afterword: Spirits and their histories. In *Spirits in culture, history, and mind*, ed. Jeanette Marie Mageo and Alan Howard, 237–49. New York: Routledge.

Lan, David. 1985. *Guns and rain: Guerrillas and spirit mediums in Zimbabwe.* Perspectives on Southern Africa. Vol. 38. London; Berkeley: J. Currey; University of California Press.

Landes, Ruth. 1994. *The city of women.* 1st University of New Mexico Press ed. Albuquerque: University of New Mexico Press.

Lave, Jean. 1988. *Cognition in practice: Mind, mathematics, and culture in everyday life.* Cambridge; New York: Cambridge University Press.

Lawson, E. Thomas. 2001. Psychological perspectives on agency. In *Religion in mind: Cognitive perspectives on religious belief, ritual and experience*, ed. Jensine Andresen, 141–72. Cambridge: Cambridge University Press.

Lawson, E. Thomas, and Robert N. McCauley. 1993. Crisis of conscience, riddle of identity: Making space for a cognitive approach to religious phenomena. *Journal of the American Academy of Religion* 61 (2): 201.

Leach, Edmund. 1982. *Social anthropology.* New York: Oxford University Press.

Leacock, Seth, Ruth Leacock, and American Museum of Natural History. 1972. *Spirits of the deep: A study of an Afro-Brazilian cult.* 1st ed. Garden City, N.Y.: Published for the American Museum of Natural History by Doubleday Natural History Press.

Lehrer, Paul, Robert Woolfolk, and N. Goldman. 1984. Progressive relaxation then and now: Does change always mean progress? In *Consciousness and self regulation: Advances in research and theory.* Vol. 4, ed. Gary Schwartz, David Shapiro, and Richard J. Davidson, 183–216. New York: Plenum Press.

Leiris, Michel. 1958. *La possession et ses aspects théâtraux chez les Éthiopiens de Gondar.* Paris: Plon.

Lenski, Gerhard E. 1953. Social correlates of religious interest. *American Sociological Review* 18 (5): 533–44.

Lerch, Patricia B. 1982. An explanation for the predominance of women in the Umbanda cults of Porto Alegre, Brazil. *Urban Anthropology* 11 (2): 237–61.

Lerner, Melvin J. 1980. *The belief in a just world: A fundamental delusion.* Perspectives in Social Psychology. New York: Plenum Press.

Leslie, A. M. 1996. A theory of agency. In *Causal cognition: A multidisciplinary debate*, ed. D. Sperber, D. Premack, and A. J. Premack, 121–47. New York: Oxford University Press.

Lett, James. 1997. Science, religion, and anthropology. In *Anthropology of religion: A handbook*, ed. Stephen D. Glazier, 103–20. Westport, Conn.: Greenwood Press.

Leveroni, Catherine L., Michael Seidenberg, Andrew R. Mayer, Larissa A. Mead, Jeffrey R. Binder, and Stephen M. Rao. 2000. Neural systems underlying the recognition of familiar and newly learned faces. *Journal of Neuroscience* 20:878–86.

Lewis, Gilbert. 2000. *A failure of treatment*. Oxford Studies in Social and Cultural Anthropology. Oxford; New York: Oxford University Press.

Lewis, Ioan M. 1971. *Ecstatic religion: An anthropological study of spirit possession and shamanism*. Pelican Anthropology Library. Harmondsworth, Eng.: Penguin Books.

———. 1983. Spirit possession and biological reductionism: A rejoinder to Kehoe and Giletti. *American Anthropologist* 85 (2): 412–13.

Lewis, Ioan, Ahmed Al-Safi, and Sayyid Hurreiz. 1991. *Women's medicine: The Zar-Bori cult in Africa and beyond*. International African Seminars New Series. Vol. 5. Edinburgh: Edinburgh University Press for the International African Institute.

Livingston, Kenneth. 2004. Religious practice, brain and belief. *Journal of Cognition and Culture* 5 (1–2): 75–117.

Luca, Taissa Tavernard de. 1999. Devaneios da memória: A história dos cultos afro-brasileiros em Belém do Pará na versão do povo-de-santo. Belém: Departamento de Antropologia/UFPA.

Luckmann, Thomas. 1967. *The invisible religion: The problem of religion in modern society*. New York: Macmillan.

Luig, Ute, and Heike Behrend. 1999. *Spirit possession, modernity and power in Africa*. Oxford: James Currey.

Lum, Kenneth Anthony. 2000. *Praising his name in the dance: Spirit possession in the spiritual Baptist faith and orisha work in Trinidad, West Indies*. Studies in Latin America and the Caribbean. Vol. 1. Australia: Harwood Academic Publishers.

Maffesoli, Michel. 1996. *Ordinary knowledge: An introduction to interpretative sociology*. Cambridge, U.K.: Polity Press.

Mageo, Jeannette Marie, and Alan Howard. 1996. *Spirits in culture, history, and mind*. New York: Routledge.

Malinowski, Bronislaw. 1954. *Magic, science and religion, and other essays*. Garden City, N.Y.: Doubleday.

Malle, Bertram, and Joshua Knobe. 1997. Which behaviors do people explain? A basic actor-observer asymmetry. *Journal of Personality and Social Psychology* 72 (2): 288–304.

Marks, M. 1992. Amazonia: Festival and cult music of northern Brazil. Available: http://www.lyrichord.com/refw/ref7300.html. Accessed 8 November 2002.

Martin, David. 1967. *A sociology of English religion*. New York: Basic Books.

Matta, Roberto da. 2001. *O que faz o Brasil, Brasil?* Rio de Janeiro: Rocco.

Matute, Helena. 1994. Learned helplessness and superstitious behavior as opposite effects of uncontrollable reinforcement in humans. *Learning and Motivation* 25:216–32.

————. 1995. Human reactions to uncontrollable outcomes: Further evidence for superstitions rather than helplessness. *Quarterly Journal of Experimental Psychology* 48:142–57.

Maués, Raymundo Heraldo. 1990. *A ilha encantada: Medicina e xamanismo numa comunidade de pescadores.* Coleção Igarapé. Belém: Centro de Filosofia e C. Humanas, NAEA/UFPA.

————. 1995. *Padres, pajés, santos e festas: Catolicismo popular e controle eclesiástico: Um estudo antropológico numa área do interior da Amazônia.* Belém, PA: Editora Cejup.

————. 1999. *Uma outra "invenção" da Amazônia: Religiões, histórias, identidades.* Belém: Editora Cejup.

Maués, Raymundo Heraldo, and Gisela Macambira Villacorta. 2001. Pajelança e encantaria Amazônica. In *Encantaria brasileira: O livro dos mestres, caboclos e encantados,* ed. Reginaldo Prandi. Rio de Janeiro: Pallas.

McIntosh, Janet. 2004. Reluctant Muslims: Embodied hegemony and moral resistance in a Giriama spirit possession complex. *Journal of the Royal Anthropological Institute* 10:91–112.

Messing, Simon. 1958. Group therapy and social status in the Zar cult of Ethiopia. *American Anthropologist* 60:1120–26.

Michotte, Albert E. 1963. *The perception of causality.* London: Methuen.

Miller, Alan S., and John P. Hoffman. 1995. Risk and religion: An explanation of gender differences in religiosity. *Journal for the Scientific Study of Religion* 34:63–75.

Mithen, Steven J. 1996. *The prehistory of the mind: A search for the origins of art, religion, and science.* London: Thames and Hudson.

Moberg, David O. 1962. *The church as a social institution: The sociology of American religion.* Prentice-Hall Sociology Series. Englewood Cliffs, N.J.: Prentice-Hall.

Modarressi, Taghi. 1968. The Zar cult in south Iran. In *Trance and possession states,* ed. Raymond Prince. Montreal: R. M. Bucke Memorial Society.

Mol, Hans. 1985. *The faith of Australians.* Studies in Society (Sydney, N.S.W.). Vol. 25. Sydney; Boston: Allen & Unwin.

Monfouga-Nicolas, Jacqueline. 1972. *Ambivalence et culte de possession; contribution á l'étude du Bori Hausa.* Paris: Anthropos.

Murdock, George, P. 1962–67. Ethnographic atlas 1962–1967. *Ethnology* 1–6.

————. 1968. World sampling provinces. *Ethnology* 7:305–26.

Murdock, George, P. and Caterina Provost. 1973. Measurement of cultural complexity. *Ethnology* 12: 329–69.

Nabokov, Isabelle. 1997. Expel the lover, recover the wife: Symbolic analysis of a south Indian exorcism. *Journal of the Royal Anthropological Institute* 3 (2): 297–316.

Neher, Andrew. 1962. A physiological explanation of unusual behavior in ceremonies involving drums. *Human Biology* 4:151–60.

Nelson, Cynthia. 1971. Self, spirit possession and world view: An illustration from Egypt. *The International Journal of Social Psychiatry* 17 (3): 194–209.

Nelson, H. M., and R. H. Potvin. 1981. Gender and regional differences in the religiosity of protestant adolescents. *Review of Religious Research,* 22:268–85.

Norbeck, Edward. 1963. African rituals of conflict. *American Anthropologist* 65 (3): 1254–79.

Nourse, Jennifer W. 1996. The voice of the winds versus the masters of cure: Contested notions of spirit possession among the Lauje of Sulawesi. *Journal of the Royal Anthropological Institute* 2 (3): 425–42.

Oesterreich, Traugott Konstantin. 1930. *Possession, demoniacal and other, among primitive races, in antiquity, the middle ages, and modern times.* New York: R. R. Smith.

Ohayon, Maurice M., Robert G. Priest, Malijai Caulet, and Christian Guilleminault. 1996. Hypnagogic and hypnopompic hallucinations: Pathological phenomena. *British Journal of Psychiatry* 169:459–67.

Oliveira, Rafael Soares de. 2003. *Candomblé: Diálogos fraternos contra a intolerância religiosa.* Rio de Janeiro: DP & A Editora: Koinonia.

Ong, Aihwa. 1988. The production of possession: Spirits and the multinational corporation in Malaysia. *American Ethnologist* 15 (1): 28–42.

Oohashi, Tsutomu, Norie Kawai, Manabu Honda, Satoshi Nakamura, Masako Morimoto, Emi Nishina, and Tadao Maekawa. 2002. Electroencephalographic measurement of possession trance in the field. *Clinical Neurophysiology* 113:435–45.

Padgett, Vernon R., and Dale O. Jorgensen. 1982. Superstition and economic threat: Germany 1918–1940. *Personality and Social Psychology Bulletin* 8:736–41.

Paranaguá, Patrícia, Paula Melo, Eleneide D. Sotta, and Adalberto Veríssimo. 2003. *Belém sustentável.* Belém: Imazon.

Parker, Sue Taylor, and Michael L. McKinney. 1999. *Origins of intelligence: The evolution of cognitive development in monkeys, apes, and humans.* Baltimore: Johns Hopkins University Press.

Persinger, Michael. 1989. Geophysical variables and behavior: LV. predicting the details of visitor experiences and the personality of experients: The temporal lobe factor. *Perceptual and Motor Skills* 68:55–65.

Piaget, Jean. 1929. *The child's conception of the world.* International Library of Psychology, Philosophy and Scientific Method. New York; London: Harcourt, Brace; Paul, Trench, Trubner.

Popper, Karl Raimund. 1959. *The logic of scientific discovery.* New York: Basic Books.

Prandi, J. Reginaldo, and André Ricardo de Souza. 2001. *Encantaria brasileira: O livro dos mestres, caboclos e encantados.* Rio de Janeiro: Pallas.

Premack, D. 1990. The infant's theory of self-propelled objects. *Cognition* 36:1–16.

Pressel, Esther. 1980. Spirit magic in the social relations between men and women. In *A world of women*, ed. Erika Bourguignon, 107–28. New York: Praeger.

Prince, Raymond. 1968. *Trance and possession states.* Montreal: R. M. Bucke Memorial Society.

Raybeck, Douglas, Judy Shoobe, and James Grauberger. 1989. Women, stress, and participation in possession cults: A re-examination of the calcium deficiency hypothesis. *Medical Anthropology Quarterly* 3 (2): 139–61.

Reber, Arthur S., and Emily Sarah Reber. 2001. *The Penguin dictionary of psychology.* 3rd ed. London; New York: Penguin Books.

Reynolds-White, Susan. 1991. Knowledge and power in Nyole divination. In *African divination systems: Ways of knowing*, ed. Philip M. Peek. Bloomington: Indiana University Press.

Ribeiro, Darcy, and Gregory Rabassa. 2000. *The Brazilian people: The formation and meaning of Brazil* [Povo Brasileiro.]. Gainesville: University Press of Florida.

Ribeiro, René. 1952. *Cultos Afrobrasileiros do Recife: Um estudo de ajustamento social.* Recife: Instituto Joaquim Nabuco.

Robb, Peter. 2004. *A death in Brazil: A book of omissions.* 1st American ed. New York: H. Holt.

Rosenthal, Judy. 1998. *Possession, ecstasy, and law in Ewe voodoo.* Charlottesville: University Press of Virginia.

Ross, Colin A., Shaun Joshi, and Raymond Currie. 1990. Dissociative experiences in the general population. *American Journal of Psychiatry* 147:1547–52.

Ross, Lee D. 1977. The intuitive psychologist and his shortcomings: Distortions in the attribution process. In *Advances in experimental social psychology*, vol. 10, ed. Leonard Berkowitz, 173–220. New York: Random House.

Rothbart, Myron, and Mark Snyder. 1970. Confidence in the prediction and postdiction of an uncertain outcome. *Canadian Journal of Behavioral Science* 2 (38): 43.

Rouget, Gilbert. 1985. *Music and trance: A theory of the relations between music and possession* [Musique et la transe.]. Chicago: University of Chicago Press.

Sales, Nívio Ramos. 2001. *Búzios: A fala dos orixás: Caídas, significados, leituras.* Rio de Janeiro: Pallas.

Sanders, Todd. 2000. Rains gone bad, women gone mad: Rethinking gender rituals of rebellion and patriarchy. *The Journal of the Royal Anthropological Institute* 6:469–86.

Santos, Jocélio T. dos. 1998. A mixed-race nation: Afro-Brazilians and cultural policy in Bahia, 1970–1990. In *Afro-Brazilian culture and politics—Bahia 1790s to 1990s.*, ed. Hendrik Kraay. Armonk, N.Y.: M. E. Sharpe.

Sargant, William. 1973. *The mind possessed: A physiology of possession, mysticism and faith healing.* London: Heinemann.

Sarges, Maria de Nazaré. 2002. *Belém: Riquezas produzindo a belle-époque (1870–1912).* 2nd ed. Belém: Paka-Tatu.

Saunders, Lucie Wood. 1977. Variants in Zar experience in an Egyptian village. In *Case studies in spirit possession*, ed. Vincent Crapanzano and Vivian Garrison, 177–91. New York: John Wiley.

Sered, Susan Starr. 1999. *Women of the sacred groves: Divine priestesses of Okinawa.* New York: Oxford University Press.

Shaara, Lila, and Andrew Strathern. 1992. A preliminary analysis of the relationship between altered states of consciousness, healing, and social structure. *American Anthropologist* 94 (1): 145–60.

Shah, Nadim, J., John C. Marshall, Oliver Zafiris, Anna Schwab, Karl Zilles, Hans J. Markowitsch, and Gereon R. Fink. 2001. The neural correlates of person familiarity: A functional magnetic resonance imaging study with clinical implications. *Brain* 124:804–15.

Shapiro, Dolores J. 1995. Blood, oil, honey, and water: Symbolism in spirit possession sects in northeastern Brazil. *American Ethnologist* 22 (4): 828–47.

Sharp, Lesley A. 1999. The power of possession in northwest Madagascar. In *Spirit possession, modernity and power in Africa*, ed. Heike Behrend and Ute Luig, 3–19. Madison: University of Wisconsin Press.

Silverman, David. 1975. *Reading Castaneda: A prologue to the social sciences.* London: Routledge and Kegan Paul.

Silverman, Julian. 1979. Shamans and acute schizophrenia. In *Consciousness: Brain, states of awareness and mysticism*, ed. Daniel Goleman and Richard J. Davidson, 120–25. New York: Harper & Row.

Simons, Ronald C. 1985. The resolution of the Latah paradox. In *The culture bound syndromes*, ed. Ronald C. Simonsand Charles C. Hughes, 43–62. Boston: Reidel.

Simpson, George Eaton. 1978. *Black religions in the new world.* New York: Columbia University Press.

Skinner, Ellen A. A guide to constructs of control. *Journal of Personality and Social Psychology* 71 (3): 549–70.

Slone, D. Jason. 2004a. Luck beliefs: A case of theological incorrectness. In *Religion as a human capacity: A festschrift in honor of E. Thomas Lawson*, ed. Timothy Light and Brian C. Wilson, 375–94. Leiden and Boston: Brill.

———. 2004b. *Theological incorrectness: Why religious people believe what they shouldn't.* Oxford; New York: Oxford University Press.

Smith, E. 1998. Mental representation and memory. In *Handbook of social psychology*, vol.1, ed. Daniel Gilbert, Susan T. Fiske, and Gardner Lindsey. 4th ed., 391–445. Boston: McGraw-Hill.

Smith, Frederick M. 2001. The current state of possession studies as a cross-disciplinary project. *Religious Studies Review* 27 (3): 203–12.

Spanos, Nicholas P. 1994. Multiple identity enactments and multiple personality disorder: A sociocognitive perspective. *Psychological Bulletin* 116:143–65.

———. 1996. *Multiple identities and false memories: A sociocognitive perspective.* Washington, D.C.: American Psychological Association.

Spelke, Elizabeth S. 1988. The origins of physical knowledge. In *Thought without language*, ed. Lawrence Weiskrantz, 168–84. Oxford: Clarendon Press.

———. 1990. Principles of object perception. *Cognitive Science* 14:29–56.

———. 1991. Physical knowledge in infancy: Reflections on Piaget's theory. In *The epigenesis of mind: Essays on biology and cognition*, ed. Susan Carey and Rochel Gelman, 133–69. Hillsdale, N.J.: Erlbaum.

Sperber, Dan. 1996. *Explaining culture: A naturalistic approach.* Oxford, U.K.; Cambridge, Mass.: Blackwell.

Sperber, Dan, and Deirdre Wilson. 1986. *Relevance: Communication and cognition.* Oxford: Blackwell.

Spiegel, David. 1994. *Dissociation: Culture, mind, and body.* 1st ed. Washington, D.C.: American Psychiatric Press.

Spring, Anita. 1978. Epidemiology of spirit possession among the Luvale of Zambia. In *Women in ritual and symbolic roles*, ed. Judith Hoch-Smith and Anita Spring, 165–90. New York: Plenum.

Staal, Franz. 1979. The meaninglessness of ritual. *Numen* 26:2–22.

Stark, Rodney. 2002. Physiology and faith: Addressing the "universal" gender difference in religious commitment. *Journal for the Scientific Study of Religion* 41 (3): 495–507.

Stirrat, R. L. 1977. Demonic possession in Roman Catholic Sri Lanka. *Journal of Anthropological Research* 33:33–57.

Stoller, Paul. 1989. *Fusion of the worlds: An ethnography of possession among the Songhay of Niger*. Chicago: University of Chicago Press.

———. 1995. *Embodying colonial memories: Spirit possession, power, and the Hauka in West Africa*. New York: Routledge.

Taussig, Michael T. 1993. *Mimesis and alterity: A particular history of the senses*. New York: Routledge.

Thompson, E. H. 1991. Beneath the status characteristics: Gender variances in religiousness. *Journal for the Scientific Study of Religion* 30:381–94.

Thompson, Suzanne C., Alexandria Sobolew-Shubin, Michael E. Galbraith, Lenore Schwankovsky, and Dana Cruzen. 1993. Maintaining perceptions of control: Finding perceived control in low-control circumstances. *Journal of Personality and Social Psychology* 64:293–304.

Thompson, Suzanne C., and Shirlynn Spacapan. 1991. Perceptions of control in vulnerable populations. *Journal of Social Issues* 41:1–21.

Toneatto, Tony. 1999. Cognitive psychopathology of problem gambling. *Substance Use and Misuse* 34 (11): 1593–1604.

Tooby, John, and Leda Cosmides. 1992. The psychological foundations of culture. In *The adapted mind: Evolutionary psychology and the generation of culture*, ed. Jerome Barkow, Leda Cosmides, and John Tooby. New York; Oxford: Oxford University Press.

Tupinambá, Pedro. 1973. *Batuques de Belém*. Belém: Academia Paraense de Letras.

Turner, Edith. 1992. *Experiencing ritual: A new interpretation of African healing*. Series in Contemporary Ethnography. Philadelphia: University of Pennsylvania Press.

———. 1993. The reality of spirits: A tabooed or permitted field of study? *Anthropology of Consciousness* 4 (1): 9–12.

Turner, Mark. 1996. *The literary mind*. New York: Oxford University Press.

Turner, Victor Witter. 1969. *The ritual process: Structure and anti-structure*. The Lewis Henry Morgan Lectures. Vol. 1966. Chicago: Aldine Pub. Co.

———. 1982. *From ritual to theatre: The human seriousness of play*. Performance Studies Series. New York: Performing Arts Journal Publications.

———. 1986. *The anthropology of performance*. 1st ed. New York: PAJ Publications.

Velho, Yvonne Maggie Alves. 2001. *Guerra de orixá: Um estudo de ritual e conflito*. Coleção antropologia social. 3rd rev ed. Rio de Janeiro: J. Zahar Editor.

Verger, Pierre, and Carybé. 1997. *Lendas africanas dos orixás*. 4th ed. São Paulo, S.P.: Corrupio.

Vergolino e Silva, Anaíza. 1976. *O tambor das flores: Uma análise da Federação Espírita Umbandista e dos Cultos Afro-brasileiros do Pará (1965–1975)*. Master's diss., UNICAMP.

————. 1987. A semana santa nos terreiros: Um estudo do sincretismo religioso em Belém do Pará. *Religião e Sociedade* 14:56–71.

Vergolino-Henry, Anaíza, and Arthur Napoleão Figueiredo. 1990. *A presença africana na Amazônia colonial: Uma notícia histórica.* Documentos históricos. Vol. 1. Belém: Governo do Estado do Pará, Secretária de Estado de Cultura, Arquivo Público do Pará: Falangola Editora.

Vyse, Stuart A. 1997. *Believing in magic: The psychology of superstition.* New York: Oxford University Press.

Wafer, James William. 1991. *The taste of blood: Spirit possession in Brazilian Candomblé.* Contemporary Ethnography Series. Philadelphia: University of Pennsylvania Press.

Wagley, Charles, Maxine L. Margolis, and William E. Carter. 1979. *Brazil, anthropological perspectives: Essays in honor of Charles Wagley.* New York: Columbia University Press.

Ward, Colleen. 1989. The cross-cultural study of altered states of consciousness and mental health. In *Altered states of consciousness and mental health,* ed. Colleen A. Ward, 15–35. Newbury Park, Calif.: Sage.

Wegner, D. M., and J. A. Bargh. 1998. Control and automaticity in social life. In *Handbook of social psychology,* vol. 1, ed. D.aniel Gilbert, Susan T. Fiske and Gardner Lindsey. 4th ed., 446–98. Boston: McGraw-Hill.

Westermeyer, J., and R. Wintrob. 1979. "Folk" criteria for the diagnosis of mental illness in rural Laos: On being insane in sane places. *American Journal of Psychiatry* 136:755–61.

Whitehouse, Harvey. 1995. *Inside the cult: Religious innovation and transmission in Papua New Guinea.* Oxford studies in Social and Cultural Anthropology. Oxford; New York: Clarendon Press; Oxford University Press.

————. 2000. *Arguments and icons: Divergent modes of religiosity.* Oxford; New York: Oxford University Press.

————. 2004. *Modes of religiosity: A cognitive theory of religious transmission.* Cognitive Science of Religion Series. Walnut Creek, Calif.: AltaMira Press.

Wilder, J. 1975. The lure of magical thinking. *American Journal of Psychotherapy* 1:37–55.

Willis, Roy G. 1999. *Some spirits heal, others only dance: A journey into human selfhood in an African village.* Oxford, England; New York: Berg.

Wilson, Peter J. 1967. Status ambiguity and spirit possession. *Man (NS)* 2:366–78.

Winkelman, Michael. 1986. Trance states: A theoretical model and cross-cultural analysis. *Ethos* 14 (2): 174–203.

————. 1990. Shamans and other "magico-religious" healers: A cross-cultural study of their origins, nature, and social transformations. *Ethos* 18 (3): 308–52.

————. 1997. Altered states of consciousness and religious behavior. In *Anthropology of religion: A handbook,* ed. Stephen D. Glazier, 393–428. Westport, Conn.: Greenwood Press.

————. 2002. Shamanism and cognitive evolution. *Cambridge Archaeological Journal* 12: 71–101.

Winkelman, Michael, and Douglas White. 1987. A cross-cultural study of magico-religious practitioners and trance states: Database. In *Human Relations Area Files research series in quantitative cross-cultural data.* vol. 3, ed. David Levinson and Roy Wagner. New Haven: HRAF Press.

Yoshiaki, Furuya. 1986a. *Caboclos* as possessing spirits: A review of two models in Afro-Bhrazilian religious studies. *Minzokugaku-Kenkyu (The Japanese Journal of Ethnology)* 51 (3): 248–51.

———. 1986b. *Entre "Nagoização" e "Umbandização": Uma sintese no culto Mina-Nagô de Belém, Brasil.* Tokyo: University of Tokyo.

Zempleni, A. 1966. La dimension therapeutique du culte des Rab, Ndop, Tuuru, et Samp: Rites de possession chez les Lebou et Wolof. *Psychiat. Afr.* 11:295–439.

Index

M93024

L40101

LaVergne, TN USA
08 October 2010
200081LV00001B/6/P